In the Shadow of the General

In the Shadow of the General

Modern France and the Myth of De Gaulle

Sudhir Hazareesingh

OXFORD

UNIVERSITY PRESS

OXFORD
UNIVERSITY PRESS

Oxford University Press, Inc., publishes works that further
Oxford University's objective of excellence
in research, scholarship, and education.

Oxford   New York
Auckland   Cape Town   Dar es Salaam   Hong Kong   Karachi
Kuala Lumpur   Madrid   Melbourne   Mexico City   Nairobi
New Delhi   Shanghai   Taipei   Toronto

With offices in
Argentina   Austria   Brazil   Chile   Czech Republic   France   Greece
Guatemala   Hungary   Italy   Japan   Poland   Portugal   Singapore
South Korea   Switzerland   Thailand   Turkey   Ukraine   Vietnam

Copyright © 2012 by Sudhir Hazareesingh

Published by Oxford University Press, Inc.
198 Madison Avenue, New York, NY 10016

www.oup.com

Oxford is a registered trademark of Oxford University Press

Library of Congress Cataloging-in-Publication Data
Hazareesingh, Sudhir.
In the shadow of the general : modern France and the myth of De Gaulle / Sudhir Hazareesingh.
p.   cm.
Includes bibliographical references and index.
ISBN 978-0-19-530888-4 (hardback : alk. paper) 1. Gaulle, Charles de, 1890–1970—Influence.
2. Myth—Social aspects—France. 3. Memory—Social aspects—France.
4. Political culture—France—History—20th century. 5. Political culture—France—History—21st century.
6. National characteristics, France. 7. France—Civilization—21st century. I. Title.
DC420.H39   2013
944.083'6092—dc23   2012001182

1 3 5 7 9 8 6 4 2
Printed in the United States of America
on acid-free paper

For Martha Dewell, with all my love.

CONTENTS

ACKNOWLEDGMENTS

I would first like to express my gratitude to all the institutions that welcomed me during my research on this vast, and initially daunting, subject, especially to the archivists who greatly facilitated my task: General Robert Bresse, director of the Musée de l'Armée at the Invalides; Françoise Gicquel, divisional commissioner and deputy head of department at the Archives of the Prefecture of Police in Paris; Christian Oppetit, director of the twentieth century section at the Archives Nationales; Philippe Oulmont, director of research at the Fondation Charles de Gaulle in Paris; François Petrazoller, director of the departmental archives of the Haute-Marne; and Vladimir Trouplin, curator at the Museum of the Order of Liberation.

I also benefited enormously from the wisdom of colleagues who kindly agreed to read some of my work (and, for the less fortunate, the entire book). For their careful reading, their critical comments and suggestions, not to mention their fraternal encouragements, I thank very warmly Claire Andrieu, Henri Bovet, Alain Chatriot, Jean-Louis Crémieux-Brilhac, Marc Fumaroli, Christophe Prochasson, Pierre Rosanvallon, Michael Sheringham, Anne Simonin, and Philippe Oulmont. A big thank-you to Pierre Nora, who shared his remarkable knowledge of the Gaullist phenomenon; our exchanges were fruitful and stimulating both in relation to the overall framework of the book and a number of specific issues.

I also had the good fortune to discuss the project with many experts and key witnesses of the Gaullist era. For these contributions, which have nourished my thinking and enriched the book, I therefore thank Maurice Agulhon, Jean-Pierre Azéma, Simone Brunau, Jean-Claude Casanova, Jean Daniel, and Régis Debray. Early drafts of some chapters of the book were presented at seminars at the Maison Française of Oxford; the Charles Baudelaire Cultural Center in Beau-Bassin, Mauritius; the Department of History at Princeton University; the Remarque Institute at New York University; the Institute of Political Studies in Paris; and Trinity College in

Dublin. I am very grateful to the colleagues who invited me and to all those who attended and participated in the discussions.

Much of this work was completed during the academic year 2008–2009, during which I was on sabbatical leave. For this privilege I thank the Master and Fellows of Balliol College and the Department of Politics and International Relations at the University of Oxford. Thank you, too, to Kate Candy and Janice French for helping secure some financial assistance from the department. Without all this support, neither the research nor the writing could have been possible. I am also very grateful to my literary agent, Jim Gill of United Agents, for his efficiency and professionalism. Carol Clark assisted me with French-to-English translation, and did so with grace and effortless superiority; I am very much in her debt.

My greatest thanks go to Karma Nabulsi, my companion and my accomplice, who encouraged and supported me all the way through. I have also drawn much inspiration from her own work on the history of republican resistance in Europe and the Middle East—from this tradition of which the General was one of the most recent (and brilliant) incarnations.

Sudhir Hazareesingh,
Oxford,
July 2011

PRELUDE

London, 18 June 2010

On a typically overcast morning in the city of London on June 18, 2010, the governments of Great Britain and France assembled in the imposing courtyard of the Royal Hospital Chelsea, a home for former soldiers, to mark a special World War Two anniversary. Seventy years earlier, on the evening of June 18, 1940, General Charles de Gaulle had broadcast an Appeal to the French nation, transmitted on the airwaves by the BBC in London. It was a stirring and often poignant commemoration, with a declamation of de Gaulle's magic words, a performance of a celebrated French war hymn, flyovers from World War Two fighter planes, and rousing speeches by President Nicolas Sarkozy and Prime Minister David Cameron. Commemorations are as much about the present as the past, and both men seized the opportunity to reaffirm the close bonds between their two countries and to salute the efforts of their respective armed forces in Afghanistan. But the anniversary was above all a tribute to Charles de Gaulle's statesmanship and its enduring qualities: his sense of vision, his unbending commitment to national sovereignty, his belief in decisive leadership, and his personal integrity.

As I watched the proceedings from my seat in the courtyard—by a piece of good fortune, I was sitting with the French military delegation— I was struck by another thought. Like many great French providential figures (Napoleon Bonaparte is another good example), Charles de Gaulle was confident in his destiny and believed that he would be vindicated by posterity. In the General's case, there was an added twist: He thought not only that everyone would agree with his judgments but that the French people would come to see themselves, and the wider world, through Gaullian eyes. In other words, de Gaulle sensed that he would one day become a mythical figure. And it was hard not to conclude, from the vantage point of Royal Hospital in 2010, that his hunch had been accurate. The grandiose celebration organized by the French and British governments in London—mirrored by a series of commemorative events all over France during the summer of 2010—attested to the General's posthumous glory, as did the General's extraordinary popularity in France, where opinion polls consistently place him as the nation's favorite historical figure. This encomium is not limited to France, however; across Europe, Africa, and Latin America, there are numerous streets and monuments honoring the General's memory. But the real measure of de Gaulle's power was that, seventy years after the event, it was his speech of June 18, 1940, that was being celebrated as a founding event, his version of the past that was being narrated—not that of his adversaries, or of his old (and now largely forgotten) rivals, the communists. History, as the saying goes, is written by victors.

Yet the outlook for de Gaulle was not very promising in June 1940. A month earlier, France had been invaded by Hitler's Germany, and in a lightning campaign Nazi troops had overrun French defenses. The military situation seemed hopeless, and on June 17 the new French government led by Marshal Philippe Pétain—a prestigious war hero from the 1914–1918 era—announced that it was seeking an armistice. Charles de Gaulle, at the time a relatively unknown junior minister in the French government, disagreed fundamentally with this capitulationist policy. He felt that France could and should fight on, as she still had resources on which she could draw (notably in her vast colonial empire), as well as the support of her key allies—in particular, Great Britain and the United States. Indeed, de Gaulle presciently understood that this was not merely a Franco-German conflict: It was a world war, which meant (as he stated in a proclamation that went up on the streets of London) that "France had lost a battle but had not lost the war." And so on the 18th of June, having traveled to London and enlisted the critical support of British prime minister Winston Churchill, de Gaulle delivered his fateful Appeal, calling on his countrymen and -women to continue the struggle against the German invaders. "The flame of the French resistance," he stated, "must not be extinguished and will not be extinguished." Reflecting on the events of June 18, 1940, in his *War Memoirs* a decade later, de Gaulle would describe his entry into dissidence as a watershed moment, which had propelled him into the uncertain existence of an "adventurer."

De Gaulle's Free French movement gradually established its leadership over the French Resistance. The General was recognized by the Allies as the legitimate representative of the French people, as opposed to the Vichy government set up by Marshal Pétain, an authoritarian regime that collaborated with the Nazi occupiers of France. In the summer of 1944, as Allied and Free French troops, in coordination with internal Resistance organizations, began to free French territory from the yoke of Nazis and their Vichy acolytes, the General returned triumphantly to his country. The adventurer, who had been sentenced to death in absentia in 1940, had now become a national liberator. His march down the Champs-Elysées in Paris in August 1944 remains one of the iconic moments in modern French collective memory. De Gaulle went on to preside over the provisional government, which restored democratic institutions in France. He governed until January 1946, when he resigned over the issue of France's future constitution. Contrary to his coalition partners, who favored a parliamentary system, de Gaulle believed that only a "strong State" could provide the leadership necessary for France to retain her "grandeur" as a nation. The General also believed that French political parties were too weak to cope with the domestic and international challenges France faced in the postwar era.

However, in the short run de Gaulle's political challenge failed, and he retired to his country home in the village of Colombey-les-Deux-Eglises, settling down to writing his *War Memoirs*. It was only in May 1958, in the wake of the crisis provoked by the brutal and fratricidal colonial war in Algeria, that the General was able to return to power to implement his vision of a presidential republic. After the ratification of a new Constitution by referendum, de Gaulle thus became the first president of the Fifth Republic. He dominated French politics for the following decade, uniting conservative and liberal political factions under his leadership, rebuilding a stable political order in France and national prestige abroad, and adding the accolade of founding father to his titles as national liberator and prophet. His final years in power were increasingly fraught: He had to fight a runoff against Socialist candidate François Mitterrand in 1965 to be reelected to the presidency, his coalition only narrowly won a majority in the 1967 parliamentary elections, his rule was vigorously contested by students during the events of May 1968 in Paris, and in April 1969 he resigned from the presidency after failing to gain a majority in a referendum he had organized. Nonetheless, at the time of his death in November 1970, Charles de Gaulle had become one of the towering figures of twentieth-century world politics.

This takes us back, neatly, to the Royal Hospital ceremony in 2010. What is analyzed in this book is not Charles de Gaulle's life but the legend he created and that survives him to this day. This myth-making was well in evidence at the London ceremony, notably in the speech of President

Sarkozy, who described the General's June 18, 1940, broadcast as an act that had "cleansed France of the dishonour of collaboration": a striking but also mystifying formula, attributing almost supernatural powers to the General's utterance (which, to be historically accurate, very few people actually heard on that day). And yet this is exactly how political myths function, making contingent events appear as if they were part of a necessary and logical scheme of things.

As we noted, an important part of the Gaullian myth also resides in the General's enduring capacity to shape the way the French people see the world—and de Gaulle's legacy remains potent here in respect to France's dealings with the United States. De Gaulle had a famously awkward relationship with his American ally, starting with President Franklin D. Roosevelt, who he believed hostile to the very principle of an independent and sovereign France (FDR returned the compliment, believing de Gaulle was delusional and suffered from a Joan of Arc complex). The General did have many admirers in the United States, most notably President Richard Nixon, who credited de Gaulle with inspiring his China policy. However, de Gaulle's later efforts to make the most of France's position on the global stage (and in particular his withdrawal from the integrated military command of NATO and his stinging criticism of the Vietnam War) were never much appreciated in the corridors of Washington. But even here, as we still occasionally experience the brittleness of the Franco-American relationship (recent instances would include the Iraq war in 2003 and the Dominique Strauss-Kahn affair in 2011), de Gaulle might savor his posthumous triumph. For the General now has streets and public squares named after him in no fewer than five American states: Colorado, Texas, Iowa, Louisiana, and Ohio—evidence of the universality of de Gaulle's fame, no doubt, but also of the accuracy of his prophecy: "Everyone has been, is, or will be a Gaullist."

In the Shadow of the General

ᴄᴧᴐ

De Gaulle, a French Passion

The announcement of France's return to the integrated military command of NATO in March 2009 was widely commented on, both at home and abroad. At the Royal Hospital ceremony in June 2010, British prime minister David Cameron warmly congratulated his French counterpart for taking this step. And even though opinions back in France have varied as to the meaning, the implications, and the appropriateness (or otherwise) of the measure, all have agreed on one point: President Sarkozy's move marked the end of a tradition, that of a certain autonomous French position on the international stage, first taken up by General de Gaulle in the 1960s and then maintained, in its most important aspects, by all his successors up to the end of President Chirac's term of office in 2007. In fact, in the new millennium, France seemed to be moving quietly away from de Gaulle's political heritage. The deaths of most of the great historic figures of Gaullism, the three successive "cohabitations" (shared governance) between parties of the Right and Left in the 1980s and 1990s, the official winding-up of the Gaullist party, the increasing absence of the General from political discourse, and, finally, the opening of new de Gaulle museums, first at the Invalides in Paris and then at Colombey, all seemed to indicate that the Man of the 18th of June was slipping peacefully into the long night of memory.

But appearances can be deceptive. The writer François Mauriac said it long ago: "When de Gaulle is gone, he will still be here."[1] There remains first, and most obviously, the imprint left by de Gaulle on the political institutions of the Fifth Republic, and particularly on the presidency.

The General had his own notion of legitimacy, which was intrinsic and "above universal suffrage," as was said of the Republic itself in the past. His reelection to the presidency in 1965 was not so much the source of his legitimacy as a sign of recognition of that legitimacy.[2] But even if this conception—an authentically democratic one but essentially neo-Bonapartist—was endorsed by the General's successors in the presidency, these men still inherited an institution whose identity was fundamentally ambiguous. Elected by universal suffrage but required in the nature of things to be the leader of a political faction, the President of the Republic represents two contradictory figures: one embodying national consensus and the other of a partisan character—or, to use more metaphysical terms, following Kantorowicz's classic distinction between the two bodies of the king—one timeless (a function of his office) and the other transitory (relating to his corporeal person).[3] From Georges Pompidou to Nicolas Sarkozy, all the General's successors have had to face up to this schizophrenia of the kingly role, which has become, as it were, inherent in the presidential function in France.

The General, then, has left the world of things only to enter into the order of symbols. Once the dominant political figure of his generation, he has passed into an ideal incarnation, transcending the political sphere. He is now an example, a model to be followed—in a word: a political myth. One could even say *the* French national political myth, because, since at least 1990, de Gaulle has sat on the summit of Mount Olympus, looking down on all other national historical figures in surveys taken among the French. He brings together in himself all the great forms of exemplarity: liberator of the fatherland, founding father of the Republic, educator in civic virtues, and protector of the nation, together with—thanks to his unceremonious eviction from power in April 1969, after his referendum defeat—a touch of the martyr, a compulsory element of legend in a country that is still heavily impregnated with Catholic symbolism.

Touched by de Gaulle's magic wand, the 18th of June has passed from being the symbol of a humiliating defeat (Napoleon's rout at the battle of Waterloo in 1815) to that of a rebirth, a truly French dynamism and obstinacy. In fact, the General's shade hovers over the whole of France: first, literally, because he is present everywhere, on commemorative monuments and in the names of thousands of streets and public squares,[4] and second, philosophically, as his views of the world, his preferences and prejudices, remain dominant. It is thanks to him, or at any rate because of him, that French people instinctively recoil against the so-called Anglo-Saxon model; that they relegate the unfortunate Fourth Republic—now universally perceived as a symbol of weak, ineffectual party government—to the dungeons of political memory; and that they are inclined, one could almost say genetically programmed, to call down plagues on all the houses of politics.

Evidence of the stature of the General in French national culture is the colossal, extraordinary volume of Gaullian literature extant: thousands of magazine and newspaper articles and books of all kinds, including memoirs of real and would-be intimates, pamphlets supporting and attacking him, studies of particular historical episodes and subjects, constitutional and legal treatises, essays in political science and the history of ideas, portraits of the public and private man, inventories, dictionaries, analyses of his vocabulary and rhetoric, collections of aphorisms and *pensées*, books of photographs and exhibition catalogs, novels, and strip-cartoon albums.[5] And that is only the beginning, for there are also the sizable archives of sound material, available online on the website of the Institut National de l'Audiovisuel (INA),[6] and above all the enormous corpus of private and public documents deposited in the French national and departmental archives[7] and in the Charles de Gaulle Foundation in Paris.[8] The public archive sources are only beginning to be exploited—many documents are not yet accessible,[9] but they have already given rise to works of the highest quality. Let us mention in particular Jean Charlot's classic study of the Gaullist movement in the 1940s and 1950s, Jean-Louis Crémieux-Brilhac's remarkable work on Free France, Jean-Luc Barré's book on de Gaulle during the Second World War, and Eric Roussel's impressive biography—all of which have thrown new and often demystifying light on the Gaullian phenomenon.[10]

Demystification: the key word has been spoken. One of the great tasks of the de Gaulle historiography has indeed been to pierce the mystery that surrounded, often at his own behest, the figure (and the policies) of the General, with the aim of revealing what had been hidden, correcting what had been exaggerated, and placing in a more collective context things that the Great Man (*noblesse oblige*) had presented as pertaining only to himself. Behind these reconsiderations one could sometimes sense a deliberate will to set France free from the ideological systems and readings of the past constructed by or inherited from the General.[11] This more complex historiography was made possible in the first place by the wealth of eye-witness accounts of de Gaulle, which have left us pictures of him that are as fascinating as they are varied. From the "tall, chilly prelate"[12] of the Resistance period depicted by Emmanuel d'Astier de la Vigerie, to the man "of great sensibility behind his proud, marble demeanour"[13] by Claude Bouchinet-Serreulles, to this "prisoner of his own, self-imposed solitude,"[14] whom Pierre-Louis Blanc knew in his last days, de Gaulle was a favorite subject of memoir writers. Let us simply mention the most famous examples: the legendary hero "haunted by France" of André Malraux's *Fallen Oaks;*[15] the attractive, shadowy figure of the Liberation era and the postwar years painted by his aides Claude Mauriac, Olivier Guichard, and Claude Guy;[16] the quasi-royal sovereign of the Fifth Republic, as depicted by his closest political associates, from Michel Debré to Alain Peyrefitte and Jacques Foccart;[17] and finally, most recently, the portrait of a caring and protective father drawn by his son admiral Philippe de Gaulle.[18]

These accounts have cast light on many aspects of the public and private life of the General. But we must recognize that this eyewitness material has also, in some respects, reinforced the Gaullian myth. Another way of making the same point, and which indicates the complexity of the work awaiting the historian of the Gaullian epic, is to recognize that unlike other great political legends—that of Napoleon, for example—the General's myth is entirely coterminous with the Gaullian phenomenon. To return to our opening example, the Appeal of the 18th of June 1940, the founding moment of the Gaullian legend, was at one and the same time an immediate reaction, prompted by a specific political context (Marshal Pétain's speech of June 17 announcing the cessation of hostilities); a highly symbolic staged performance, in which every word was carefully weighed; and, as we shall see presently, an "invented tradition," which eventually transformed an absence, an emptiness (to repeat: very few people heard de Gaulle's original broadcast) into a shared collective norm. The line between myth and reality in the Gaullian story should therefore not be drawn too strictly. Understanding how de Gaulle is imagined requires a reasoned, measured (yes, let us say it—scientific) analysis of the Great Man's propensity to be, as the historian Maurice Agulhon put it,[19] "a myth-maker." The ambition behind this book is, therefore, not to sidestep the Gaullian myth or to reduce it to manageable size but on the contrary to enter fully into it, to try to occupy the whole of its physical, intellectual, and emotional space. To do so, we focus in part on the General himself, to try to see how (and using what ideological and memory tools) he "constructed" his public character and his vision of things.[20] The chief monument of this heroic exemplarity was the *War Memoirs,* but it was also displayed in other, more mundane, arenas: his television speeches and press conferences, in which he made use of genuine dramatic talents (already those who encountered him in London had been astonished to discover "'a great actor'");[21] his voluminous correspondence; the often remarkable speeches of wartime Gaullism; or even his ways of commemorating June 18, the totemic date in the Gaullian calendar. From all these sources we shall derive a complex picture of the General: that of a figure who saw himself as an incarnation of providence and who was inhabited by the conviction of representing national legitimacy in himself alone, but also of a sometimes vulnerable man, tormented by contradictory impulses and instincts, who was even capable of great humility.

But the Gaullian myth did not belong only to its creator. To understand what de Gaulle represented in the French collective imagination, we must also view the legend of the General in all its contexts—political, intellectual, and sociological. Such a multidimensional approach allows us to grasp the myth in its objective nature: how it took form, the institutions that transmitted it, its emotional and memory vectors, its hypnotic repetitions, and its modulations, without forgetting its dissonances. With this in mind, we shall try to reconstruct Gaullian popular culture as it manifested itself in a multitude of registers from 1940 until the present day: in the acclamations with which the General was received on his provincial tours; in the memories of war veterans; among the expressions of grief at the time of his death, as they were inscribed in town and village condolence books; in the steps of the thousands of men and women who made the pilgrimage to Colombey-les-Deux-Eglises between the early 1970s and the end of the millennium, which marked the apogee of a neoreligious cult of the General; and among the various objects that constitute the pious trinkets of Gaullism. Through and beyond this colorful collection, we also note how de Gaulle was appropriated, even posthumously reinvented, by conservative and progressive politicians alike, and among elites as well as in French popular imagination. For, while staying true to themselves, great mythical figures (think of Charlemagne or Joan of Arc or, in the American context, Jefferson or Lincoln) have the power to adapt themselves—and to be adapted—to particular political and cultural contexts.[22]

This malleability of the Gaullian image can be seen with remarkable clarity in one of the original sources we consulted in the research for this work: the letters sent to the General from members of the public. De Gaulle was a prolific correspondent, and toward the end of his life he calculated that he had sent more than 35,000 letters;[23] these writings, of which the published part already fills thirteen volumes,[24] can be most revealing, especially when they are compared with newly available documents. We have found, for example, in the Paris archives of the Order of the Liberation (the decoration created by de Gaulle during the Second World War), an unpublished letter of the General's that casts a whole new light on his conception of the 18th of June celebrations. However, we have mainly focused on the letters received by de Gaulle. For here, in contrast with the Great Man's own writings, very little of the surviving material has been published. The few collections of letters from notable French and foreign figures to the General do, however, bear witness to the richness of these exchanges and their potential contribution to our understanding of the Gaullian phenomenon.[25] While waiting for the eventual publication of more of these documents, we have chosen to work on a source of material completely unexploited until now: the letters written to de Gaulle by ordinary men and women, particularly between the 1950s and his death in November 1970. We have been able to view a large number of originals, held in the Charles de Gaulle Foundation, and to consult the reports on this correspondence prepared by the General's secretariat from 1958 onward; these are available in the French National Archives in the "Elysée" collection.[26]

This mass of documents offers precious food for thought about the phenomenon of "ordinary" writing.[27] For between these pen-wielding citizens and the General, a remarkable epistolary relationship grew, which broke with one of the founding principles of the genre: reciprocity, even though the General did sometimes reply directly to his correspondents. Each week his private secretary, Xavier de Beaulaincourt, selected a few letters for him, and he would take them off to Colombey on the weekend and reply to them there.[28] These letters sent to de Gaulle prove most valuable precisely because they were not intended to be read by the public. Their authors reveal their undisguised, private thoughts about the General. Every kind of letter is represented among them, from the confessional letter, in which the writers tell the often poignant story of their lives to the General, to the hostile missive in which de Gaulle's words and deeds are roundly denounced.[29] But the most common type is certainly the letter of admiration, in which de Gaulle is assured of the writer's affection, respect, friendship, brotherly feeling, and often love. Here, in contrast with the letters, notebooks, and memoirs of members of the Resistance, who sometimes strongly distanced themselves from the trappings of heroic discourse,[30] it is clear that these letters addressed to de Gaulle were at the heart of his myth. Taken as a whole, these writings throw a fascinating light on how the General was represented in the public imagination and are above all evidence of his astonishing ability to incarnate both the most absolute remoteness and the most touching intimacy.

We analyze the Gaullian myth in this work as a pattern of representations: complex enough to constitute an intelligible system; concentrated enough to appear in the simplest forms—an inscription on a monument, a preserved memory, a letter—and coherent enough to remain intact and survive adaptation, change, and metamorphosis through time.[31] Complexity, concentration, coherence—these terms apply equally well to the figure of de Gaulle and to the Gaullian system of representation, including his vision of the past (recent and distant), his choice of symbols (such as his characteristic gestures, but also his anniversaries and political emblems, like the cross of Lorraine, already chosen as the banner of Free France in 1940–1944),[32] and his mode of expression. In a twentieth century whose political vocabulary was strongly marked by ideological passion, de Gaulle's discourse constantly relied on epic dramatizations; hence the recurrence of notions related to the sacred, forms of heroism, and manifestations of collective enthusiasm. Gaullism was, as one of his followers rightly said, an "enormous adventure."[33] But in the background of this Promethean discourse, darker figures were lurking: the danger of corruption, the fear of national division, or simply the pull of doubt— doubt about whether he could achieve his ends but above all doubt in himself, aligned with a sense that the French did not love him as they should, or as much as they should. A year before his final retirement in 1969, de Gaulle publicly admitted that he had thought of "leaving the stage" on many occasions since 1940.[34]

Through the example of de Gaulle, and following on from our work on the Napoleon legend, we therefore aim to deepen our reflection on the phenomenon of the myth in France. This subject has generated a rich and diverse historiography that has singled out all kinds of mythogenic objects and forms, including Roland Barthes's celebrated description of the beard of a famous French clergyman.[35] It is true that the General's *képi* could be an excellent subject for political psychoanalysis: in schoolchildren's drawings, as in contemporary caricatures, his headdress often appeared as the distinguishing mark of the General—along with his nose.[36] But one of the aspects that interests us most is the myth's ideological dimension, which can add force to it or delegitimize it. At the heart of the system of representations of great national myths, we often find positive idealizations: the nobleman of the monarchist, the "new classes" of the republican, the "working people" of socialist and communist traditions, and the individual of laissez-faire economics. But for Gaullism, which always rejected anything that might fragment the body politic, the "nation" was the supreme sociological myth and the pursuit of national "grandeur" one of the enduring objectives. National myths also carried along with them negative representations and great fears: The Gaullian proclivity for creating anxiety often played upon the great French pathologies—apprehension of death, fear of disorder, and anguish at national weakness and decline. At the same time, the General was himself demonized using classic figures from the nation's stock of phobias: fear of dictatorship, apprehension of conspiracies, and the influence of occult forces (ever since the French Revolution, these demons have haunted the nation's political culture, and progressives were especially wary of de Gaulle because he came from the military, which has a long history of antagonism with the republican tradition). That is why Gaullism occupies a special place in the pantheon of political myths: It is the perfect illustration of the description given by the historian Raoul Girardet as "a kind of cross-roads of the collective imagination, where the most varied, and sometimes the most contradictory, aspirations and demands meet and intermingle."[37]

This notion of a "cross-roads of the collective imagination" expresses very well the methodological approach adopted in this work, which stands at the interface between cultural and political history. We attempt to observe the Gaullian phenomenon through this range of different fields of study of the political, foregrounding concepts, such as memory, symbolism, ritual, mediation, and sensibility.[38] The history of the Gaullian myth shows first of all the strong heuristic value of the notion of sensibility. Especially during the war years and at the Liberation, but also in later decades, de Gaulle's voice and his physical image played a major role in the creation of his legend. It must be remembered that a large number of people knew him only by his radio broadcasts during the 1940–1944 era. De Gaulle was above all the last great historic avatar of what was a key phenomenon in the political history of the twentieth century: passion. As with its political antithesis (communism), affiliation to Gaullism was often likened to joining a religious cult,[39] and the notions of "faith" and "faithfulness" were long to remain (even after the death of the General) the defining characteristics of Gaullist sensibility—and also an essential criterion distinguishing true Gaullists from opportunists. De Gaulle himself attached great importance to the notion of "sentiment," and his speeches drew on the register of extreme emotions. As Jean-Luc Barré has rightly observed, the word "grief" recurs with striking frequency in the vocabulary of wartime Gaullism.[40] We too shall come to recognize the extent to which—despite his apparent hard shell—the General's sensibility influenced his behavior and his view of the world. Indeed, our reading of the *War Memoirs* is largely framed around the Gaullian conception of sentiment.

But passion was also, and principally, a component of the popular Gaullian myth: passion in the form of gaiety, hope, gratitude, disappointment, depression, sorrow, and love—love such as that of Claude Mauriac, private secretary to the Great Man from 1944 to 1948, who realized that he "loved [the General] tenderly,"[41] or that of the progressive journalist Jean Daniel, who, after hearing that de Gaulle had escaped an assassination attempt in 1961, recorded in his diary "I realise now how much I love this man and what he represents, expresses, incarnates."[42] This "love affair"[43] that de Gaulle carried on with those around him could also interact with a wider range of feelings. In a letter that he wrote to the General after he had left power in 1969, the historian Fernand Braudel stated that "all that is best in France will continue to think of you with emotion, love and pride."[44] These feelings came together for the last time on the death of the General in November 1970, marking one of the most intense moments of collective emotion of the second half of the twentieth century in France.

At the same time, this passion could also take far less pleasant forms, such as mistrust, anger, hatred, and even attempts at physical elimination. The repeated attempts of assassination of the president, and the floods of angry and threatening letters received at the Elysée, bear witness to such feelings. No political figure of the twentieth century inspired such dislike, even loathing, as Charles de Gaulle, among soldiers and civilians, among militants and intellectuals, on the extreme Right as well as the extreme Left, among his former supporters and longtime opponents, and finally and above all, among the *pieds noirs*, the descendants of white Algerian settlers.[45] As Régis Debray rightly insisted, these negative representations, wrapping as they did the Man of the 18th of June in "a protective cloak of ambiguities," greatly contributed to the growth of the Gaullian myth.[46]

But there was also, in the passionate relationship between de Gaulle and his opponents, something special: an imitative fascination, founded in part on a shared reliance on the charismatic phenomenon.[47] In this context, Pierre Nora has penetratingly shown how Gaullism and communism constructed themselves as "sites of memory," antithetical yet often complementary.[48] Both ideologies aspired to represent the essence of the French nation and at times demanded the ultimate sacrifice from their members; both also believed that history was on their side and that this would eventually guarantee their triumph over their adversaries. It is perhaps this latent connivance that explains how the most virulent negative feelings toward the General could fade away with time and how the most spectacular reversals could be observed, on the Left as on the Right, in the face of de Gaulle's legacy. These reversals are examined in the last chapters of this book. As in all legends, the concept of time plays an essential role in the Gaullian myth.[49] Gaullism operated on several different, overlapping time scales: a long view, as when the General pronounced that France was the cumulative product of fifteen centuries of collective endeavor; a median view, as when he used the notion of a "thirty years' war" to explain the conflict of 1940–1944, presenting the Second World War as the continuation of the historic French battle against Germanic expansionism; but also a very short view—intense moments when history seemed to speed up, as in the first months of the Liberation in the summer of 1944, or again in May 1958, when de Gaulle returned to power in the wake of the Algerian crisis and within a matter of weeks laid the foundations of a new political order. In this context, one of the major aims of this work is to view the Gaullian phenomenon in its wider historical context. To do so, we must go back well beyond June 18, 1940, that heavily symbolic date on which the Gaullian myth has tended to locate its origins, to find the real influences on the General's historical imagination. It has often been said, although the idea has never been fully developed, that de Gaulle was really a man of the long nineteenth century, that formative period of modern French political culture. It was in the light of that experience, from the disastrous fall of the Napoleonic Empire to France's triumph in the First World War, that de Gaulle developed his own historical vision of a France eternally torn between grandeur and humiliation. It was there too that he found the figures who most inspired him, political (republican war leaders such as Léon Gambetta and Georges Clemenceau), military (Marshal Foch, the heroic symbol of French military valor during the First World War), and literary (the writer, diplomat, and historian François-René de Chateaubriand, one of the founders of French romanticism). It was from the same rich source that his opponents drew the range of negative representations that always haunted Gaullism, from the Bonaparte of the first coup d'état in 1799 to General Boulanger, whose nationalist challenge threatened the Republic in the late nineteenth century, and of course the supreme villain in France's national demonology, Louis Napoléon, whose coup overthrew the Second Republic in 1851.[50] Sometimes, in an ultimate refinement, these monstrous figures were coupled with the memory of the Vichy era, as when the socialist leader François Mitterrand declared in 1967, "the Right, the beastly Right, has found in the General its strong man, after failing with Boulanger and Pétain."[51]

The Gaullian myth also cultivated a particular relationship with space. Like its Napoleonic predecessor, the Gaullian legend took on global dimensions, which, sadly, we do not have time to explore fully in this work. Let us simply quote, for example, a letter received in 1969 by the General from one of his admirers in Toulon, who had spent thirty-eight years of his life in the Middle East and in North Africa: "Everywhere I went," he states, "I heard people speak of de Gaulle with fervour, emotion, gratitude, and envy of France for having such a prestigious leader."[52] Reference to the affective dimension, we note again, was all-important. But space also meant distance and alienation: exile abroad, as in 1940–1944 (and, in the black legend of Gaullism, the tribulations of the French settlers in Algeria); exile at home, during the years of "crossing the desert" and then the period from April 1969 to November 1970; and also (more speculatively) exile as a feeling of distance in the face of power. De Gaulle literally never felt at home at the Elysée; he did not keep any personal belongings in the place that he always called "a stranger's palace."[53] This was more so because of his dear village of Colombey, situated in the eastern department of the Haute-Marne, a symbol of a well-protected private life but also of a Gaullian association with locality and territoriality that has remained deeply fixed in France and has been further accentuated by the proliferation since 1970 of plaques, public squares, and streets named after the General.

This inscription of de Gaulle's name in space is the logical counterpart of Gaullian imagery itself, which was always marked by a passion for territorial symbolism. A sign of this is the great number of sites that have acquired a normative significance in the Gaullian vocabulary and that the historian Philippe Oulmont justly describes as "holy places".[54] the retreat in Carlton Gardens, in London, where the Free French Movement began its life in exile in 1940; the good city of Bayeux, from where the plan of the new Gaullian republic was first proclaimed in 1946; the five communes decorated with the Order of the Liberation for their exceptional contribution to national liberation;[55] the mont Valérien, a place of painful contemplation after the war, where more than a thousand Resistants were executed by the Nazis during the Second World War; and the ever-faithful political strong-holds of Gaullism, such as Alsace, Brittany, and, above all, the North, where one in every five communes has a De Gaulle Street.[56] There were also the lesser sites, notably the hundreds of towns and villages that enjoyed official visits from the General between 1958 and 1969. Even though these were flying visits, these pilgrimages through France could—thanks to a single speech, a factory visit, a simple handshake—fix his image forever in local collective memory. To this space-memory was added a virtual dimension: de Gaulle was the first French president of the television age, and some of his performances (and that is the right word for them) left an indelible imprint on his viewers. When asked to name an image of the General that they spontaneously recall, many of those who witnessed it mention his speech of April 23, 1961, at the height of the Algerian War, when he appeared in military uniform to pour scorn on the "handful of retired generals" who had attempted a military coup against him (the mere appearance of the General on television, and his stern denunciation of the plotters, caused the coup to crumble rapidly).

To these temporal and spatial components of the General's legend we add a last key element: the epic register. De Gaulle's mythical power appears in his ability to produce sacredness in all its forms: in his own person, as in "I, General de Gaulle" (transcendence is already present in the 18th of June Appeal); in his invocation of the symbols of national glory that open the *War Memoirs,* such as Notre Dame, Versailles, the Arc de Triomphe, and the vault of the Invalides; and in the great moments of collective emotion, such as his walk down the Champs-Elysées in 1944 or, in more private moments of commemoration, the 18th of June anniversaries at the mont Valérien. And what does the huge cross of Lorraine erected at Colombey after the General's death represent, if not a symbol of de Gaulle's hallowed status? This sacredness was reinforced by the constant invocation of its opposite—profanation. Like all great political legends, Gaullism knew how to make use of negative representations, drawing the line between good and bad Frenchmen, between grandeur and mediocrity, honor and humiliation, renewal and decadence. Behind these antinomies lay the specter of the old eschatological opposition—firmly rooted in the traditions of his "old and dear country"—between Good and Evil, which was already apparent in the discourse of wartime Gaullism and was revived under the Fourth Republic in certain aspects of the language of the Gaullist movement.[57] Even after 1958, after de Gaulle's return to power, this tendency did not completely disappear. As we noted earlier, the General could use demonization so effectively that he created a long-standing hostility toward the Americans and even managed to revive the old tradition of Anglophobia in certain layers of public opinion. Among the 40,000 or so letters he received on his resignation in April 1969, we quote from this one: "Perfidious Albion may be crowing now, but one day we'll knock her off her perch. She destroyed the Emperor Napoleon, now she wants to destroy France. But the time is coming when we'll make her pay."[58] Let us note in passing—this is one of the recurring themes of our work—the comparison with Napoleon, which often occurred in popular representations of the General, alongside (notably) Joan of Arc and Louis XIV, but also republican heroes such as Carnot and Clemenceau, war leaders who had defended French soil against foreign invasion.

This range of historical references shows the great adaptability of the mythical General. If de Gaulle could be, as the above example shows, the emblem of jingoistic patriotism, he could also be transfigured as a universal symbol of humanistic values. Juan Rousseau Portalis, a decorated veteran from the Resistance era, found himself in a little up-country village in Venezuela at the time of the General's death in 1970. He was astonished to discover that the local schoolmistress, as soon as she heard the news, had flown the school flag at half-mast and dictated to her pupils a eulogy of the Great Man.[59] Such symbolic combinations were by no means the result of chance. On the contrary, one of the great diachronic forces of the Gaullian myth was its ability to carry on a creative dialogue, both explicit and latent, with all the great components of the French political tradition, from monarchism to communism, as well as the Revolution of 1789 and the Napoleonic legend: hence its ability to assimilate and then to synthesize in the General's person the continuing ideals of French political culture. As we shall see in the following pages, de Gaulle could embody, at the same time and sometimes in the same set of representations, a whole array of contrasting figures: the haughty monarch and the homely head of state; the symbol of grandeur and the image of Christian humility; the face of authority and the voice of insubordination; the ideal of the just and the figure of the avenger; the standard of chivalric values and the personification of popular sovereignty; the example of military glory and the pacifier of a wounded nation; the providential man and the guarantor of public interest; the prudent legislator and the prophet of apocalyptic fury; the cold-hearted monster and the man of passion.

CHAPTER 2

✿

Hail to the Liberator

"Having the chance to write to you, to let you know something of our admiration and gratitude, to cry aloud the faith we have in you, is a dream come true. But how can we begin to tell you everything that has been filling our hearts since that dreadful evening in June 1940, when everything we loved, everything we hoped for, seemed to be disappearing for ever? Ever since then, you have been the incarnation of France for us, a France true to herself, to her past, her traditions, her heroes, her thinkers, immortal France, France, in a word."[1]

At the time, in 1942, when he received this fervent expression of support from "a group of Frenchwomen in the occupied zone," General de Gaulle, the head of the Free France movement,[2] was still little known inside the country. Two years after his appeal to continue the struggle in 1940, the Man of the 18th of June was isolated in his London exile. Denounced by the Vichy government, where Marshal Pétain was still genuinely popular, and viewed with increasing suspicion by Washington, de Gaulle was supported only by the British government and some parts of the French overseas empire that had rallied to his cause. Even British support was conditional and intermittent, and by 1943 Churchill was attempting to have de Gaulle "eliminated" from the leadership of the Free French, calling him a "marplot and mischief-maker" and a "vain and malignant man who hates England." Not surprisingly, the General confessed later that his memory of the early years of Free France was one of "unbelievable loneliness."[3] The war years were therefore marked by a quest for three kinds of recognition: first, of his political authority over the Resistance; second, of his exclusive right to represent France on the international stage; and third, of his own popular legitimacy in France itself. We concentrate on the last of those here. This domestic legitimacy was essential for de Gaulle, who wrote: "the effective support, freely given, for Free France of thousands of French citizens and millions of French subjects [in the overseas empire], along with the evident sympathy of the great majority of French men and women in France itself, constitute a kind of ongoing election which justifies our authority."[4] We see how, through his deeds, speeches, and messages, de Gaulle constantly sought this support, notably by elaborating an heroic and idealized vision of France. It was from this double movement—the charismatic discourse of the General and the multiple echoes it found in the French collective imagination—that the mythical figure of Charles de Gaulle first emerged, finding its consecration as Liberator during the summer and autumn of 1944.

The letter of 1942 points to the development of this heroic image of de Gaulle. Here the chief of Free France already appears as the "only spokesman and representative of the nation" and also as the incarnation of its strongest values (courage, loyalty, steadfastness, justice, freedom) and as the savior of the fatherland, "sent by Providence." The letter dwells especially on the General's voice, whose particular tones, "warm and commanding," had sounded in the darkness to "save the honour of the French name."[5] In the construction of this first messianic persona, a decisive part was played by Charles de Gaulle's voice, transmitted to France thanks to his wireless broadcasts. Between 1940 and 1944 de Gaulle spoke sixty-seven times on the radio (first from London and then from Algiers) and no fewer than twenty times in the months of June and July 1940 alone.[6] It is not surprising, therefore, that the qualities of the General's voice were singled out in the early formulations of his legend. "Your voice is the only one to speak out firmly and clearly,"[7] a school headmistress wrote to him in August 1940; an "incisive and sonorous voice," which had "awakened France," an anonymous poem added.[8] For one group of refugees in the Auvergne, the General's voice could "restore the morale of Frenchmen" but also "destroy the lies planted by the Germans in the newspapers."[9] Another correspondent summed up public feeling in his neighborhood in this way: "When they know you are going to be speaking on the radio, they are all there to listen, their ears stuck to the set, feverishly waiting to hear your voice which gives them the sublime hope of deliverance near at hand." That letter concludes: "They would like to hear your voice more often, they have placed all their hopes in you, they await you like the Messiah."[10]

To raise such a sense of optimism and defiance among the people, while rallying the French under his banner, was the program de Gaulle set for himself from the very beginning of his odyssey. In 1940, in his Appeal of June 18th, which sought to "stir up the flame of Resistance,"[11] de Gaulle tried to keep hope alive by exhorting the French to continue the struggle against the German occupier and the collaborators of Vichy. At the same time, the head of Free France was careful to define himself as the incarnation of all the living forces of the country: "In the face of the confusion of French spirits, in the face of a government fallen into dissolution under the enemy's heel, I, General de Gaulle, as soldier and French chief, am conscious that I speak in the name of France."[12]

This representation of the charismatic figure of the "chief," which is a key concept in wartime Gaullist discourse, is also to be found, in fascinating and complex forms, in the General's public utterances—fascinating because it is here, in the speeches and messages of the 1940–1944 period, that the real Gaullian doctrine on this point took shape. It differed both from that of his prewar writings, notably *The Edge of the Sword* (where the word *chief* was essentially understood in its military application), and from the smooth formulae of the later *War Memoirs*, where de Gaulle was already addressing posterity. It was complex because although he had to affirm his authority, de Gaulle also had to proceed carefully: first, in order not to offend the susceptibilities of the Resistance inside France, and second, to avoid any disagreeable echoes of the "providential" rhetoric of Petain's Vichy supporters (to say nothing of the fascist model). After all, in an article published in 1943, which referred to the Bonapartist tradition but was obviously aimed at de Gaulle, Raymond Aron warned against "the adventure of a single man," which had so often led to "the tragedy of a nation."[13]

De Gaulle presented himself above all as a war leader, who had "picked up the broken sword"[14] let fall by the men of Vichy; in August 1940, having signed an agreement with the British government, he undertook to "organize a French land, sea and air force to fight alongside the Allies."[15] All the armed actions of the Free French were greeted as real military feats achieved under his command—notably the taking of Tobruk in January 1941, when de Gaulle underlined explicitly, not once but twice, that he and he only was "their Chief,"[16] and in May 1943, when he saluted "the important and glorious part" played by French troops in the final defeat of the German and Italian forces in Africa.[17] Gaullist propaganda never tired of representing de Gaulle as a great military leader. Two examples come to mind: first, the BBC broadcast *Les Français parlent aux Français* of May 20, 1941, which was devoted to General de Gaulle's actions during the fighting around Laon in 1940. The portrait painted was an epic one, as the following extract shows: "On the May 16, General de Gaulle establishes his headquarters at Bruyères, near Laon. As he stands there in his leather coat, a helmet on his head, his tall figure is silhouetted against the sky like, in the distance, the twin gothic towers of Laon cathedral. He smokes one cigarette after another and his binoculars never leave his eyes."[18] Another example is the BBC's first program in Arabic about the Free French Forces, broadcast in 1943. It opened with: "What is Free France? First and foremost, it is its chief, young, energetic and already venerated, General Charles de Gaulle. Wounded and taken prisoner in the last war, he is the first military chief to have understood the importance of motor transport, tanks and aeroplanes in modern war."[19]

A young war leader and a great strategist, de Gaulle also put himself forward as the protector of the French Empire, a "vital element" for France's future grandeur.[20] At Brazzaville he saluted the Empire's "civilizing mission,"[21] and all attempts by America and Britain to question France's "rights" over her foreign territories were energetically repulsed.[22] This warlike, individualistic, and heroic discourse was sometimes replaced by more collective language. Before the Franco-British Committee of the House of Commons in February 1941, the General cast himself as a "soldier" who might have "felt some reluctance to raise his voice in this place, had he not known that his mouth, left free exceptionally and by chance, could speak for a gagged nation."[23] Above all, when speaking of the Resistance, the General tended to use the first-person plural: The military chief's "I" then became a collective "we."[24] In Cairo, in April 1941, he declared to journalists: "We are the temporary but determined trustees of the French patrimony."[25] But that this title to legitimacy had come about by chance in no way diminished its strength—quite the opposite, in fact. For de Gaulle had a profound sense that he was expressing the collective sentiment of the nation. He declared as much on the fourth anniversary of his rebellion, in 1944: "If the appeal of the 18th of June has taken on the meaning that it has, it is simply because the French nation chose to listen and respond to it; it is because, in spite of the nation's sufferings, honour, victory, freedom remained at the heart of its instinctive will."[26] It is worth noting here, as the war was drawing to a close, the incipient mythologization of the 18th of June: A broadcast that had been heard by only a very small minority of French people in 1940 had now become, by the magic wand of de Gaulle's rhetoric, a speech that had been heard and acted on by the entire "French nation."

It is this same context that allows us to grasp the pedagogic dimension of Gaullian wartime discourse, for the chief's role was not only to lead but to explain and clarify, first, the meaning of the conflict. Three notions are recurrent in this Gaullian didacticism: the idea that this was a world war, which still gave France a chance of victory despite its painful military defeat in 1940; that it was part of a long history of military conflict (de Gaulle declared in September 1941, "In fact the world has been at war for thirty years, for or against the universal domination of Germanism"[27]); and that what was ultimately at stake in the conflict was "the life or death of Western civilisation."[28] And what was the basis of this civilization? Throughout the whole war, de Gaulle hammered out the same reply: "freedom"[29]—a political principle founded by the French Revolution and shared by all the democracies[30] and a moral principle that bound together all the forces fighting against Hitlerian "slavery."[31] Inspired by his wartime readings, this contrast—classically republican, we should note—between liberty and tyranny was the foundation stone of Gaullian thought. It also allowed the General to draw from the rich national store of exemplary historic figures and to define the true moral and political values that should inspire the action of the chief. Thus, from the very first weeks, de Gaulle was appealing to and mobilizing French history to condemn the shameful terms of the armistice signed by the Pétain-led French government in 1940: "Would Joan of Arc, Richelieu, Louis XIV, Carnot, Napoleon, Gambetta, Poincaré, Clemenceau, Marshal Foch ever have agreed to hand over all France's arms to her enemies, to be used against her Allies?"[32] Obviously a rhetorical question.

In fact, this kind of recourse to history had a threefold purpose for de Gaulle. It allowed him to stigmatize Vichy and highlight its "anti-French" character and to project an idealized image of the "soul of France,"[33] so as to encourage hope and promote political commitment. But the exercise was also, and primarily, an autobiographical one: By means of his gallery of tutelary figures, de Gaulle was defining himself and drawing his own portrait, and revealing (in a subliminal fashion) his political and moral ideas to his fellow citizens. Before the war, his favorite historical icon had been Joan of Arc, and de Gaulle constantly referred to her image after

1940, the more determinedly as Vichy tried to claim her for itself. The Marshal's regime went on celebrating the Festival of Joan (an official anniversary of the Third Republic) as a means of cultivating nationalism, Anglophobia, religious piety, and monarchist feeling.[34] In town halls, certain enthusiastic followers of the new regime even tried to replace the busts of Marianne with those of Joan of Arc, "saint of the fatherland."[35] In Gaullian discourse, it was a very different Joan who appeared: a symbol of national unity, of course, but above all a sublime incarnation of the "holy fury of France,"[36] which inspired the resistance and the military combat against the Germans. She also personified two key virtues in the Gaullian scheme of values: "intransigence in honour."[37] On May 10, 1942, the celebration of the Festival of Joan of Arc allowed the revelation of the perfect osmosis between de Gaulle and the Maid of Orléans, whose political mission exactly reflected his: "to open the eyes of the nation, oppressed by the enemy and divided against itself."[38]

However, de Gaulle was aware that Joan of Arc, even dressed in the martial garb of the Resistance, was a figure of the nationalist ideological heritage—or, more precisely, she personified the conservative turn taken by French republicanism after 1919. Thus so as not to be trapped in a purely traditionalist symbolic system, his speeches also appealed to the progressive aspects of the republican heritage in France[39]—not the reified tradition of the waning Third Republic, with which de Gaulle felt little sympathy, but that of the "fatherland in danger" personified first by Danton and the Committee of Public Safety and then in 1870 by Gambetta and the "men of National Defence," who "took power temporarily in the name of the Republic so as to direct the nation's efforts in war."[40] Already, at the beginning of June 1940, de Gaulle had drawn upon this Revolutionary heritage when he urged Paul Reynaud to maintain his resolve: "We are on the edge of the abyss [...] Be Carnot or we shall perish."[41] But this invocation of the French Revolution's successful defeat of foreign invaders was not simply a defensive posture. De Gaulle wanted to "re-establish all French liberties in their totality and have the laws of the Republic observed"[42] so as to form a "true democracy" with a "new leadership"[43] drawn from the Resistance. Defining in 1942 his political aims for the renewal of France, de Gaulle did not hesitate to appeal directly to the memory of the "great French Revolution": "It is a revolution," he noted, "the greatest in her history, which France, betrayed by her ruling élites and her privilege-holders, is beginning to accomplish."[44]

With Joan of Arc on his right hand and the Revolution on his left, de Gaulle completed his imaginary pantheon with Clemenceau and Foch, two emblematic heroic figures of the great war—an inevitable historical reference for his generation and the determining period in forming the General's imagination. Often cited alongside Joan of Arc, the Tiger (as Clemenceau was affectionately known) was also called upon at particularly dark moments, as in October 1941, when the Wehrmacht was making its lightning advance on the Soviet Union: "This is the time to grit our teeth, to keep our nerves and tongues under control, and to redouble our efforts on all fronts, as we did before at Clemenceau's behest."[45] In March 1942, de Gaulle explicitly compared the situation to 1917, warning that "Clemenceau's hour would soon strike" and calling for "the attacking, intransigent spirit without which any war is lost."[46] If the "Père-la-Victoire,"[47] to whom the speech of November 11, 1941, was dedicated,[48] personified the civilian side of this tenacity, its military aspect was represented by Marshal Foch. The "exemplarity" of the victor of November 11 was often celebrated by de Gaulle during the war years, and not only in the national context: De Gaulle used the anniversary of his death to remind the Americans that "united effort" under his leadership had allowed the Allies to triumph in the Great War.[49] Foch was therefore presented as the symbol of French courage and military genius but also of a truly Gaullian obstinacy: Had he not won the war "by sheer force of will"?[50]

In contrast with his June 18, 1940, broadcast, General de Gaulle's ensuing speeches and messages were widely echoed in French public opinion during the occupation years, though it is impossible to measure the scope of their impact precisely. People listened to de Gaulle's voice in private, often in secret (beginning in October 1940 the Vichy authorities forbade any listening to the British radio in a public place).[51] Furthermore, according to the intelligence of the Vichy authorities, Gaullist propaganda was not as well structured as the communists' and circulated chiefly by word of mouth.[52] The General's speeches on the BBC also became less frequent: In 1943—more evidence of his troubled relationship with his allies—he was even banned from the airwaves as a result of his disagreements with London and Washington, and it was only later in that year that Radio-Brazzaville acquired a transmitter strong enough to reach mainland France.[53] It is nevertheless true that signs of enthusiasm for the Gaullist cause were observable everywhere in France: This symbolic fervor was marked by the sending of letters to London, as well as various gestures of support and anti-Vichy speeches.

The most direct sign of support took the form of letters sent to the General by individuals. They began to arrive—in small numbers—in the summer of 1940, and some were read on the BBC radio program *Les Français parlent aux Français.*[54] Maurice Schumann, one of the main broadcasters, made them the subject of one of his radio talks at the beginning of August: "Your letters have reached us. We read them and re-read them every day. And simply reading the place-names at the head of your messages—Grenoble or Albi, Bourgueil or Sainte-Suzanne—we feel our strength redoubled as we touch the earth—the earth of France."[55] An important point to note is that radio propaganda, overseen by a London Committee, struck an essentially "republican and democratic" note, tending to dwell on the signs of support given for Free France as a collective entity, rather than marks of enthusiasm for the General in person.[56] But such enthusiasm did exist. As well as expressing gratitude to de Gaulle, the letters talked about a variety of other subjects. The General's broadcasts were commented on ("we listen with interest to your daily broadcasts");[57] he was informed of the difficulty of finding food or was given detailed advice, for example, about the best way of having propaganda dropped by Free French pilots or the Royal Air Force.[58] Above all, he was informed about the high politics of the day: In January 1941, a correspondent in Lyon denounced the behavior of "unworthy Frenchmen" (an expression regularly used by de Gaulle during the early years of the occupation), while rejoicing in the "failing morale" of the Germans and the spread of "passive resistance" in France, together with the support for Free France being given by "Mr Churchill and President Roosevelt" (this last no doubt prompting a bitter smile from de Gaulle).[59] Someone writing from the Haute-Savoie referred to the approaching discomfiture of the occupying Italians: "The 'Eyeties' have all got long faces: they took us Savoyards for biscuits but now they're learning different."[60] Brave estimates were also put forward about the state of local public opinion: The same Savoyard writer thought that "eight out of ten peasants are thinking and acting like Frenchmen, real Frenchmen,"[61] while another letter suggested that "in Auvergne 75% are for you."[62] These figures obviously cannot be verified and were almost certainly inflated, but they expressed the fervor of these ordinary correspondents and their wish to send useful and uplifting information to the General.

These letters often offered remarkable personal testimonies. One that obviously held General de Gaulle's attention[63] was written on March 15, 1942, by an elderly inhabitant of Grasse, Gervaise Carminat. She painted a detailed picture of the situation in the Alpes-Maritimes: If her assessment of the movement of opinion in favor of the Free French was no doubt optimistic ("the great majority of people of the worker and peasant classes are fervent supporters of the Gaullist cause"), she also spoke precisely and eloquently about the brutal exploitation of artisans, the shortages of coal and basic foodstuffs, the working of the black market, and the frightening increase in tuberculosis among children. Picking up on a point in one of de Gaulle's recent radio broadcasts about the treachery of the men of Vichy who were "dismembering France physically and morally in order to sustain the enemy,"[64] she told how the local authorities were surreptitiously sending wheat to Italy packed in wine barrels. She also drew a vivid picture of the feasting habits of the local dignitaries: "I saw the gentlemen from the Prefecture sit down to an elaborate luncheon, with oysters, snails, veal cutlets, carrots in cream, sauerkraut, salad, cheese, fruit—apples, pears, mandarins, grapes, almonds and figs—all washed down with vintage wines, while the poor souls at the neighbouring tables had to make do with a few tasteless plain boiled vegetables." She concluded ironically, "To think that our new masters in the New Order accuse the Third Republic of having been the 'Old Pals' Republic!!!"[65]

An iconography of the General rapidly took shape after June 1940, organized by the various information and propaganda arms of Free France,[66] but also more spontaneously in France itself, at the initiative of groups and individuals. De Gaulle was so little known in 1940 that some of his first supporters did not even know how to spell his name: We find them writing "Degaulle," "De Gaule," or even "Degaul."[67] At the Liberation, among the thousands of letters received by the General's secretariat, we find even quainter variants: "Henri de Gaulle," "Général Dugaul," or "Charles De Gull."[68] Many had not the least idea what he looked like. To see the General's image, they had to wait until it was circulated in *Le Courrier de l'Air*,[69] a periodical produced by the British propaganda services and dropped over France every week by the Royal Air Force.[70] Others found more ingenious methods, like the young resistance fighter Lucien Neuwirth, who went to visit Marie-Agnès Cailliau, the General's sister, who, like Neuwirth, lived in the town of Saint-Etienne. She dug out a photograph of the then-Colonel de Gaulle for Neuwirth, taken when de

Gaulle was commanding the garrison at Metz. Thus the first portraits of the General began to circulate in the free zone.[71] These images, often of poor quality,[72] were sometimes decorated with the cross of Lorraine (the symbol of Free France). They were distributed throughout France, often through clandestine networks, and were used in various symbolic demonstrations of Gaullism. During the occupation, for example, Alice Bornet's husband was a prisoner of war in Austria, and she worked in a business under German administration. She pinned up a picture of the General inside a cupboard in her office, under the German manager's nose; she said afterward that looking at this portrait had given her the "hope and strength" to "carry on and win."[73] Portraits of their hero were even hidden by prisoners of war in Germany. One former prisoner, imprisoned in Germany with two comrades in 1941–1942, would afterward describe their lives in a letter to the General:

> How could we spend the endless hours of Sunday? Well, in the afternoon we would all get onto the top bunk of a three-decker, and there we would open a suitcase with a false bottom where there was a fine big picture of General de Gaulle that one of my friends from Le Havre had got hold of. We would sit and look at the photograph and talk about how the war was going: we were sure it would end in the defeat of Hitler's armies. These long discussions made us optimistic about the outcome of the war, and we tried to spread this optimism among our fellow prisoners. Every Sunday for two years we looked at the hidden picture, and the Germans, in spite of all their searches, never got hold of it.[74]

Alongside this private cult, General de Gaulle also inspired various public forms of symbolic resistance. Recent scholarship on the early history of the French Resistance has underlined the strength of Gaullist popular support, as expressed for example through seditious inscriptions and the dissemination of flysheets in public areas.[75] The General's name was repeatedly shouted at the first street demonstration against the Germans, on November 11, 1940, in Paris;[76] on the same occasion the high-school boy Igor de Schotten laid out an enormous wreath in the shape of the cross of Lorraine, prepared by the florist Charles Landrat.[77] As for the leader of the Free French, although de Gaulle had stated in 1940 that there "could be no more celebrations for a great people enslaved,"[78] he did not hesitate later to recommend the observance of important events in the commemorative calendar, notably July 14, the anniversary of the French Revolution, and June 18, the launching date of his odyssey.[79] Above all, he took his inspiration from a classic tactic in the French repertoire of protest: the taking-over and subversion of official events. Specific instructions were given. Thus de Gaulle called upon the French—it was his own idea[80]—to mark the date of January 1, 1941, by an "hour of hope," asking those living in the free zone to stay at home between 2:00 and 3:00 in the afternoon and those in the occupied zone to do the same between 3:00 and 4:00.[81] The great success of this operation encouraged the General to continue. In 1942, on the occasion of the First of May celebrations (a national holiday under Vichy), he asked Frenchmen and women to walk past the statues of the Republic and the town halls from half past six in the evening onward—we note here not only the republican symbolism but the recognition of communal institutions as sites of popular sovereignty.[82] On November 11, 1942, the actions planned for Victory Day had to be suspended because of the German invasion of the free zone, but de Gaulle expressed the wish that, between midday and half past, the French would all bring together their thoughts and prayers "for the freedom, the integrity and the greatness" of their country.[83]

Beyond their political character, these gestures had wider aims: to disseminate the Gaullist message while refusing to surrender the public space completely to the Germans and their Vichy henchmen—or to the French Communist Party, which was traditionally very active in commandeering public events for protest purposes. The object was also to show the effectiveness of "civil resistance"—a less dangerous method than the armed struggle the Communists were demanding and that provoked harsh reprisals by the Germans throughout the war. Joan of Arc's Day, celebrated with splendor by Vichy, thus became the favorite occasion for affirming the presence of Gaullism on the ground. In 1941, the General had the BBC broadcast messages appealing for "a huge demonstration of national unanimity" on May 11, with these clear instructions: "On that day, from three to four in the afternoon, Frenchmen and women will be on all the public walks of our towns and villages. They will go individually, or in families, or in groups of friends; they will not form processions; they will walk in complete silence, but as they look into each other's eyes their looks will express their common determination."[84] The appeal met with a considerable response in the parts of France where Gaullism was strong, notably in the Paris region and in Bordeaux. In Rennes, thousands of people walked back and forth between the Place de la Republique and Valton's grocery in the rue d'Antrain, carrying bunches of red, white, and blue flowers. The furious local authorities arrested more than 100 people.[85]

Actions like these—sometimes spontaneous, sometimes inspired from abroad or masterminded by local Gaullist organizations—marked all the Vichy public rituals until 1944. The 11th of November commemorations (marking the end of the First World War) could thus be transformed into moments of Gaullist affirmation. Leaflets, pictures, stickers, wreath-layings at war memorials, singing the Marseillaise, displaying the cross of Lorraine banners (in 1943, a group of underground fighters turned up in Bourg-en-Bresse and hung one around the bust of Marianne, the feminine allegorical symbol of the Republic)[86]—all these served to reclaim the public space, sometimes with dramatic results. On November 11, 1943, after the laying of wreaths, which the Germans considered a provocation, several hundred demonstrators were arrested in Grenoble and deported.[87] Historic monuments were also the scene of Gaullist demonstrations—both implicit, like the theft by the underground fighters at Le Puy of the statue of Lafayette, the hero of the American and French Revolutions, which the Germans were intending to melt down (it was solemnly returned to its pedestal at the Liberation, in the presence of two representatives of General de Gaulle),[88] and explicit, as when on one 11th of November the lawyer André Weil-Curiel laid a wreath at the statue of Clemenceau in Paris with a gigantic white card a meter long bearing this simple message: "From General de Gaulle."[89] If such gestures were impossible, as they were for most people, the General's fervent supporters could fall back on an enduring element of the national antifestive tradition: the writing of seditious inscriptions in public places. In 1941, in the Alsatian town of Hochfelden, under German occupation, an anonymous hand wrote "Avenue Général de Gaulle" on the wall of the priest's house. The gesture was prophetic: Four years later the street would be officially renamed in honor of the Liberator.[90]

"We have been recognized." These were de Gaulle's typically laconic words when, on his arrival on French soil in June 1944, he was saluted by two gendarmes on the road to Bayeux.[91] Already the virtual incarnation of "republican legality," the General became its effective symbol when he showed himself in the Paris uprising in 1944, confirming his political triumph by highly symbolic gestures like reoccupying Clemenceau's old office in the War Ministry[92] and leading the march down the Champs-Elysées—as well as by a gesture he did not make: his refusal to proclaim the Republic. In his view, the Vichy regime had been illegal: During the four years of the occupation, national sovereignty had been devolved to the Free French, who had become its temporary custodians. In 1944, the Republic did thus not need to be proclaimed: It had never ceased to exist. This remained the official French view of the 1940–1944 period until the late twentieth century.

If this Parisian period confirmed his occupation of power in two crucial aspects (the international recognition of his legitimacy and the neutralization of any attempt to establish an insurrectionary government), one essential dimension of de Gaulle's political authority remained to be secured: recognition by the people. For the military chief who had become president of the provisional government of the Republic was perfectly conscious of a key fact in French political history: Though power could be seized in Paris, it would not hold for any length of time unless it was anchored in the "real country." Between September and October 1944, de Gaulle therefore undertook a series of journeys through the provinces. Beyond his immediate political aims (to impose his authority on the local authorities and resistance groups), the essential objective was to show himself to his compatriots (most of whom knew him only as a disembodied voice on the airwaves) and by this means to seal the mystical union between his person and the French people. As he declared in Nancy, in September 1944, "I have had the honour of seeing you, you have seen me, you have heard me speak. We are in agreement, aren't we, just as we are in agreement with Paris, Marseille, Toulouse, Bordeaux, Lille, Strasbourg?"[93] He was given a prodigious reception everywhere and was welcomed by huge crowds of men and women who sometimes made exhausting journeys to set eyes on him. In early October 1944, a woman wrote to him before his arrival in the town of Lisieux, "Tomorrow my daughter and I will get on our bikes and come to see you pass by; riding the eleven miles will be a pleasure, for we are coming to cheer you on."[94]

What did all this popular enthusiasm signify, and what does it reveal about de Gaulle's place in the collective imagination during these summer and autumn months of 1944, as his wartime legend was crystallizing? Some answers can be found in the torrent of homages addressed to the Liberator during this period by men and women of all political persuasions. In these thousands of letters and poems, the effusive addresses from local councils, and also in the absolute determination to name public squares and avenues, and even fishing boats,[95] after him, an heroic image of the General was taking shape throughout France: strikingly resplendent in some respects, yet at the same time fluid, fragile, and contradictory, and already foreshadowing the dissonances to come.

An example is a typical speech such as that delivered by Monsieur Roche, mayor of Courbevoie in the Paris suburbs, on November 11, 1944, to mark the inauguration of the new Avenue Charles de Gaulle connecting his locality to the neighboring commune of Puteaux. In his celebration of the Liberator, the mayor faithfully rehearsed all the themes of the Gaullian legend: his "military genius" in the realm of strategy, which had particularly shown itself in his "victorious advance" during the battle of Crécy-sur-Serre in May 1940; his refusal to see the nation "enslaved" after the armistice of 1940; his appeal of the 18th of June (already an obligatory reference), in virtue of which the General had been "officially delegated by the Republic to carry on the struggle" (an elegant turn of phrase, whose vagueness probably reflected the embarrassment of this good republican in the face of political and military insubordination); and finally his emergence as the "undisputed chief of all the French resistance." In his peroration, the mayor drew abundantly from the fund of images of wartime Gaullism, describing de Gaulle as the "worthy successor" of a long line of French civilian and military heroes from the 1790s to the First World War, including Carnot and Foch.[96]

Throughout France, these local manifestations of recognition and gratitude all had a common foundation: the recovery of national sovereignty, celebrated in the heroic figure of the General, the illustrious Liberator, about whose martial qualities the mayor of Sète waxed lyrical in December 1944: a "great soldier," "far-sighted" and "unyielding," whose claims to glory were "too fresh in all our minds for me to have to list them."[97] In Ligny (Meuse), the authorities renamed one of the main streets after General de Gaulle, "the first voice of the French Resistance, and the first to put his hand to the liberation of the soil of the fatherland." The Allies were not forgotten, and the road from which the "glorious American liberators" had entered to take the town was renamed "Rue des Etats-Unis."[98] But such broad-mindedness was not the rule everywhere: In the collective consciousness a myth was already taking shape of a country "freed by its own people," helped only by "the armies of France," as de Gaulle had boldly insisted in his populist speech at the Hôtel de Ville in Paris in August 1944.[99] The idea was taken up again by the commune of Palavas-les-Flots (Hérault) when it decided to name its main street after the chief of the Free French "since General de Gaulle and his armies liberated France from the German invader."[100] At Bazas (Gironde), to give their full significance to the events of 1944, the former Cours Thiers, named after the French leader who reconstructed the country after the ravages of the 1870–1871 conflicts, was rechristened after General de Gaulle: a symbolic replacement of one national liberator by another.[101] At Toulouse, it was the magnificent Place du Capitole that the mayor proposed to rename after the Liberator, so as to "symbolise the resurrection of France, and the immutable continuity of her historic mission."[102] The language of the commune of Cappelle (Nord) was even more grandiloquent, as it paid homage to General de Gaulle, "that great soldier of the Resistance, who through his great love of France has saved not only our beautiful country and our beloved Republic, but Europe, the World and civilisation from the *Boches* and from the poison of Nazism."[103]

As liberator and savior, de Gaulle also symbolized a sentiment that occurs repeatedly in the discourse of local officials: pride—pride in national sovereignty regained, of course, but also the flowering through the figure of de Gaulle of a whole range of local patriotisms. Alongside the General, municipal councils often honored leading figures of the local resistance: Toulouse, for example, named streets of the city after Captain Pélissier, François Verdier, Lucien Cassagne, and Jacques Sauvegrain, all "martyrs of the Liberation."[104] Sometimes this desire for exemplarity struck a discordant note, as at Cysoing (Nord), where the mayor could not conceal his anger from the Prefect, who seemed to want to deny him the right to honor the Liberator, even though neighboring communes had been allowed to do so. "Cysoing, which made a large contribution to the resistance, should at least have the honour of naming one of its streets after the General. You will note that the communes of Louvril and Bouvines, particularly the latter, which never produced a group of resistance fighters, have been allowed to give the General's name to one of the streets of their commune. I do not see, therefore, why Cysoing [the main locality in the canton] should be denied the same privilege."[105] Some refusals produced real psychodramas in the locality, as at Fontaine-sous-Préaux (Seine-Inférieure), where the mayor's deputy addressed a long complaint directly to the Liberator: "I take the liberty of informing the General that as a result of the refusal we have suffered we are all somewhat at a loss." He stressed that "the square we have chosen is thoroughly suitable, for where could the names of our heroes who fell in defence of the sacred soil be better placed than next to that of our great and venerated chief?" before concluding with an almost desperate plea: "We have already bought the plaque and the pillars needed for the inauguration—must they go to waste? Surely not."[106]

Such local pride could also be incarnated in de Gaulle himself. In his home region of the Nord, an inhabitant of his native town of Lille sent him a poem in September 1944 that expressed the feeling of the locals: "France is the country of your birth:/And all free France shares in your joy./But prouder still are we of the North/To see her freed by a Northern boy."[107] Not to be outdone, the city council of Lille announced to all and sundry its intention to inaugurate a "Place du Général de Gaulle" in October 1944.[108] The decision snowballed, and in the following months several communes of the Nord hurried to give the name of the local boy, now the "great chief and symbol of the French nation,"[109] to their avenue, street, or main square; this pride of the "people of the Nord" in the prodigious epic of the Man of the 18th of June also recurred often in letters to the General. Another source of their delight was the return of the "republican spirit," of "democracy," which now, thanks to the General, as the mayor of Villeveyrac reminded his audience, "could take its rightful place once more in a commune which had too long remained in the hands of its enemies."[110] It was a pride sometimes tinged with embarrassment, even with remorse, since the streets now being named after the General were often those that during the occupation had borne the name of Marshal Pétain. At Villeveyrac, in fact, the Place du maréchal Pétain was quickly rechristened Place de la République—but in Bordeaux and Fronsac (Gironde), in Alès (Gard) and Loulay (Charente-Maritime), the General replaced the Marshal from one day to the next. Sometimes local people took the initiative, as can be seen from the minutes of the town council of Villeneuve-la-Comtesse (Charente-Maritime), which on September 24, 1944, unanimously ratified "the population's wish, expressed on the seventeenth of September, to change the name of the main square from 'Place Maréchal Pétain' to 'Place Charles de Gaulle,' this to remain its name in perpetuity."[111]

These changes of nomenclature are evidence of a variety of things: of a certain feeling of guilt at having succumbed to the prevailing *pétainisme* of the first years of the war, but also of a certain abiding providentialist sentiment in France. A mere few months apart in 1944, had not the Paris crowds cheered first Marshal Pétain and then General de Gaulle? At the same time, France, which gave its overwhelming support to de Gaulle in the first months of the Liberation, did so in the hope, first, of a rapid improvement in its living conditions. The fulsome tributes from the communes sometimes barely concealed demands for assistance. Thus, the mayor of Wissant (Pas de Calais) wrote to "Général de Gaule" [*sic*] in

January 1945 to tell him that the town hall square had been renamed after him (one hopes the plaque was correctly spelled on this occasion), before adding,

> I take this opportunity of humbly informing you of the present state of our village, whose fields, gardens, dunes, beach and houses are still mined and covered everywhere with traps of all kinds. All these devices prevent us from resuming normal life and are a danger for our children. Our beautiful seaside villas, the part of the village towards Calais from the Bellevue hotel and the part on the Marquise road have been destroyed by the enemy. Our church and the houses around it have been damaged. All we want is to bring all this back to life. With that aim in view, we beg you to use your high authority to help us rebuild our dear Wissant.[112]

Between the summer of 1944 and the end of the war in May 1945, de Gaulle the Liberator also represented for thousands of women, wives, and mothers a supreme hope: that of seeing the return home of their beloved combatants and prisoners of war, many of whose families had had no news of them for years. These relatives wrote the General hundreds of letters, many of them heartbreaking, asking for his help in finding a son in the navy, not heard of since 1943,[113] or the body of a husband, head of the resistance in Lisieux, shot by the Germans in November 1943 and whose place of burial remained unknown.[114] Pathetic evidence of the dreadful anguish caused by the war, these letters also expressed hope in a miraculous intervention by the head of government. And when, from May 1945 onward, the prisoners did begin to return to France from their captivity in Germany, their formal welcome by the local authorities often combined a tribute to their courage and sufferings with a demonstration of gratitude to General de Gaulle. At Saint-Magne, in the Gironde, the official unveiling of the plaque for the new Avenue du general de Gaulle coincided with the celebration of the "prisoners' return."[115]

The expectations were also, and above all, political. This was where tensions soon appeared—muted at first, it is true, but already suggestive of a certain fragility of the Gaullian image in public opinion. In his speech of November 11, 1944, the mayor of Courbevoie expressed his deep satisfaction "with the constitutional, political and economic commitments made by General de Gaulle" and added, "We know that in this area there may be resistance from the big bosses and backward-looking capitalists. There is still a battle to be won. But with General de Gaulle we shall win it, working together, driven by the love of our country and the ideal of social justice."[116] But while in September 1944 in his major speech at the Palais de Chaillot de Gaulle had indeed placed himself within the republican tradition, and had promised "profound reforms"[117] when the time was ripe (that is, the whole of France had been liberated), he had been careful not to give a precise definition of his political objectives. This vagueness allowed the local elites to represent the figure of de Gaulle in contrasting fashions: In one place, he was the "guarantor of republican legality," defined by the Prefect of the Nord region, Françis Closon, as "de Gaulle's greatest promise: to let the voice of the French people be heard again."[118] Elsewhere, the General's image was more ideologically robust, as at Saint-Macaire, in the Gironde, where the council displayed his portrait in the town hall, before writing to express the local population's entire confidence in him to "continue the work of reviving the greatness and prestige of France as a pure and uncompromising Republic."[119] In simpler terms, they expected him to carry out the program of the National Council of the Resistance, which had promised widespread economic and social reforms once French territory had been liberated.

One symbol of this hesitation between the stick and the carrot was the mayor of La Réole (Gironde), when announcing the naming of the new Esplanade du général de Gaulle in his commune, calling upon the head of the government to "punish without mercy all traitors, collaborators, black marketeers and hoarders" but at the same time to "silence our hatreds, our personal resentments, and to call on all Frenchmen of goodwill to build a new, republican France."[120] In more flowery language, a female social worker at Argenteuil expressed the same mixed feelings in a poem addressed to the General:

> We can't forget the failures, the defeats,
> The fatal selfishness of yesterday.
> But still your people lift their eyes and say,
> "They did not die in vain, our martyred men.
> General, with you to lead, a glorious day
> Awaits us: France will be great again."[121]

At the moment when these popular tributes were descending on him, de Gaulle could savor his triumph. The man who in London had been only a "pauper king"[122] had now brought off his wild gamble: to become the political and military chief of the Resistance, the only legitimate interlocutor with the great Allied powers, and the incarnation of the general will of the French people. The men who had followed him in the adventure of

Free France had very quickly grasped his unique powers: "that excessive quality that comes to him from being a visionary; he transcends the reality of the moment with a curious mixture of realism and prophetic inspiration."[123] But these political successes, remarkable as they were, had given birth to something even more prodigious: De Gaulle had become a living legend or, as Claude Mauriac, his private secretary, noted with wonder, "a kind of myth."[124] This phenomenon was illustrated by Lucien Nachin's book *Charles de Gaulle, General of France*, which had already gone through thirty editions by the autumn of 1944,[125] or the hagiographies that were already appearing, such as the *Extraordinary Life of General de Gaulle*,[126] or Robert Perrein's *A Great Frenchman, General de Gaulle*,[127] or Ludovic Bron's book, whose title says it all: *General de Gaulle, The Man Sent by Providence*.[128]

The new myth could most clearly be seen in the popular acclamations that met the General everywhere he went in France, in the flood of letters, addresses, and laudatory poems poured out in his honor, which rehearsed, often with great amplifications, the already classic themes of Gaullian messianism. In these tributes to the "man of miracle," the first thing celebrated was usually de Gaulle's voice, those "manly, prophetic tones that had revived our faith and our patriotic fervour."[129] A great chief appearing in the heavens "to guide our beloved France in the path traced out by Providence,"[130] the General was even compared for his military genius (legend demands exaggeration) to the "daring military strokes of Napoleon."[131] De Gaulle could also tickle the nationalist chords: He was "the reincarnation of our beloved Joan of Arc,"[132] in the direct line of those great figures that arise "throughout history to save the nation's soul."[133] The republican tradition was not left out: De Gaulle was celebrated as the glorious successor to such revolutionary military heroes as Lazare Hoche, Jean-Baptiste Kléber, and François-Séverin Marceau,[134] and as the man who would plant in the soil of France "a true, strong peace, Peace as the Republic once wanted it to be."[135]

Above all, he was the undisputed master, the Father, "standing in the sublime light of a triumph which will shine forth in History for ever."[136] Heedless of the "roll and crash of gunfire"[137] at Notre Dame in August 1944, the newly arrived General was "our leader, our Knight of Glory, our symbol, our God."[138] This was the most striking difference between the legend constructed by wartime Gaullism and the popular myth that sprang up at the Liberation. During the years 1940 to 1944, partly out of respect for the traditional republican separation between church and state and also in contrast to Vichy's self-flagellating rhetoric of a "sinful" France,[139] de Gaulle's speeches usually avoided overt references to religion. But now this did not prevent a host of representations of the General as an incarnation of the divine, a "superman sent by God"[140] to free France and the world from the "Satan who arose in 1939,"[141] or, in a common variation on the same theme, an almost Christ-like figure: "Alas, we saw him not, but still our hearts/Found out the way to him, and like a draught/ Of healing waters, then he gave us life/To follow in his footsteps."[142] Among the Frenchmen and -women who had heard the apostle of the 18th of June were many nuns, like the headmistress of a convent school at Le Dominelais (Ille-et-Vilaine), who heard the voice of the General on a clandestine radio and recognized in him the man "chosen by God to save France."[143]

How and why had this messianic cult emerged with such lightning speed? French national political culture had no doubt contributed to it, as a fighter in the French Resistance opportunely recalled: "At the most perilous moments of its history, France has always found the providential man."[144] This was as much as to say that if de Gaulle had not existed, someone would have had to invent him. Circumstances had certainly favored the Man of the 18th of June: Next to a Marshal Pétain whose prestige was fatally damaged by collaboration, a discredited republican political class, and a Communist Party whose general secretary Maurice Thorez had taken refuge in Moscow during the war years (and which, in any case, in the name of progressive values, rejected the very idea of providentialism), de Gaulle was the only man of any political standing who could play the part of national savior at the Liberation—and all the more so because he was new to politics, a "General above reproach bearing a name given by Destiny."[145] But the main reason for his success was the deliberate creation, by the General himself, of a specifically Gaullian mystique, a mixture of the symbolic and the discursive as powerful as it was subtle. Out of this compound, put together from scratch during the war years, de Gaulle built a system of representation that was taken up ever more enthusiastically by French public opinion and allowed him to stand out as a unique figure against his rivals and opponents while also appearing as the man who could bring together the values of all his fellow citizens. For if the Resistance expressed, in its diversity, the great collective ideals of the national tradition, de Gaulle represented its indispensable complement: the authority principle.[146] The use he made of the heroic figures of French history clearly reveals the astonishing political instinct of this newcomer to public life; his appropriation of them played a key role in the early years of the war, giving the General a historic solidity and also allowing him to put forward his own ideas and values. It is also notable that his historical references became increasingly less frequent, before disappearing almost completely in 1944. De Gaulle had acquired so much momentum of his own by then that he could afford to make history start on June 18, 1940.

The Gaullian myth thus represented both a continuity and a break with French political tradition. The continuity was in form, since the symbolic repertory of wartime Gaullism redeployed the classic elements of French providentialist mythology: the founding moment (the 18th of June), the symbolic apparatus (the cross of Lorraine), charismatic oratory, and miraculous apparitions (the town of Bayeux, when he first reappeared on French soil in the summer of 1944, then in liberated Paris), to which would soon be added the annual rituals and the scriptural writings of the *War Memoirs*. Nevertheless, the content represented a profound rupture. De Gaulle could personify the various facets of providentialism—military, nationalist, republican-patriotic—but he was above all its only truly successful synthesis since the French Revolution. For though he based his appeal on the great political and military figures that he liked to cite as his models, he also stood apart from them—or rather, above them—by his own particular virtues. De Gaulle had the military skills of Foch but with an added geostrategic vision and a more acute sense of the political; he had the cult of willpower of Carnot and Gambetta, but with powers of organization and a tactical instinct that were far superior; he incarnated the Napoleonic sense of authority and the cult of the State, but without any hint of despotism.

The most instructive comparison was with his idol Clemenceau, the man who led France to victory in 1918. Both men were venerated war leaders, and they both personified in the public mind the indomitable will to triumph over the German enemy and to reclaim the lost provinces. We have seen how readily wartime Gaullism identified with the Tiger: This equation occurs again in the popular tributes to the General, as in a poem written as early as the summer of 1940, which represents the appeal of the 18th of June as "an echo" of the fiery words of Clemenceau.[147] De Gaulle always remained faithful to the Tiger's memory: In May 1946, on the first anniversary of the end of the war, he paid a solemn visit to the tomb of Clemenceau and hailed him as the formidable leader who had remained "unwavering in the midst of all the storms"; after his return to power in

1958, he always marked the November 11 ceremonies in Paris by stopping to lay a wreath before Clemenceau's statue.[148] Nevertheless, Clemenceau's legend never became as powerful as the myth of the General. De Gaulle tried to explain why: "I can see an essential difference between Clemenceau's undertaking and ours. Clemenceau never developed a mystique. His was the breath that stopped the pendulum, that made victory change from one camp to the other. He was the *fact* of victory. While we, in everything we did, were carried forward by a great wave of support which I was able to generate, and which was infinitely larger than my own person."[149] De Gaulle was right to observe that, once set in motion, great political myths no longer belong completely to their originators. The celebration of the General as religious savior at the Liberation is a good example of this, and we shall find many others as we take this narrative forward.

But there were more fundamental and perhaps more disturbing differences. The Gaullian myth rested on public feelings a good deal more ambiguous than those of the generation of 1914–1918. The Great War had demanded terrible sacrifices of the French Army and the nation, which had come close to disaster in 1917—but the conflict had awakened, and even strengthened, national unity, while the events of 1940–1944 had had the opposite effect. Above all, at no time had the Great War produced a disaster equal to the utter French humiliation of 1940. Behind the wave of providentialism, which was "infinitely larger" than the General's person, there was also this dark shadow that Clemenceau had never had to confront. For the Tiger personified victory at a moment when the republican ideal was still strong (and it was this same ideal, with its hostility to "strong men," that turned against him in 1918 and finished his political career), whereas de Gaulle came to prominence at a time when the republican ideal was remarkably enfeebled. It was because of this political vacuum, which had also allowed the Marshal's providentialism briefly to triumph, that he could impose his own mystique and become the supreme incarnation of the "chief"—or, as he would say later in his *Memoirs*, "a somewhat legendary character."[150]

CHAPTER 3

❧

Sentiment and Reason

All my life, I have thought of France in a certain way. This is inspired by sentiment as much as by reason. The emotional side of me tends to imagine France, like the princess in the fairy stories or the Madonna in the frescoes, as dedicated to an exalted and exceptional destiny. Instinctively I have the feeling that Providence has created her either for complete successes or for exemplary misfortunes. If, in spite of this, mediocrity shows in her acts and deeds, it strikes me as an absurd anomaly, to be imputed to the faults of the Frenchmen, not to the genius of the land. But the positive side of my mind also assures me that France is not really herself unless in the front rank; that only vast enterprises are capable of counterbalancing the ferments of dispersal which are inherent in her people; that our country, as it is, surrounded by the others, as they are, must aim high and hold itself straight, on pain of mortal danger. In short, to my mind, France cannot be France without greatness.[1]

Charles de Gaulle's legend was born, as we saw in the previous chapter, in the 1940–1944 period, when he emerged as France's national liberator. The next phase in the crystallization of this legend came a decade later, with the publication of his *War Memoirs*. Its opening passage, quoted in the epigraph above, is one of the most celebrated pieces of prose in modern French political literature. Indeed, on the appearance of the first volume in 1954, the work enjoyed a triumphal, almost excessive reception. The public rushed to the bookshops, as the first volume achieved one of the highest print runs since France's Liberation in 1944 (equaled only by Jean-Paul Sartre's *Dirty Hands*).[2] The aesthetic quality of de Gaulle's writing was also praised by the critics, sometimes in hyperbolic fashion; as his panegyrist François Mauriac wrote, "like Caesar and Napoleon, General de Gaulle has the style to match his destiny, a style in tune with history."[3] It is true that the author had carefully built up the suspense about his book: Banned from the airwaves since leaving the government in 1946, on the grounds of his implacable hostility to the "regime of parties" that ruled France under the Fourth Republic, de Gaulle had remained for the majority of his fellow citizens—and even for many of his old Resistance colleagues—"a mystery."[4]

The General was all the more keen to cultivate this enigmatic side of his image that represented, in his eyes, an essential quality of leadership.[5] Indeed, after the painful failure of the revisionist political movement he set up in 1947, the Rassemblement du Peuple Français (RPF), which had marked for him the "end of illusions,"[6] he had completely retired to his country mansion at Colombey. Between 1953 and 1958, de Gaulle made few public appearances and did not comment on the major domestic and international events of the time; historians such as Jean Lacouture have likened this period to his "crossing of the desert." Making the best of a bad situation, part of the national press declared that, for de Gaulle, silence was "the best means of expression."[7] The theme of the "flawed saviour,"[8] which had already been heard in the immediate postwar years, notably in the classic (and faintly Vichyite) text by Arouet, *Life and Adventures of General de la Perche*,[9] was now trumpeted more insistently. His opponents were preparing to lay him to rest, like the former Vichy sympathizer who triumphantly attacked him, saying, "You have done too much damage to France. The country is finished with you."[10] All kinds of rumors were circulating about de Gaulle. In 1956 the London *Sunday Express* even reported that the General would soon be entering a monastic order.[11] In this context, there was a touch of the sublime about the volumes, which recalled the *Mémorial de Sainte-Hélène*, the greatest French political memoir of the nineteenth century, written in the final, exiled years of Napoleon Bonaparte's life. The banished Emperor and the self-exiled Liberator wrote in a similar vein about a glorious but already distant past. They also shared a similar remoteness from day-to-day events, the same melancholy in the face of "the nature of things," and the same bitterness tinged with admiration for English perfidy (multiplied tenfold, no doubt, for de Gaulle by the Nobel Prize for Literature recently won by Winston Churchill). Finally, and in spite of everything, they also shared same certainty that the future would prove them right—indeed, would belong to them. Like Napoleon, who had proclaimed himself "the Messiah of new ideas," de Gaulle enthroned himself as the country's providential hero: His action as the first voice of resistance in France made him not only "the obvious bearer of sovereignty" but also the "saviour to whom all were bound to turn."[12] And, as if by magic, the prophecy seemed to be realized again just in time for the third volume, whose appearance in 1959 coincided with de Gaulle's return to power and the establishment of the Fifth Republic.

It seemed a miraculous text, but the *War Memoirs* were also highly topical. They were addressed to a France that was losing its way in the 1950s in a succession of disastrous colonial wars (most notably in Indochina and then in Algeria) and whose sense of itself had not yet recovered from the wounds of 1940–1944. The General's purpose must also be understood in the context of the ideological battle that had begun in France around how the events of the war years should be represented. On one side was Communist memory, vehement and uncompromising, which saw the Party as the vanguard of the "spirit of resistance," while on the other were the first cautious articulations of a Vichyist memory, which found some echoes even in de Gaulle's own camp.[13] Faced with these dissonances, and mindful of how he would be perceived by posterity, de Gaulle had to offer his own version of history—as he might have said himself, honor and good sense required him to do so. So it was that the Gaullian myth, unfolded in the pages of the *War Memoirs*, which offered a comprehensive vision of recent French history centered around the General's three chief roles as war leader. First, de Gaulle cast himself, as a result of his Appeal of the 18th of June, as the only legitimate expression of the national will. There was no providentialism in this assertion, it is true, but a truly prodigious self-identification becomes clear when he writes: "Suddenly my mission appeared to me, clear and terrible. At that moment, the blackest in her history, it fell to me to take responsibility for France."[14]

Second, de Gaulle presented Free France as the single pivot of the Resistance, celebrating the "key unification"[15] achieved by his envoy Jean Moulin, who brought together the different components of the French Resistance in 1943 in the face of communists who were certainly brave and devoted but who always tried to turn circumstances to their own advantage, "while never losing an opportunity," the General continued, "to sound off against the 'de Gaulle myth.'"[16] Finally, the leader of Free France presented himself as the unyielding defender of the national interest against British and American allies who sought to "vassalize" France. Although he wrote a fulsome tribute to Churchill, he had much to say about British designs on Syria, Lebanon, and Madagascar;[17] as for President Roosevelt, his gestures and actions made plain (says de Gaulle) his hostility toward the very idea of a "sovereign and independent" France.[18] In the General's view, his resistance against the Allies was one of the key elements of his successful leadership of Free France. Also, to make sure that this part of his story would not pass unnoticed, he agreed at the time his second volume appeared in 1956 to give an interview to Jacqueline Piatier, who was to review it for *Le Monde*.[19] Clearly taking her lead from the author's presentation of his work, Piatier summed up the second volume of the *Memoirs* as follows: "It tells the story of two campaigns: one, open, clear and above-board, the resumption of the struggle against Germany, and the other muted, full of intrigue and concealed blows, the hidden struggle against the Americans. For it was in fact against them that the General eventually triumphed."[20]

This head-on opposition between France and the Anglo-Saxon world would become even more evident under the Fifth Republic in the 1960s, when de Gaulle would challenge American hegemony and (twice) oppose British entry into the Common Market on the grounds that she was a "Trojan Horse" of the United States. It also marked the strongest break between the legend of the war years and the narrative constructed by the *Memoirs*, where all the conflicts with the British and the Americans were deliberately foregrounded. The time was long past when de Gaulle would pay tribute to the "fine and worthy Allied armies and their chiefs"[21] and when popular addresses to the General were everywhere accompanied by naming of streets after the United States or lyrical hymns in praise of the "free, noble soul"[22] of "splendid England"[23] (as late as the mid-1950s de Gaulle was still receiving poems celebrating him as "the great friend of Great Britain").[24] The shifting of Gaullian discourse toward a prickly nationalism was part of a larger phenomenon that underlay the General's mythogenic writing: the appeal to a dramatic sensibility. From the very beginning of the *Memoirs*, de Gaulle strongly defined a series of binary oppositions: He described a France torn between death and resurrection, between honor and humiliation, between renewal and decay. This eschatology derives from Providence, which had created France "for striking successes or resounding failures."[25] Even the "*grandeur*" without which "France [could] not be France" could be seen only in the mirror of its opposite, "mediocrity."[26] In these contrasts, de Gaulle was already anchoring his narrative to an essential element of legendary folklore: the "titanic fight"[27] that must precede final victory. Yet that victory was assured, because de Gaulle, even though driven from power in January 1946, was the incarnation of the supreme teleology. Leaving power, he "took away with him something primordial, something permanent and necessary, which he personified through his role in History, and which the regime of parties could not represent."[28]

A text both timeless and topical, the *Memoirs* invite, indeed require, more than one reading. Like all the great founding tracts of political traditions, the work is marked by a multiplicity of meanings. It is both a personal apologia and expressive of a collective undertaking; a contextual political intervention and a contribution to the philosophy of history; a dispassionate, empirical study based on a mass of unpublished material and an ideological manifesto, at times tendentious to the point of outrage; the starting point of a new departure in French history and the apotheosis of an intertextual genre of State memoirs that begins as far back as the Sun King, Louis XIV.[29] In 2000, after sales totaling more than 2.5 million copies in France, the *War Memoirs* were published in the prestigious *La Pléiade* collection by Gallimard, providing the work with its ultimate literary consecration. This accolade is especially fitting given the heroic genesis of the text itself, in an extraordinary labor of composition. The final form of the work was preceded by two manuscript versions, followed by two typescripts, each of them reworked, to a greater or lesser degree, in the General's own hand. Nor should we forget his frequent readings of the text aloud to his close friends (notably the writer André Malraux, one of de Gaulle's closest intellectual companions and his Minister of Culture under the Fifth Republic;[30] in January 1957, de Gaulle read his portrayal of the Soviet leader Joseph Stalin, whom he had met during a visit to Moscow in late 1944, to his private secretary Olivier Guichard.[31] Held in the Bibliothèque Nationale de France, these early drafts, with their indentations and crossings-out, offer a moving contrast between the clear, logical construction of the final version and the "stripping of the self bare"[32] that accompanied de Gaulle's writing until the very last stages.

The *Memoirs* also instituted a Gaullian Word: a personal style, deploying a particular range of rhetorical figures; a sense of the lapidary phrase, with a constant use of metaphors, abstractions, and balanced oppositions; a rich imaginative power, based on a heroic ontology; and a dogma based on revealed truths about France, the nation, and the State. The most perfect example of this Gaullian language is the *Memoirs of Hope*. Though unfinished at the time of de Gaulle's death in 1970, it clearly represents a return to the aesthetic model of the *War Memoirs*, whose matrix is constantly apparent in this later work. If the trials facing France were now somewhat different, the characterization of the General was the same: He is the "saviour,"[33] the "obvious instrument"[34] to serve the country's need. There is the same certainty that de Gaulle was the only person able to "take responsibility for France" ("if it was a question of serving France, the whole of France and nothing but France, a strong enough drive to do so could come only from me");[35] the same telling understatements to designate the General as the incarnation of the general will ("it comes to be felt that de Gaulle is on the right track");[36] and the same irritation with national political divisions, the product of the "everlasting French propensity to dissipate our energy in battles of words."[37]

Above all, the usual binary oppositions constantly return to life in the text: in the contradictory inspirations that guided the General's action ("it is in a time everywhere drawn to mediocrity that I shall have to act for greatness");[38] in his vision of the "clash" between two conceptions of the Republic ("the republic of yesterday which we can see aspiring to be reborn behind the squabbles of party politicians, and that of today which I represent, and which I am trying to ensure survives beyond tomorrow"),[39] and most of all in the proud contrast between the role of a president "devoted to what is essential and permanent" and his prime minister "who has to deal with day-to-day events."[40]

To measure how strongly these Gaullian stylistic effects established themselves in French national discourse and imagination, let us look for a moment at the legacy of the celebrated opening words of the *War Memoirs*: "All my life, I have thought of France in a certain way."[41] The expression struck contemporary observers, who noted the allusion to Marcel Proust's opening in *Remembrance of Things Past* ("For a long time I used to go to bed early") and was often quoted in reviews of the first volume.[42] It also haunted the imagination of the General's followers, who often summed up the Gaullian philosophy in these terms. In fact, one admirer saluted him as "the representative of an idea, a certain idea of France, who placed above the party battles which represent only particular interests, the interest of France herself."[43] Another declared, "You have given to many Frenchmen an 'Idea of France' based on unity, greatness and thoughtful, effective social progress."[44] Above all, the expression was the mark of the Gaullist tradition, from stalwarts such as Michel Debré, de Gaulle's first prime minister under the Fifth Republic, to the death throes of the Gaullist movement under Jacques Chirac in the early twenty-first century.[45] It was also appropriated by all politicians in search of inspiration, who used the expression to introduce their various visions of Paris,[46] of the political center,[47] of the Left,[48] of the Republic,[49] of Europe,[50] and even of the Indian Ocean island of Mauritius.[51]

With its epic dramatization of time, the Gaullian phrase has also obsessed the General's successors as president of the Republic, from the deliberate simplicity of Georges Pompidou, who immediately followed de Gaulle as president ("however far back I go, the lessons I received were always those of honesty, decency and hard work")[52] to the high-flown words of Jacques Chirac, who admitted that he always kept by him a document "briefly listing the chief stages of the evolution of Life, the Earth and the Universe."[53] We also note, in a parallel register, the colorful and somewhat superior prolixity of François Mitterrand, stressing the multiplicity of his ideas of France ("I have more than just one"), while carefully reducing the General's vision to the outdated world "when we learnt history dates by heart, the births of crown princes, the engagements of princesses."[54] The stylistic contagion even spread to Nicolas Sarkozy, who candidly admitted to a youth without political ideals but nonetheless could not resist the magnetism of the Gaullian sentence pattern: "As far back as I can remember, I have always wanted to *do something.*"[55] A key element of the Gaullian vision that pervades the *War Memoirs* is the idea of "two Frances," to which French president Valéry Giscard d'Estaing returns in his speech at Verdun-sur-le-Doubs in 1978: "It has always seemed to me that France's future could go in two different directions: sometimes, when she organises herself, she is a brave, strong-willed, effective country, capable of facing the worst and of going far; at other times, when she lets herself go, she is a country which quickly slides into laziness, confusion, selfishness and disorder. The strength and weakness of France is that her fate is never finally decided, as between greatness and the danger of mediocrity."[56]

This "de Gaulle-speak," drawn from the *War Memoirs*, took on almost the authority of holy writ in the memoirs of the Gaullist "companions." This copious literature, which began to appear soon after the Liberation and became even more voluminous after the General's death, recounts the lives of men (and they were nearly all men) who took some part in the Gaullian epic, from the great fight of the Resistance to his departure in 1969: whether the partisan battles of the late 1940s and early 1950s, the "'crossing of the desert'," the founding of the Fifth Republic in 1958, the ending of the Algerian War in the early 1960s, or the tempestuous events of May 1968, in which de Gaulle was confronted by France's protesting youth. Despite their very different characters and the various, sometimes contradictory, judgments they passed on the conflicts in which they were involved, these supporters of the General, whether militants, soldiers, ministers, civil servants, or simple eyewitnesses, all agree on one thing: the "spell-binding"[57] power of the Gaullian Word. Evidence of its magic is often found in the titles of their works, which are one tribute after another to the central metaphors of the Gaullian imagination: combat,[58] action,[59] hope,[60] rebirth,[61] deprivation,[62] and, virtue of all virtues, loyalty.[63] On August 10, 1953, at La Boisserie, de Gaulle read the beginning of his *War Memoirs* to his brother-in-law, Jacques Vendroux: The first words "took his breath away."[64] It became a totemic opening phrase, which enabled former collaborators of de Gaulle to launch all kinds of fulsome rhetoric, as when Olivier Guichard wrote, "Down all these years, I have carried with me a certain idea of the General; and now, ten years after his death, I realise that he is as present to me as the dearest of my living friends. My memory is short, but not for him: I carry him within me, for ever unchanging."[65] Pierre Messmer, as if in echo, replies: "All my life, I have dreamed of an independent, strong and fraternal France."[66] The first sentence of the *War Memoirs* was enough for Pierre Lefranc, who immediately recognized the "masterwork"[67] of Gaullian writing; the same words led Yves Guéna to conclude that de Gaulle "incarnates our language, just as he is our History."[68]

No politician better exemplifies this almost mimetic devotion to the General's memory than Michel Debré, whose memoirs, published between 1984 and 1994, undoubtedly mark the apotheosis of the Gaullian Word in this literary genre. In a striking about-turn, the writer appropriated the opening words of the *War Memoirs* to affirm his faith, not so much in France as in the person of the General: "If defining oneself in terms of him meant defining oneself in terms of a certain idea of France, I have always known that de Gaulle ought to be at the head of our country, and I have always wished it to be so."[69] The whole plan of Debré's memoirs seems to be designed to recall the *War Memoirs*: the General's portrait, placed at the head of the first volume (just next to the author's father, Dr. Debré); the titles of the different volumes (five, as in the General's *Memoirs*) and their form, which includes documentary annexes at the end of each volume; the striving for narrative exemplarity, shown both in the constant references to "destiny"[70] and in the victory of reason over sentiment[71] and in the refusal to mention any political disagreements within the government ("The State has its secrets and should keep them"),[72] as well as the very Gaullian refusal to reveal anything about private life, which also belongs to the realm of "secrets."[73] In his portrait of the providential hero, Debré defined the General as "one of a kind,"[74] "a legend in his lifetime," a phenomenon that de Gaulle himself could not entirely explain and of which he was sometimes the "prisoner"[75]—all formulae taken over and slightly adapted by the disciple from the Messianic originals in the *War Memoirs*.

The opening phrase of the *War Memoirs* therefore illustrates something remarkable enough in itself: the potency of the Gaullian Word. The use of the first person ("I have carried with me . . .") also raises the problem often noted by commentators: the apparent absence of emotional elements or expressions of personal feeling in the Gaullian narrative. André Malraux expressed it in a famous formula in his recollections of his last visit to de Gaulle, shortly before the General's death: "Charles is not there in his *Memoirs*."[76] It is true that de Gaulle often refers to himself in the third person (as he also did in conversation) and that the story is constantly being brought within a cosmogony of "destiny" or, more prosaically, one of order or instrumental rationality: hence the famous "realism" of Gaullian analysis, in which states behave like "sacred egotists"; hence too the celebration of authority and the explicit cult of "public interest."[77]

However, to grasp the excitement inspired by the *War Memoirs* and their profound meaning, we must stop at the following phrase in which de Gaulle explained the two elements making up his vision of France: "Sentiment inspires me as much as reason."[78] We note that feeling precedes reason, but this by no means suggests that it occupied a secondary role. This is all the more likely as de Gaulle had already spoken on this subject in 1925, in a lecture at the Saint-Cyr military academy. He then suggested, following Bergson, that "in their thinking, men are not influenced by rational logic, but by emotional logic, or rather, they make from their emotions and physical sensations a kind of logic which they regard as rational."[79] Thirty years later, had he changed his view on this point? On the contrary, he was all the more convinced of it, as we see from the earliest passages of the *War Memoirs*, in which de Gaulle engages in a veritable phenomenology of his own emotional nature. It was this nature that allowed him "naturally to imagine" France. In the same way, the notion that his country was made for great successes or great failures came to him from his "instinct." If France wallowed in mediocrity, de Gaulle had "the feeling of an absurd anomaly." Even the famous phrase "France cannot be France without greatness" was preceded by "In a word, I feel that. . . ."[80] And the emotional wave continued to unfold through the second paragraph, with the Gaullian tribute to his father, "filled with the sense of France's dignity"; his mother, who "had an unyielding passion for her country equal in strength to her religious piety"; and his three brothers and sister, all marked by "a certain anxious pride" when their country was in question.[81]

In fact, though de Gaulle placed his early years spent in the family under the sign of exemplary virtue—there is no mention of walks, meals, or family disagreements—it is more a question for him of exemplary sentiments: enthusiasm or sadness, excitement or despair, fascination or horror.[82] And that is not an exception to the general structure of his book; on the contrary, most of the great portraits in the *War Memoirs* are supported by, if not based on, representations of affectivity—his portrait of Churchill, for example: His "almost unfailing power over others" came, de Gaulle thought, from the "original, poetic, moving flow of his ideas, arguments and feelings."[83] Pétain seemed to him "too proud for plots, too strong for mediocrity, too ambitious for petty self-advancement." De Gaulle added that "in his solitude he was cherishing a passion for domination, long strengthened by his sense of his own worth, the setbacks he had encountered and his contempt for others."[84] Stalin, "possessed by the will to dominate," was in his turn "trained by a life of plotting to hide his features and his soul behind a mask, to live without illusions, without sincerity or pity, to see in every human being an obstacle or a danger, everything in him was manoeuvre, mistrust and stubbornness."[85] Finally Roosevelt, the most awkward ally, who had wanted to send de Gaulle as governor of Madagascar, "had a star's readiness to take offence at the parts given to others"[86] (de Gaulle, it should be said, had great personal familiarity with this last character trait).

To return to Malraux's remark: If "'Charles is not there'" in his *Memoirs*, his sentiments are present on every page. A figure of great significance for him allows us to focus more precisely on this emotional register of Gaullian writing: the nineteenth-century writer François-René de Chateaubriand, one of de Gaulle's great literary inspirations. Both the writings of the General (especially his letters) and his personal conversations make clear to what extent, throughout his whole life, de Gaulle remained under the spell of Chateaubriand, whose *Memoirs* were one of the great landmarks of nineteenth-century French literature. In a letter to the Comtesse de Durfort, he describes how the writing of her illustrious ancestor had "haunted him for forty-eight years."[87] A further indication is that we know—the General himself had allowed the rumor to spread—that Chateaubriand's *Memoirs* were the General's "bedside book" through the composition of his own *War Memoirs*.[88] How did this source of inspiration make itself felt in the Gaullian text? We can, first of all, note a certain stylistic convergence, especially in de Gaulle's fondness for archaic-sounding expressions, and also the central place held in the imagination of both men by aquatic metaphors. The "troubled waters"[89] into which Chateaubriand plunged (the vicissitudes of his own era) are echoed by the Gaullian ocean, the symbol of his apprehension in 1940: "I seemed to myself, alone and lacking everything, like a man standing at the edge of an ocean and planning to swim over to the other side."[90] But the sea could also symbolize hope and the inspiration of thought: It was when flying low over the ocean that de Gaulle, remembering the words of Chateaubriand, declared that he wanted to "lead the French through dreams."[91] However, the decisive element here was the General's observation in the course of a literary discussion with his private secretary Claude Guy in 1947, when de Gaulle described his relation to Chateaubriand's writings in these revealing terms: "I *feel* like him."[92] One can therefore, in spite of Malraux's view to the contrary,[93] put forward the hypothesis that this shared romantic sensibility, reflected in Chateaubriand's *Memoirs*, was really at the emotional core of the *War Memoirs*.

This sensibility sprang from character traits shared between the two men, such as the appeal to both of contemplative solitude; a powerful though largely concealed introspective drive (Chateaubriand liked to speak of his "'heart of hearts'");[94] and above all the same bipolar tendency: Each of the memoir writers was constantly torn between optimism and despair, between dream and reality. Chateaubriand foreshadows the General most clearly when he writes, "In my inner, theoretical life, I am an inveterate dreamer; in outward, practical life, the complete realist."[95] De Gaulle in turn was in direct line of descent from the *Memoirs* when he took leave of his readers, at the end of the third volume of his own *War Memoirs*, by communicating his strong sense of the "meaninglessness of things."[96] This shared sensibility can also be observed in the underlying inspiration of both men, where the parallels are as numerous as they are striking. Chateaubriand's *Memoirs* were the work of a writer who would have liked to be a great statesman; the *War Memoirs* is the story of a soldier who aspired to equal his greatest literary inspirations. One allowed the expression of an inner narcissism: of the extraordinary range of figures with whom he came in contact, from the Ancien

Régime to the July Monarchy, Chateaubriand thought none his equal but Napoleon (and he was so determined to rise to his level that he changed his own birth date to bring it closer to the Emperor's), while the other projected his narcissism on the outside world. For the General, the universe really had meaning only to the extent that it worked out the Gaullist teleology. This principle is the only explanation of the breathtaking spatial displacement operated by the *War Memoirs,* as they tell the story, not of metropolitan France during the war years, but of Free France.

Finally, the two men, royalists at heart but republicans by reason, took up similarly ambiguous attitudes toward history. Was not de Gaulle, heir to a range of political traditions but not tied down to any single one, the successor to Chateaubriand, who had found himself "between two centuries as if at the confluence of two rivers"?[97] The connection is all the more obvious because the two works shared the same fear of the standardizing effects of democracy. As with Tocqueville, Chateaubriand bewailed the tendency of democracy to make "a single man out of the whole human race," sweeping away "great individual existences."[98] A major part of the dramatic tension of the *War Memoirs* comes from de Gaulle's attempt to give a positive answer to the inescapable question: Where, in the "mediocrity" inseparable from modern democracy (which had just been glaringly demonstrated by Winston Churchill's electoral defeat in 1945),[99] could there be a place for greatness, as incarnated in those "superior human types" whom the *Memoirs* already saw as belonging to the past?[100]

How one can create and manifest, but also be inwardly conscious of, greatness: That is what the narration of the *War Memoirs* must try to demonstrate. To do so, Gaullian discourse employed an essential device, used almost to excess throughout the text: distanciation. De Gaulle constructed his own character by manipulating his environment so as to differentiate himself from it by isolating and elevating himself—a process that owed as much to reason as to sentiment.

This setting himself apart was deliberate and constantly foregrounded: in his relationship with political institutions (the discussions of the Consultative Assembly at Algiers, with their endless controversies, inspired the lapidary saying, "Discussion is for many: action is for one");[101] in his portrait of a constantly fragmented, constantly ineffective Resistance, dwarfed by the providential figure of General de Gaulle ("I began to wonder whether, among all these people talking about revolution, I was not in fact the only revolutionary");[102] and in his vision of a republican political class incapable of conceiving of the general interest (a cruel instance of this incapacity was his exchange with Edouard Herriot: "I asked him to help rebuild France, and he answered that his job was to rebuild the Radical Party").[103] The final and greatest distance was the extraordinary gap he discovered on his return to Paris in 1944 between the appearance and the reality of power. Reoccupying his old office in the War Ministry, de Gaulle described a striking contrast between "the figure and the authority of the State," incarnated in himself, and the absolute power vacuum that it would be his job to fill: "Nothing is lacking, except the State. I shall have to recreate it."[104] He allowed himself few personal friendships, even with his close collaborators. A picturesque detail is that during the Free France years de Gaulle kept the outside world at bay by not accepting telephone calls.[105] To stress the uselessness of this mode of communication, he made it the symbol of republican impotence. After describing his fruitless meeting with the socialist head of government Léon Blum in 1936, de Gaulle concludes by observing sourly that "the telephone had rung ten times."[106]

But this distance, an indispensable condition of the chief's "grandeur," revealed its true meaning only in the light of a deeper sentiment, which also appears as a leitmotif in Chateaubriand's *Memoirs*: that of solitude. Speaking of his entry into rebellion in 1940, de Gaulle presents himself as "alone and lacking everything" but at the same time as the "unyielding champion of the nation and the State." In fact, the first was the necessary condition of the second: "Constrained and alone as I was, *and precisely because I was so alone,* I had to reach for the heights and stay there."[107] Solitude was therefore the foundation of Gaullian grandeur and a key feature of de Gaulle's myth (this is doubly true, both in his memory of the events and in the contemporary experience of the narrator, for the man writing the *Memoirs* in the 1950s was also on his own, physically and politically). It was this retreat into himself that allowed de Gaulle to give free rein to his most intense feelings, like that "boundless fury" inspired by the humiliation of France in 1940, which made him resolve to fight "wherever I have to, for as long as I have to, until the enemy is defeated and the stain on the nation washed clean."[108] Wartime Gaullism had raised the "holy fury of France" to the rank of a cardinal virtue. In a broadcast in November 1940, de Gaulle had invoked a "saving passion" that would bring about the deliverance of France: "fury, good fury, a productive fury against the enemy and his collaborators."[109] This fury was all the more necessary because the very future of France was at stake, "as a nation and as a State."[110] It is here too, in this world of extreme feelings, that the theme of death found its place—death that, under the darkling inspiration of Chateaubriand, haunts the pages of the *War Memoirs*. In the face of the "shipwreck"[111] represented by the old age of Marshal Pétain, de Gaulle felt new life stirring in himself in 1940 and, above all, the unshakable confidence that France would not "pass away."[112]

A comparison of the sensibility of the *War Memoirs* with that of the *Memoirs* also throws light on de Gaulle's silence about one of the topics that most preoccupied Chateaubriand, which was that of religion. It is a deafening silence for anyone familiar with de Gaulle's "heart of hearts" and particularly in light of his declarations to his inner circle after the war, when he bewailed the "levelling" of public opinion in the Western world, which he explained largely by the decay of Christian sentiment: "There is no more Christianity, or at least almost no Christianity any more. When it disappears completely, the spirit of resistance will disappear with it."[113] How, then, can we explain the apparent lack of explicitly Christian references in the *War Memoirs*? De Gaulle was perhaps inviting us to read between the lines: When he says, for example, that the atomic bombs that reduced Hiroshima and Nagasaki to dust "shook me to the depths of my soul," perhaps we are supposed to see a barely disguised allusion to his religious sensibility? Such a reading is all the more legitimate as de Gaulle was inclined to speak of his "emotions" when referring to his spiritual feelings; thus, he describes his "calm emotion" at the sublime moment of the popular demonstration on the Champs-Elysées in August 1944, a "miracle of national consciousness" whose effects on him were similar to a religious revelation: "In this communion of all in a single thought, a single enthusiasm, a single cry, differences are resolved and individuals disappear."[114] A transcendent moment that, we note, somewhat recalls the moment of "religious awe" experienced by Chateaubriand as he looked over Golfe-Juan, the site of Napoleon's miraculous landing in 1815, when he returned from the island of Elba successfully to reclaim his throne from the Bourbons without firing a single shot.[115]

In fact, the General's religious sensibility constantly appears through gaps in the text, notably in his accounts of popular feeling. Thus, the "astonishment" that struck the good people of Bayeux at the sight of the General in 1944, when he returned to France shortly after the Normandy landings, followed by waves of cheers and tears, leaves little room for doubt: They had been present at a miracle,[116] a religious revelation brought

about by what de Gaulle had earlier called "the sudden and rare intervention."[117] Such prodigies were connected with the Gaullian ability not only
to understand collective feeling but to relate to it. Speaking of his journeys into the provinces, and his constant seeking out of contact with the
crowd, we note how de Gaulle believed he could see "beyond the shouting and the eager looks, the reflection of their souls."[118] It was moments
like these that drove Malraux, an unequaled interpreter of Gaullian mysticism, to conclude that the Man of the 18th of June had much in common
with the "great religious solitaries," and there was even "something of the
wizard about him."[119] But if this spiritual communion gave the shaman a
tremendous sensation of power, it also made terrible demands on him.
Greatness, with the responsibilities it brought with it, thus became a "per-
petual burden" for the chief: "The fact of personifying, in my companions' eyes, the destiny of our cause, and representing for the mass of the
French the symbol of their hopes, and for foreigners the figure of a France
unbowed amid all its trials, would determine my conduct and require me
to adopt an attitude which I could never afterwards change. All this
imposed an unrelenting control on my inner life, as well as being a heavy
yoke to bear."[120] No need for de Gaulle to say he was carrying a cross: His
description is evocative enough without the metaphor.

The *War Memoirs* are conceived as a treatise on the theme of grandeur.
This greatness—and the work recalls in this regard the *Memoirs* of Louis
XIV—attaches in the first place to the public persona of the General. He
personified it by the action he took, by his ideas, and by his values (notably his conception of authority), but also by his sensibility and his style;
even when de Gaulle was leaving power in 1946, the communist minister
Maurice Thorez could not help exclaiming, "Even as he leaves, there is a
greatness about him."[121]

Greatness, however, is not a straightforward phenomenon. Here, more
than ever, the Gaullian contrasts proved all-important: between reason
and feeling, between what could be clearly seen in the outward appearance
of things and what belonged to their inward, hidden essence. Nazism and
Communism also offered greatness of a sort, but de Gaulle distinguished it
from his by drawing on the order of the emotions. That is why, in spite of its
grandiose scale, he called Hitler's power "sombre" and why Stalin's foreign
minister Molotov, symbol of the unquestionable greatness "of the totali-
tarian system," inspired in him only "melancholy."[122] In these various evocations of the complexity of greatness, one figure stood out in the Gaullian

imagination: Napoleon. In the *War Memoirs*, Bonaparte appears in various guises: as one of the greatest incarnations in history of national unity (this particularly on the occasion of the August 1944 demonstration on the Champs-Elysées);[123] as First Consul, excelling in "his legislative and administrative functions";[124] but above all as the supreme symbol of glory. De Gaulle cites Churchill's testimony to this; when he visited the Invalides in November 1944, the Englishman exclaimed, "Nothing in the world has such grandeur."[125] As reported by de Gaulle, no tribute could have carried more weight, for the memoirist had already declared Churchill "the great champion of a great undertaking and the great artist of a great history."[126]

Napoleon and de Gaulle: an inescapable subject for anyone trying to understand the Gaullian sensibility, but also a subject that is almost impossible to broach, so numerous are the polemics and fantasies that have been woven around it—by de Gaulle's inveterate enemies, always ready to apply the "Bonapartist" label to condemn one aspect or other of his politics, but also by his most fervent admirers, like Malraux, enthusiastically reviving the Napoleon legend to try to capture the essence of the Gaullian myth.[127] To find our way through this labyrinth, we need a few guidelines. First, de Gaulle, in his imaginative life, carried on a close, emotional relationship with the history and memory of Napoleon. To be convinced of this, one needs only to leaf through the collection of de Gaulle's *Letters and Notebooks*, or to note the numerous Napoleonic references in his conversations with those close to him. One example, among many, is the fine phrase addressed one day to Michel Debré: "Not everyone can die on St Helena."[128] Contemporary cartoonists did not miss the comparison; they constantly represented the General in Napoleonic guise. De Gaulle's idea of presidential power was often compared to the Emperor's; for example, his official visit to the USSR represented the peaceful counterpart to the Napoleonic expedition of 1812, and, at the end of the Algerian War, de Gaulle was depicted as a human Vendôme Column, the iconic Parisian symbol of Napoleonic military glory.[129] More seriously, the memoirs of the General's companions, and those of Admiral de Gaulle, his son, all make quite clear the extent of de Gaulle's fascination with the work of "the father of the modern French state."[130] Note, too, that de Gaulle's judgment of Napoleon was complex and careful. One example of this is this passage in *France and Her Army:*

Faced with such a prodigious career, our judgment remains suspended between condemnation and admiration. Napoleon left France crushed, over-run, bled white of her bravest men, smaller than he had found her, confined within bad frontiers (a fault which has not yet been corrected), suffering the mistrust of all Europe (a weight which she still bears a century later); but must one overlook the incredible prestige with which he surrounded our arms, the sense he gave the nation, once and for all, of incredible aptitude for war, the reputation of power that the fatherland gained from his victories, the echo of which can still be heard?[131]

We note again the different appeals made by de Gaulle here to reason and to sentiment. This ambivalence was always to mark the General's attitude to the Emperor. In his last conversation with Malraux, after having said that one should not "haggle over greatness," he asked what was for him the crucial question: "Did Napoleon have a true 'calling' to lead France, that is, did he love the country?"[132] Greatness achieved through reason and greatness based on feeling—the distinction takes us right back to Chateaubriand's *Memoirs*. For de Gaulle's view of the imperial epic corresponds to a large degree with Chateaubriand's, who, as we have already indicated, made the Emperor the central figure of his book, the sublime symbol of the grandeur and decadence of his time. Dazzled by this "immense genius for war," the memoirist nevertheless had deep misgivings about the "wretched results" of Napoleon's political initiatives.[133] But what truly obsessed Chateaubriand in Napoleon's greatness was his ability to "impose himself, to force other soldiers, his equals, his captains superiors or his rivals, to bend to his will," and even that "a man without background, without any authority but that of his genius, should have been able to make thirty-six million subjects obey him, at a time when no mystique surrounds even thrones."[134] Was not that the chief comparison and the ultimate challenge that the Napoleon legend set for de Gaulle: to impose his will in a democratic age when the mystique of power had disappeared and any assumption of authority would be condemned as authoritarianism?

It is this challenge that gives meaning to the two most eloquent passages on the subject of Napoleon in the *War Memoirs*. One appears toward the end of the second volume, at the moment of the liberation of Paris in 1944, where de Gaulle defines his state of mind in these terms: "I was both happy at the fighting spirit shown and confirmed in my determination not to accept any kind of investiture of power, except that given me directly by the voice of the crowds."[135] This last formula is drawn from a Napoleonic axiom that would always be present in the General's thought from 1944 onward: Whatever democratic legitimacy republican political institutions might enjoy, his own was greater, since it rested on a direct, personal, ontological relationship with the people, established on June 18, 1940.

But where should he let this Napoleonic logic take him? The General gave his own answer toward the end of the third volume, in the course of his reflections on the political and constitutional future of France at the time of his leaving power in 1946. While nominally speaking about the recent past, and in particular trying to counter the charges of authoritarianism made against him at the time of the Liberation, de Gaulle was really commenting on the present; his real subject, treated here in a veiled fashion, was the events of May 1958. For at the time the third volume was appearing, the General was back in power, and the specter of dictatorship was again being paraded by his opponents. Looking at this passage in detail, we see that de Gaulle offers a careful analysis of the conditions under which dictatorial power can emerge. He thought there were two such circumstances: "a great national ambition" and "the fears of a threatened people." France, he continued, had had two empires under these conditions during the 19th century: "She acclaimed the First Empire at a time when she felt herself capable of dominating Europe and where she could no longer tolerate the prevailing disorder and confusion. She consented to the Second in her desire to erase the humiliation of the treaties that had sealed her defeat, and in the state of anguish to which social upheavals of the day had reduced her."[136]

All the ambiguity of de Gaulle's attitude toward the Bonapartist tradition, but also his feelings about the immediate present, are concentrated in this passage. He reminds the reader that in both cases the Bonapartist Empire eventually collapsed, but he also stresses that it had enjoyed a large measure of popular support and even that the people had "given consent" to Louis-Napoleon's seizure of power in 1851—a statement offensive to the republican tradition (which has viewed the 1851 coup as fundamentally antidemocratic) but that is not there by accident. In fact, when one consults the various early manuscript versions of the *War Memoirs,* one notices that this passage on the conditions that may justify a dictatorship has been heavily reworked by the General (one whole paragraph has even been completely crossed out), but the notion that the people had "consented" to the coup d'état of December 1851 is there from the beginning.[137] Its presence owes nothing to chance. In his postwar conversations, de Gaulle often spelled out that he would not have enjoyed public support if he had tried to take power by force in 1946, but that the two Bonapartist coups were legitimate because they had been approved by public opinion. Thus he asserted to his entourage in March 1946, "Napoleon I seized power on the 18th of *Brumaire* because the whole of France was pushing him forward. The 18th of *Brumaire* came about because France wanted it."[138] A few days later he added that "A coup d'état cannot succeed without public support" and that Louis-Napoleon was "called to power by the almost unanimous consent of the nation."[139] De Gaulle is therefore suggesting *sotto voce* in the *War Memoirs* that the taking of power by force can be justified at a time when public safety is threatened and public support assured. This far from uncontroversial notion of political legitimacy would surface again at the time of the General's return to power in May 1958.

For the historian today, de Gaulle's *War Memoirs*, like other works in this genre (notably Winston Churchill's celebrated recollections of the Second World War[140]), are striking as much for their testimony as for their significant elements of distortion and self-aggrandizement. But the singular power of the Gaullian writings resided in their capacity to change the way his countrymen perceived the past. Indeed, if the years of the Resistance and the Liberation gave birth to the Gaullian legend, it was undoubtedly the *War Memoirs* that carried it over the baptismal font. This work, which allowed the reader "so fully and clearly to form an idea of France,"[141] marked the true takeoff point of the Gaullian myth, whose three historic components (the Gaullian unification of the Resistance, the unyielding defense of French sovereignty by Free France, and the incarnation in de Gaulle of the general will) first appeared there in ideological form. Taken up again and amplified by Gaullist institutional memory during the Fifth Republic, this *doxa* would long remain the dominant representation of the war and occupation years in France. Above all, as Pierre Nora has noted, this popular version of history was the very foundation of the Gaullian myth, since it demanded that the national hero be judged "by the standards he had himself imposed."[142] For, simultaneously, the most important effect of the work was to present the figure of the General in a new, more brilliant light. It was this text, both mythical and prophetic, that permanently defined the providential contours of the Man of the 18th of June as chief, savior, and father of the nation. We might even entertain the thought that without the first two volumes of the *War Memoirs*, de Gaulle's return to power in 1958 would have been seriously jeopardized, for it was the recall of the General's historic services to his country that allowed the public to forget the sometimes excessively partisan Gaullism of the late 1940s and early 1950s, when his political movement (the RPF) challenged the Fourth Republic. As a recent study rightly observes, the *War Memoirs* provided an idealized narrative that could form both a consensual representation of the past and a political program for the future.[143]

It is precisely because they pointed toward the future that the evocations of Napoleon in the *War Memoirs* are so important. The General may explicitly condemn the ending in failure of the two Empires as regimes (that is, political failures in the order of reason), but a certain Bonapartist sensibility is still evident in his discussion of the means they used. He had no doubt whatsoever that, if circumstances were right and popular consent could be expected, resorting to force was not only necessary but entirely legitimate. In this sense, May 1958, which was essentially a coup d'état, retrospectively justified Napoleon's 18th of *Brumaire*.[144] There is thus a remarkable telescoping of historical narration and of the events that would bring him back to power. It further proves that, even if the author of the *War Memoirs* did not aspire, as Bonaparte had, to "take four strides to the ends of the earth,"[145] he was not yet ready to put on the peaceful garb of a French Washington. At the same time, it is undeniable that Gaullism was fundamentally different from Bonapartism in its approach to political ends: The Gaullian odyssey of 1940–1944 showed that greatness was authentic only if placed at the service of the higher national interest and not in the accomplishment of an individual epic, however glorious that might be. Even in the most adventurous and seditious aspects of his activities in 1958—and there were many more of these than his contemporaries ever knew[146]—de Gaulle and Gaullism remained much more than an expression of authoritarian, antidemocratic populism.

All the more so, his text reveals a new political sensibility. Owing much to the inspiration of Chateaubriand, it marks a deep break from the dominant prewar culture of the French Right. Attachment to the idea of the providential man is still at the heart of the Gaullism of the *War Memoirs*, but the values that flowed from this idea have been radically reordered. In De Gaulle's conception of France, there is no room for traditional hierarchies, no instinctive hostility to the State and the Republic, no celebration of God or idealization of the peasantry, no diatribes against rationalism, and no shrinking away from conflict. On the contrary, the book decisively rejects fatalism, seeking to regenerate the republican tradition and rebuild the political and social order by means of a centralized civil power capable of avoiding the excesses of the previous Republics.[147] Though a negative sensibility underlay this ambition (to quote Malraux again, the General was never happy "except when he was saying 'No'"),[148] the extraordinary skill of the Gaullism of the *War Memoirs* lies in its ability, at the very moment when the nation was looking for new inspiration, to associate itself with the imagery of energy and modernity while casting the Left as an eternal Cassandra, fixed in an attitude of "eternal dissatisfaction."[149]

Vision for the future but also faithfulness to the past: the other dimension of the Gaullian sensibility was a constant return to the experience of the years 1940–1944 as a source of legitimacy and the benchmark of loyalty. An example of this political attachment is when Jacques Chaban-Delmas, another of de Gaulle's loyal lieutenants, said "I revered General de Gaulle as the liberator of the country, the almost visionary head of state who had been able to foresee the course of History. But I also loved him as a father."[150] There was something deeper there too, something that would always mark the sensibility of "historic" Gaullism: a certain fragility. For alongside the positive elements that de Gaulle imported from the Jacobin tradition—the cult of the nation, the celebration of the State as guarantor of national unity, the praise of the willpower and of the general interest—he also incorporated some of its less admirable characteristics: a certain excessive abstraction, an obsessive fear of plots, a permanent feeling of insecurity, a fear of failure, and always the sense of something incomplete. In Gaullian demonology—one thinks, in another register, of Camus's *The Plague*—the enemy was never completely defeated, only held at bay. Or perhaps here, too, it was a question of de Gaulle's latent Christianity: Evil is always there, as we bear it within ourselves. In one of his last conversations with Michel Debré, de Gaulle explained his defeat in 1969 in these terms: "We set the country on its feet again, but we were never able to kill off the Vichy spirit completely. That is what has defeated us today."[151]

This was an overstatement, no doubt, but in this recalling of Vichy a greater truth lay hidden. For in spite of their huge success as a mythogenic text, the Gaullian myth created by the *War Memoirs* never succeeded in sweeping away the "Vichy syndrome" from French national consciousness. This failure was not surprising, since de Gaulle had refused to confront Petainism directly after the Liberation. Certainly, his vision of history was at the opposite extreme from the historical relativism of Pétainist writing,[152] and he also contradicted with the greatest vehemence anyone in his entourage who dared say anything positive about the Vichy regime's policies. The journalist Jean Mauriac found this out to his cost in 1956, when he dared to suggest in front of the General that Vichy's having kept control of North Africa had prevented the Germans from occupying it and so, objectively, had assisted Free France: "the thunder" came down on him.[153] But it is undeniable that de Gaulle showed a certain gentleness toward Pétain, even declaring after the war that the Marshal had "done great things for France."[154] He glosses over the subject of collaboration in his *Memoirs* and treats only obliquely the popular support enjoyed by Pétain's regime. In 1966, speaking on the occasion of the fiftieth anniversary of the battle of Verdun, the General went so far as to say that the "glory" that Marshal Pétain had won in that terrible battle "cannot be denied nor forgotten by his country."[155]

These choices of de Gaulle's were essentially made for tactical reasons, as well as from a desire (understandable if not altogether praiseworthy) for national reconciliation. But they also reflected, perhaps, an intuition of the General's—sentiment, again—about the hesitation that Frenchmen of his generation had felt between two models of the savior: on one hand, his own refusal, in the name of honor, to accept the nation's surrender in 1940, and on the other, the Marshal's undeniable determination, irrespective of the cost, to stay at the side of his people through their "darkest days."

CHAPTER 4

✧

The Spirit of the 18th of June

Mon Général,

Today is the 22nd of November—your birthday! May God grant you many more years, for the safety of France and her return to greatness! In June 1940 my son answered your call, and for three years he and his family were proud to think of him fighting under your command, in Africa, in his "Lorraine" squadron. You called him back to London to prepare for the invasion of Normandy; he died on the 15th of March 1943 in a dreadful tragedy at sea. Général, for Lieutenant Paul-Jean Roquère you were the man sent by Providence; that will be your name in History.[1]

S ent to the General on November 22, 1944, by a French public official whose son had died for France, this moving letter is evidence of the impact of the Gaullian image during the first months of the Liberation. De Gaulle represented, via the miraculous date of June 18, the figure of the hero on the world stage, the daring military leader, the savior sent by destiny, and finally the prophet, whose redeeming word gave meaning to the life and death of a young officer. At the same time, through its variety of registers (patrician deference, emotional closeness, epic heroism, religious providentialism, anguished suffering), the tribute revealed a certain plasticity in the representations of the General in public opinion. This fluidity is understandable, at a time when France was going through a great political transition, as the Vichy regime imploded and the republican regime was being reborn. But it was also a reminder (and this theme would later become a Gaullian leitmotif under the Fourth Republic) that the question of executive power remained unresolved in France. History was repeating itself: A century earlier, the writer and poet Victor Hugo had experienced the same uncertainty as he left the Elysée Palace. After dining with Louis-Napoleon Bonaparte, newly elected president of the Republic and (like de Gaulle in 1944) recently returned from exile in London, Hugo began to reflect:

> As I left, I was thinking: thinking about this sudden move into the palace, this attempt to establish an etiquette, this mixture of the bourgeois, the republican and the imperial, that are the surface aspects of this profound thing that we now call the President of the Republic. These are not the least of the oddities one observes, not the least characteristic of the situation of a man whom people on all sides and at the same time call prince, your Highness, sir, my Lord and citizen.[2]

If he had been able to observe Charles de Gaulle at the time of his taking up quarters in Paris at the Liberation, Victor Hugo would certainly have been struck by the same happy cacophony. In the torrent of letters that submerged his private secretariat in 1944–1945, de Gaulle was addressed by every possible title. He was called *sir, Mr. President, General, Generalissimo, Marshal,* and, in a wonderful Freudian slip, one of his earliest military companions Admiral d'Argenlieu once addressed him as *monsignor*[3]— which would not have at all astonished those (and there were many) who saw in him "the herald of the reign of Christ the King in France."[4] All the figures of the collective political imagination converged in de Gaulle. For some, he was the symbol of a pragmatic "government of experts,"[5] while for others he was the "political chief" whom they wanted to see acting with "more authority and more drive";[6] the General was the orator whose words could "fill the people with wonder"[7] but also the inquisitor who revived sinister memories of the excesses of the French Revolution in 1793 in, for example, the man who wrote protesting against the arbitrary arrests during the purges at the end of 1944 and who saw de Gaulle as threatening to repeat "the Great Terror which swept over France after Germinal."[8] All this uncertainty was aggravated by the Gaullian political topography, which was thoroughly hybrid: If his favorite places were those traditionally claimed by the Right (the Invalides, the Arc de Triomphe, Notre Dame), he was also able to go in ceremonial state to the Hôtel de Ville, on April 2, 1945, to award the Cross of the Liberation (the highest award in the Gaullist honorary order) to the city of Paris as a whole, for its "masterpiece of wonderful success"[9]—and to receive in return a virtual declaration of love from the representative of a "patriotic and revolutionary city," who presented the General's action in resisting the occupants as a continuation of the tradition of the Three Glorious Days of the 1830 Revolution and of the republican insurrections of June 1848, September 1870, and March 1871.[10]

De Gaulle was above all the Liberator, celebrated everywhere, a required presence at all the celebrations. In the wave of commemorations that unfurled over France in 1945, especially on the first anniversary of the Liberation, the Man of the 18th of June was begged to attend them all. Invitations came from the city of Le Havre, which celebrated the anniversary of its liberation on September 12, 1945;[11] from the town of Sélestat, for December 2, 1945;[12] or even from the village of Maille (Indre-et-Loire), which had been burnt to the ground by the Germans on August 26, 1944.[13] There were also all the correspondents, male and female, such as the mother from Le Havre, who desperately wanted "just a little Cross of the Liberation" for their city or town.[14] Anniversaries, unveilings of monuments, patriotic processions—everywhere the presence of the head of the provisional government was desired, hoped for, begged for. De Gaulle normally sent a representative to these local ceremonies, presiding in person only over the traditional republican festivals in Paris. Thus, he led the celebrations of the 11th of November 1944 and 1945, that of the 14th of July 1945, and the festival of Joan of Arc on the 13th of May 1946. At the same time, the chief of the provisional government did not forget to honor the internal Resistance—in all its various components. On October 12, 1944, in the courtyard of the Invalides in Paris, he praised in heroic terms the sacrifice of the 190 Paris policemen who died fighting for the liberation of Paris,[15] and on May 26, de Gaulle was present at a short ceremony to unveil a plaque at 44 rue du Four on the building that had been the meeting place of the National Council of the Resistance during the occupation.[16] Above all, on November 11, 1944, he went to the mont Valérien, a military fort to the west of Paris, near Suresnes. In this holy place of the Resistance, where more than 1,000 French and foreign patriots had been shot by the Nazis, the General laid a wreath in the shape of a Cross of Lorraine in the clearing where the executions took place.[17]

This plethora of commemorations was in part imposed on the General by the political and military circumstances and by his role as president of the provisional government, in which he combined the functions of head of government and of state. But de Gaulle, who had a keen sense of the importance of political allegory, nevertheless wanted to put his own stamp on these celebrations, right from the first moments of the Liberation. Here we analyze the design (and the practice) of Gaullian political rituals, particularly in their symbolic and ceremonial aspects and the varied reactions they could provoke, whether among his supporters or the general public. We shall also endeavor to understand what these Gaullian celebrations tell us about the General's sensibility, about his conception of his political legitimacy, and, most fundamentally, about his distinctiveness with respect to the various national political traditions. In other words, understanding Gaullian political rituals allows us to cast light on the question that preoccupied so many French citizens at the Liberation: Beyond the public tributes, and behind the extraordinarily multiform representations of the public man, just who was Charles de Gaulle?

In *Seven Times Seven Days*, published in 1947, Emmanuel d'Astier was already calling de Gaulle "the Symbol."[18] Taken up again and amplified in the years that followed the Liberation, this view of de Gaulle became current, even among his supporters. As an early member of his circle observed in his private notebook: "Everything about Free France is symbol and not power."[19] One could develop this intuition further in that, for de Gaulle, the symbolic was a necessary dimension of power. In any case, there was in his mind, and in his conception of politics, a dialectic relationship between the two notions.

A striking example of this symbiosis, from the very first days of the Liberation, was his return to Paris in August 1944, which was quickly followed by his assumption of power during August 25–26. When de Gaulle arrived in Paris, he came as the head of the Provisional Government of the French Republic (GPRF), an interim organization established in Algiers in June 1944. However, as the Allied armies approached Paris in the wake of the liberation of Normandy, the city was in a state of insurrection, and de Gaulle's power was potentially challenged by the Paris insurgents, among whom communists were preponderant. De Gaulle was able to impose himself as leader, thanks in large part to a series of symbolic gestures, such as his move back into the office he had occupied in 1940 at the War Ministry in the rue Saint-Dominique, a concrete illustration of the Gaullian doctrine of the continuity of the State between 1940 and 1944 (and the consequent entire illegality of the Vichy regime); his visit to the Paris police headquarters before crossing to the Hôtel de Ville; his refusal to proclaim the Republic from there, which showed his determination to hold back the revolutionary impetus born of the Paris insurrection; and finally his lyrical speech on the liberation of Paris, with its insistence on national unity.[20] We now know that this "improvised" speech had in fact been carefully prepared over the preceding four days. Even—and especially—during the great, heady moment of his walk down the Champs-Elysées, de Gaulle was careful to monitor any transgression of the symbolic order: When one of the leading figures in the internal Resistance, Georges Bidault, presumed to walk level with him de Gaulle sharply instructed him to "fall back a little."[21] In such gestures we can already see some of the fundamental elements of Gaullian symbolism, notably the insistence on the preeminence of the State, the representation of the General as incarnation of popular sovereignty, and at the same time—already—the mystical notion that de Gaulle possessed an intrinsic sovereignty that outranked, and logically preceded, that of any political group or institution.

The archives of the GPRF show that de Gaulle enjoyed taking on the role of organizer-in-chief of public festivities. He constantly involved himself in the planning of the Liberation fêtes, whether in the choice (and number) of those who would be decorated, in the duration of the ceremonies (the General was allergic to long rituals), and even in the precise planning of the length of stops. On November 11, 1944, his office, at de Gaulle's precise insistence, allowed five minutes for the conferring of decorations, three minutes' pause at the statue of Clemenceau, and a five-minute tribute to Marshal Foch.[22] It was also de Gaulle who personally decided that the Allies would be invited to the Paris celebrations. For July 14, 1945, the first national day to be celebrated in liberated France, de Gaulle arranged a march-past of American, British, Canadian, and Russian forces to express the thanks of the nation to the foreign troops who had fought to free France from occupation and the world from the curse of Hitler.[23] Churchill made an official visit to Paris for the ceremonies of the 11th of November 1944: The occasion marked the consecration of the Franco-British alliance. Despite the stormy moments of their past relationship, de Gaulle took particular pains to honor the man who had supported him in the face of all difficulties in 1940. The two heads of government rode up the Champs-Elysées in an open car, to the cheers of an immense crowd; they walked down together, and as they stopped in front of Clemenceau's statue, a choir performed the song "Le Père la Victoire," which the prime minister had sung for de Gaulle at Chequers one evening during the war, "remembering every single word."[24] In his message of thanks, Churchill was at pains to stress how much he had been moved by the "countless kind attentions" he had been shown during his visit and ended by saying, "I shall always remember as one of the most glorious and most moving moments of my life the magnificent reception the Parisians gave to their British guests on our first visit to the liberated Capital."[25]

If they were not yet running with perfect smoothness, the main lines of Gaullian ceremonial were already laid down by 1944–1945. Its aim was to stir up patriotic fervor and popular enthusiasm—hence the strict conception of order and protocol, improvised initially at the time of the Liberation in August 1944, then refined during the national ceremonies of 1944–1945, and particularly during the General's journeys to the provinces.[26] In this ritual, which was unfailingly repeated with each visit to a different locality, de Gaulle was first welcomed by the highest civil and military authorities; he then went to the Prefecture, where he would make a speech to an invited audience; and, finally, he would speak to the local population amassed in front of the town hall.[27] This pattern, as has often been noted, expressed the Gaullian affirmation of the importance of the State in the face of "representative" republican institutions. But de Gaulle also used it to mark his own conception of the Republic, which was founded not only on order but also on national unity and fraternal concord—notions on which he insisted ever more heavily in his public speeches from the autumn of 1945 onward, when public opinion was becoming divided (notably about the thorny question of purges of collaborators), and his own political position was being questioned by the "parties." Thus, on the 11th of November 1945, which was to be his last national ceremony before he left government, he delivered a vibrant appeal to the notion of fraternity: "We must accept the need to join hands like brothers, so as to heal wounded France. Like brothers! That means burying absurd quarrels and going forward on the same road, at the same pace, and singing the same song!"[28]

This invocation of a fraternal republic was the very opposite of the "revolutionary" republican tradition that the French Communist Party (PCF) was promoting in 1944–1945 (and which, as we have seen, had also had its moment of glory in wartime Gaullism). In this "battle of memory" engaged between communists and Gaullists, which continued through the whole year in 1945,[29] the sign that revealed the paradigm change was the General's decision not to mark the 75th anniversary of the founding of the Republic, on September 4, 1945, with public celebrations of any kind. Plans had been under way and seemed to be making good progress, largely driven by André Malraux, who had fought in the liberation of France and had joined the General's office in August 1945.[30]

The projected festival that he had helped design was something grandiose: a ceremony after dark, on the night of September 4, on the Place de la République, with searchlights placed behind the huge statue, throwing "a high and wide column of light" into the sky, and four immense pylons each bearing an oval with the founding dates of the first three French Republics: 1792, 1848, and 1870. On the last one was to be mounted a shield with the Cross of Lorraine surmounted by a cap of liberty (the traditional symbol of French republicanism)—a symbolic medley no doubt inspired by Malraux's ambition to present de Gaulle as the inheritor of the classical French republican tradition. There were also plans to install two large hoardings, one bearing the legislative texts founding the three Republics and the other with the text of the Declaration of Human Rights.[31] This project followed exactly the pedagogic tradition of French republican festivals.

However, this project for a festive celebration of the anniversary of the 4th of September never got off the drawing board, because de Gaulle vetoed its execution. An afternoon march and wreath-laying were hurriedly organized by internal Resistance groups in the Place de la République; the PCF, the trade unions, and various resistance associations took part in it.[32] De Gaulle, for his part, marked the day with a radio broadcast at 8 P.M.[33] His speech praised the "powerful, noble and productive" principles of the republican tradition; he also mentioned the great achievements of the Third Republic (its defense of liberty, the development of education, the rebuilding of the nation after 1871, imperial expansion, the victory of 1918, and the recovery of Alsace and Lorraine), while also stressing the "poor functioning" of the regime, which had led to the disaster of 1940, and which made it clear that the Fourth Republic must be organized on wholly new lines.[34] It was this Gaullian criticism that had spelled the end of the plan that involved a celebration of the founding of the Third Republic. But the other essential factor that had caused the ritual to be aborted was allegorical: De Gaulle wanted to be the symbol of republican renewal, but he would not hear of having "his" Republic associated with those of 1792, 1848, or 1870, and far less of polluting "his" Cross of Lorraine by crowning it with a cap of liberty. De Gaulle was no doubt inspired by the republican ideal, but from the very beginning he wanted, as Maurice Agulhon perfectly expresses it, to assume his republican identity "differently."[35]

This differentiation meant, above all, in the commemorative context, the establishment of a ritual that would leave the Gaullian "mystery" intact. For the Gaullist festival was also a celebration of charisma, based most importantly on the physical presence of the General. His stature was invariably imposing and inspired wonder and instant enthusiasm. Several months after having seen him, a woman living in a provincial town recalled, "We have kept our memory of him: his voice, his height, his wave."[36] Indeed, it was that famous de Gaulle gesture: a quite distinctive hand movement, directed downward and away from the body toward the crowd, in answer to its cheering. Parisians saw it for the first time in August 1944, as he came down the Champs-Elysées; after his provincial visits of September to November 1944, the "de Gaulle wave" had become an integral part of his legend; crowds expected it and the local press often picked it up.[37] Above all, in this Gaullian rapport with the crowd, there was a constant striving for consecration, for a "plebiscite every day" that could serve to anoint his power. In the Gaullian festive scheme, everything was, it seems, directed toward achieving an original balance, made up of selective borrowings from different national political traditions, including a good dose of the French revolutionary (in the cult of the state and the emphasis on fraternity), a pinch of monarchy (in its focus on mysticism, but without the sacred element or any religious trappings), and even a hint of the Napoleonic (in its celebration of the charisma of the chief and of military glory). This attempt at an original festive synthesis took concrete form in 1945 in the celebration of the anniversary of the 18th of June.

The anniversary of the London appeal had been scrupulously observed by the General throughout the war, starting on June 18, 1941, when de Gaulle spoke from Cairo, a speech broadcast by the BBC. The following year, the commemoration was marked by a major speech at the Albert Hall in London. These annual rituals were occasions for reports on the progress being made by Free France and reminders of the need for national unity, symbolized by the ideal of "fraternity."[38] In 1945, on the first 18th of June to be celebrated in a liberated country, de Gaulle could not fail to make a striking commemoration of the event; discussion among members of his staff started several months in advance. However, disagreements soon surfaced about the character and scale to be given to these ceremonies; these differences were the sign of a certain tension in the construction of Gaullian symbolism—a tension increased tenfold by the need to find a suitable tone and a distinct format for this commemoration. In fact, the festive calendar was extremely overloaded, since June

18 fell between, on the one hand, the military ceremonies of April 2 and May 8 and 9 (the victory over the Axis powers) and, on the other, July 14 and the first anniversary of the Liberation of Paris in August 1945. In this series of triumphal rites, how could the anniversary of the founding appeal in 1940 be made to stand out?

Some members of the General's entourage reacted by imagining the whole thing on the most grandiose scale. One sketch for a project dated April 30,[39] and developed in a fuller document a month later,[40] imagined the 18th of June celebrations in epic if not excessive terms. This plan involved declaring the day a public holiday and inviting the mayors of all France's great cities, as well as those of the towns that had received the Cross of the Liberation. The celebration was to be in three stages: first a commemoration of the war dead at the Arc de Triomphe on the evening of June 17; then a military parade on the morning of the 18th, on the Place de la Concorde, followed by a speech by the General; and finally a great party at the Trocadero on the evening of the 18th, with dancing in the street, fireworks, and a fly-by over the heads of the crowd by military air-craft, as well as floodlighting all the chief monuments of Paris. The details of the ceremonial reflected an explicit intention to set the Gaullian stamp upon the festivities—in particular, under the archway of the Arc de Tri-omphe, where a black curtain was to hang, bearing the Cross of Lorraine and studded with silver tears. In this plan, de Gaulle figured as a veritable demiurge: he was to preside over not only the military parade but the street party; there was talk of sending a copy of the 18th of June Appeal to every school in France, of posting it up on the walls of Paris, and even (for the benefit of the politically blind) of broadcasting it through loud-speakers set up all around the city, provided that the General was willing to make a recording of it.[41]

De Gaulle immediately vetoed this last idea (he had an instinctive revulsion of any kind of political "'marketing'," and even in London had protested against the attempts by Churchill's propaganda machine to "'sell him like a bar of soap'"). His categorical refusal was also the sign of a reluctance to give too imperial a tone to the ceremonies; as a result, others among the General's team sketched out a more modest—and more republican—plan for the festival. As a member of his staff noted, if the 18th of June was marked in too triumphal a manner, that would put the 14th of July in the shade—"which would offend a lot of people."[42] It was suggested that the two events be celebrated at the same time, and another telling argument was put forward: "The public does not, in fact, seem particularly enthusiastic about ceremonies whose lavishness and somewhat pretentious elaboration can only recall the dictatorships which have been overthrown, and not the democracies to which we are morally and intellectually related."[43] From a republican perspective, furthermore, a public festival should be instructive and not simply a moment of leisure: That was the argument put forward by Georges Pompidou—de Gaulle's future successor as president of the Fifth Republic, then a young member of his staff—who reminded his colleagues that since the beginning of April 1945, the French (and particularly Parisians) had lived in an atmosphere "of almost constant celebrations, which are difficult to reconcile with the need for self-denial and effort."[44] Pompidou also showed farsightedness in warning against the dangers of any too obvious appropriation by the Gaullists of the Resistance. If the 18th of June were celebrated in too bombastic a manner, the other resistance movements were likely to be displeased.[45]

All these arguments about the ideal way to "represent" the 18th of June illustrated the dilemmas facing the General in 1944–1945, particularly in his ambition to personify the Resistance, the nation, and the Republic without seeming to exclude all others; in his desire to bear witness to the restored grandeur of France, without forgetting the huge human tribute the nation had paid; and in his plan to graft a kind of providentialist charisma into republican rituals, without reviving any memory of Marshal Pétain's Vichy festivals, or indeed turning his back on a republican festive tradition that was more inclined to celebrate collective virtues. De Gaulle achieved this delicate balance by opting in the end for a kind of attenuated martialism. It was martialism nonetheless, for the overriding tone of the 18th of June 1945 was patriotic and soldierly, involving a huge parade lasting three and a half hours on the Place de la Concorde, at which the Sultan of Morocco was present, featuring great military chiefs like Leclerc, the liberator of Paris, but also the battalions of the First Army, the Alpine Army, the French Forces of the Far East, the colonial army, and the Foreign Legion, not forgetting the marines who brought up the rear of the parade. Airplanes let out red, white, and blue smoke over the Arc de Triomphe and traced moving Crosses of Lorraine in the sky. The headline of a Paris newspaper summed up the spirit of the day: "Paris acclaims the victorious French Army and the man who gave it back its soul."[46]

Even so, the festival had been considerably scaled down, both physically and politically. The provincial mayors were not invited, the all-night parties planned for June 17 and 18 were simply canceled, no public holiday was declared, and, despite the presence of Gaullist insignia, the predominant emblem was the tricolor flag. The most revealing program change was the Liberator's decision not to make a speech at the end of the military parade on the morning of the 18th, when it had been suggested that he might deliver "a great address to France and the Empire."[47] The setting would have seemed ideal to establish, in a moment of collective fervor, the legend of the 18th of June—all the more so as the day had been chosen for the release, in the cinemas of Paris, of a film glorifying the French military forces. Nonetheless, de Gaulle did not choose to speak that morning. No doubt he was only too aware of the contradiction between the "revolutionary" discourse of wartime Gaullism and the present need for order and reconstruction of the State's authority, which he had recognized as a priority on his return to France. Maybe there was, too, an element of prudence in his decision. It was important not to offend the Resistance or to go too far in giving the military ceremonies (which recalled the 14th of July celebrations of 1919) the look of an imperial triumph. Finally, his marble impassivity displayed one characteristically Gaullian trait: In moments of great political intensity, he would always try to preserve his mystique by retreating into what one of his companions would later call his "dominating silence."[48]

These political differences were expressed in the diverse reactions on the day following the 18th of June festivities. As one might have expected in an event of this size, there were some organizational mix-ups. The official enclosures were overrun; the police estimated that more than 5,000 holders of invitations (including hundreds of former combatants who had been seriously wounded or deported) could not reach the seats in the stands that had been reserved for them; a member of the General's staff admitted that he "had had to hand out more invitations than there were places."[49] At the military parade, parts of the First and Fifth armored divisions were cut off from the other troops by an enthusiastic crowd that broke the barriers as they were entering the Place de la Concorde; the saluting base was already empty.[50]

What was more worrying, and indicative of storms to come, was that the press fired several barbs in the direction of the General. Certainly, the socialist leader Léon Blum paid a glowing tribute, saying that the 18th of June had been "the starting point of France's resurrection" and that "this one action would earn General de Gaulle a place in history, a place alongside George Washington."[51] But other reactions were more guarded.

While saluting this grandiose celebration of "the anniversary of the Resistance," the newspaper *Combat* noted somewhat slyly that "the date of the 18th of June by no means evokes a precise memory for all Frenchmen."[52] Echoing feelings widely shared among those who had carried on the clandestine struggle in France, the leader-writer of *Résistance* was unimpressed: "We would have preferred less exclusively official celebrations. What started on June 18, 1940, was an uprising of the French people against a failed ruling class. We would have liked the 18th of June 1945 to be a day of huge gatherings, popular marches."[53] An internal note of the General's office a few days later admitted that the lack of an after-dark party had disappointed the Parisians, especially in working-class districts.[54]

Not surprisingly, it was the Communist daily *L'Humanité* that most strongly contested the political significance given to the 18th of June and the leading role implicitly awarded to the Gaullist resistance. It did so first by printing an impassioned tribute to Colonel Rol-Tanguy, a key communist figure in the insurrection of August 1944, celebrated as the liberator of Paris and decorated the same day with a "well-deserved" Cross of the Liberation;[55] then, in broader terms, the paper gave a well-judged salute to the undaunted spirit of the capital, the heroic center of the national resistance: "As well as in the industrial cities, it was above all in Paris, where the population was profoundly anti-fascist and the influence of the Communist Party was strong, that the national resistance began, and that the recovery took root in the national soil itself, while General de Gaulle was in London issuing his appeals to continue the struggle."[56] This careful syntax expressed the double denial (temporal and spatial) of the primacy of June 18, 1940—a denial that already contained the seeds of the battle for memory between Communists and Gaullists that would so heavily mark the second half of the twentieth century.

In the late afternoon of June 18, 1946, a tightly packed crowd at the Arc de Triomphe witnessed the relighting of the flame on the tomb of the Unknown Soldier by the president of the Free French Association, General de Larminat. The General also lit a torch and passed it to a disabled ex-serviceman. This torch was then carried in procession to the mont Valérien, the symbol of Resistance martyrdom on the outskirts of Paris, by representatives of various ex-combatants' associations of the two wars, and in the early evening a brief ceremony was held there to mark the anniversary of de Gaulle's Appeal.[57] At half past six precisely, General de Gaulle arrived at the fort, followed a few minutes later by the torch. The former chief of Free France took the torch and used it to light a giant flame. Then, after a one-cannon salute followed by a minute's silence, de Gaulle walked to the Martyrs' Clearing, where he laid a wreath. Before leaving the military compound, he said a brief silent prayer in the little chapel where those condemned to death used to stop before facing the firing squad. That evening, in every part of Paris, crowds were shouting for General de Gaulle.[58]

It was in the summer of 1945, a few days before June 18, that the General had had his Council of Ministers adopt the principle of a short, restrained ceremony at the mont Valérien in which, accompanied by his close companions, he would light a memorial flame to honor the dead of both wars; the journey of the torch from the Arc de Triomphe was intended to symbolize the link between the two conflicts.[59] This mont Valérien rite, observed for the first time on June 18, 1945, by de Gaulle (accompanied by 200 decorated veterans of the Gaullist Order of the Liberation), was completed on November 11, 1945, with the solemn transfer of the remains of fifteen Frenchmen who had died for France between 1939 and 1945.[60] In a moving torchlight ceremony the coffins, surrounded by a carpet of flowers, were laid in one of the underground rooms of the fortress, which had been converted into a solemn crypt.[61] The running of the ceremony was entrusted to the Order of the Liberation. The rite of the 18th of June, which took its final form at that moment, was in the best tradition of Gaullian ceremony of the early days of the Liberation, notably in the extreme shortness of its liturgy, in the stress laid on military deaths (of the fifteen chosen, nine had been uniformed soldiers),[62] and in the evident desire to honor the continuity of French sacrifice from 1914 to 1945. De Gaulle in fact had a very profound sense of this continuity, as he explained to his private secretary Claude Mauriac in 1946: "The ceremony of the mont Valérien must be re-enacted every year, every year the tomb of the Unknown Soldier and the site of the martyrs must be linked in a single symbolic ceremony, so that French people become used to considering our Thirty Years' War as a single war, with its high and low moments, certainly, but ending in victory for France. Foch, Clemenceau, de Gaulle: it's all one story."[63] The General repeated the idea in a letter to Prime Minister Paul Ramadier in 1947: "I want this rite to become a tradition, symbolising the national truth that it was one and the same flame that inspired the fighters in both World Wars."[64]

Until the end of the 1950s, this notion of a "continuity of French sacrifice" in both wars remained at the heart of the memorial arrangements for the 18th of June. The letter of invitation sent by the Grand Chancellor of the Order to individuals and associations made a specific reference to this expression every year.[65] But between the two 18th of June anniversaries in 1945 and 1946, the political situation had completely changed, since de Gaulle left power in January 1946. His resignation, and subsequent removal from political power until 1958, had three major consequences for the ceremonies. First, the governments of the Fourth Republic kept a discreet distance from any official commemoration of the Appeal.[66] In 1947, replying to a letter from Admiral d'Argenlieu requesting official authorization for the ceremony at the mont Valérien, Prime Minister Ramadier wrote that he "did not see how he could oppose it"—a form of words that clearly expressed the government's lack of enthusiasm.[67] In response, de Gaulle stayed away from all official ceremonies, even those marking the anniversaries of the Second World War, like the 8th of May or the celebrations of the liberation of Paris. These developments, in the second place, had a significant impact on the character of the 18th of June itself; not only did the rite become an essentially Gaullist celebration (and therefore less "fraternal" in the republican sense of the term), but the anniversary of the 1940 Appeal was inevitably transformed into a remembrance ceremony for "France's dead." After the triumphal, martial spirit of the ceremonies in 1945, grief became the keynote of Gaullist political rites (with the exception of the festivals of the short-lived Gaullist movement created in 1947, the Rassemblement du Peuple Français (RPF), which brought together hundreds of thousands of participants in 1947–1949).[68] This sorrowful note was accentuated by the General's deliberate withdrawal from the national commemorative stage. For, though he was repeatedly begged to honor with his presence various commemorations, de Gaulle imposed on himself a "general principle"[69] of highly restricted appearances on memorial occasions.

Under this strict code, the only rite in which Gaulle regularly participated from 1946 onward was the ceremony at the mont Valérien—a gesture that he was scrupulously to observe every year until 1969, and always in exactly the same form; and, in 1950, for the 10th anniversary of the Appeal, he published a brief message to the Free French.[70] But he systematically refused the constant demands from associations and veterans' groups that he act as their patron. The only exception, which again shows his desire to keep alive the spirit of continuity between the two wars, was his agreement to act as Honorary President of the Colombey branch of the War Veterans' Association;[71] he also supported their charity work with financial donations, especially on November 11 each year.[72] With very few exceptions (such as the naming of an avenue for General Leclerc in Paris on June18, 1949), the ex–chief of the Resistance resolutely refused the countless invitations he received to attend Free French public commemorations, whether in Paris or the provinces. Especially after the failure of the RPF, de Gaulle's allergy to "the regime of parties" was such that if he heard that a member of the government would be attending (even a Companion of the Liberation), he would immediately decide to stay away.[73]

This policy of splendid isolation was the sign of a double determination on de Gaulle's part with respect to the years 1940–1944: first, to deny any "resistance-related" legitimacy to the Fourth Republic, and second, to claim it all for Free France, symbolized by the Order of the Liberation, whose membership roll was "the beginning and the end of the history of the Resistance."[74] It is easy to imagine the conflicts produced by this Gaullian solipsism, particularly with the Communists (with whom there were serious clashes at the 18th of June observances in Paris in 1949). Everything came to a head over the extraordinary staging of the commemoration of the tenth anniversary of the Liberation in 1954, in which de Gaulle refused to take part.[75] The General did, however, try to mark the occasion with a personal gesture, laying a wreath at the Arc de Triomphe on Sunday, May 9 (the official festivity of Joan of Arc). The events of that day, coming shortly after the fall of Dien Bien Phu in Indochina, perfectly symbolize the psychodrama of the Fourth Republic, with de Gaulle on one side, proclaiming his wish to remain "alone" and in "a mighty silence" (two key components of his personal liturgy), surrounded by veterans of the two Indo-Chinese wars,[76] and on the other, a government plainly obsessed by the fear of a Gaullian pronunciamento. Leaving nothing to chance, the Minister of the Interior (François Mitterrand, de Gaulle's later adversary under the Fifth Republic) planned in minute detail the arrival of the General and his departure from the Arc de Tromphe, with the obvious aim of ensuring there could be no contact between de Gaulle and the crowd.[77] A sizable police guard was placed around the main public buildings in the capital, and the police formally demanded to be told what to do if the crowd marched on the Elysée Palace (the seat of the French Presidency)[78]—a possibility that had indeed been considered by some elements of the Gaullist movement.[79]

In the end, the 9th of May did not give rise to any notable incidents and was indeed something of a flop for de Gaulle: The president of the Republic, René Coty, drew a bigger crowd at the Arc de Triomphe in the morning than the General did in the afternoon.[80] Broadly speaking, the day's events confirmed that, in the collective imagination of the elites of the Fourth Republic, de Gaulle was now a bogeyman. The true spirit of the 18th of June would now have to go into hibernation, into a kind of internal exile, until the General's recall to power in 1958.

Beyond the official ceremonies, and the disturbances that shook the political microcosm under the Fourth Republic, the date of June 18 kept its totemic character in the circle of the General's loyal followers, like one schoolmaster who went to the Arc de Triomphe and then to the mont Valérien in 1946, after having given the text of the Appeal to his pupils as their daily dictation the same morning.[81] This popular cult flourished through the 1940s and 1950s, with resistance associations, war veterans, and those who had been deported always in the vanguard. They asked the General for signed photographs and sent him cards, letters, and telegrams from every part of France to mark the anniversary of the Appeal and convey their loyalty to him—like those veterans of the First Army who assured him of their "gratitude and respectful and devoted regards."[82] The day of the anniversary was observed in the *départements,* often under the aegis of the local branch of the Free French Association, which had 25,000 members at the end of the 1940s.[83] The 18th of June was often the trigger for local commemorative initiatives: for example, the launching of a campaign to create a Place Général de Gaulle, as at Valognes (Manche) in 1957, where the president of the veterans' association, somewhat overwrought, assured the General that "90% of the population agrees unanimously that a square in the town should bear your name";[84] or the founding of a fraternity, as at Saint-Dié, where the Association of Resistance Volunteers was formed in 1956, a few days before June 18.[85]

This institutional memory was not restricted to metropolitan France. The anniversary of the Appeal was regularly celebrated by associations abroad, notably in New York,[86] or even farther afield, by the Legionnaires and Free French Fraternity of Hanoi, which sent a telegram to the General assuring him that their "faith in France's destiny remained intact," because they were all breathing an "18th of June atmosphere"—an expression that often figured in these messages, as did a certain "18th of June spirit,"[87] about which we shall have more to say later. This shared sentiment was also reflected in material gestures: awarding a shield, or sending a parchment testimonial to the General's glory,[88] or even traveling to London for the unveiling of a commemorative plaque in Carlton Gardens, the headquarters of the Free French, on the 18th of June 1947.[89] The prize for faithful commemoration must go to Lucien Paimbeuf, a veteran of the First Army and president of the "Rhine and Danube" Association. This dedicated Gaullist chose the 18th of June 1955 as his wedding day, declaring, "I am getting married on the 18th of June to fix the date of the Appeal for ever in my memory, and so that on every wedding anniversary until my death, I shall commemorate it in my heart, and my thoughts will turn to the chief of the FFL, even after his death."[90] (The wife of this gallant veteran might well have said, with the late Diana Princess of Wales, "there were three of us in this marriage").

If such devotion was certainly the dominant tendency, the cult of the Man of the 18th of June was sometimes replaced by more ambivalent and guarded reactions—and even by criticism. During the lean years when Gaullism was in opposition, followed by a long "crossing of the desert" in the 1950s, the faithful did not always understand, or appreciate, De Gaulle's words and deeds. One of the most difficult moments occurred in 1949 when the General publicly criticized the continuing imprisonment of Marshal Pétain on the Ile d'Yeu. Among the indignant reactions, one was from a *maquisard* in the Cher, who described himself as "a Gaullist since 1940" (and whose association bore on its banner a large Cross of Lorraine). Outraged by this initiative of the General's, who furthermore was speaking at a time when a succession of collaborators had been acquitted by the French courts, this old resistance fighter publicly broke with his former chief: "You have asked for mercy to be shown to a frail old man, to Pétain? So, sir, the blood that was shed for France, the dreadful tortures endured by so many of us, the total sacrifice that we made so willingly, everything that freed France and brought you to power—all this is to count for nothing?"[91]

Less extreme, but much more widely felt, was the disenchantment caused by the General's systematic refusal to honor with his presence the commemorative rituals of Free France. In 1948, the anniversary of the 18th of June saw the inauguration of the war memorial to the dead of Free France at the Palace of Modern Art in Paris. The announcement that the General would not be coming caused "bitter disappointment" in the ranks; one Free French veteran tried to change de Gaulle's mind by making this impassioned appeal: "Our families cannot bear the thought that their loved ones who answered your appeal of the 18th of June, who fought under your orders and died for France, should not be raised to glory in your presence."[92] In 1954, for the ceremonies marking the 10th anniversary of the liberation of Strasbourg, the veterans of the 2nd Tank Regiment put similar pressure—with the same lack of success—on the General.[93] In the face of this Gaullian splendid isolation, some of his followers could not but feel themselves somewhat abandoned, like Roger Barberot, a decorated Companion of the Liberation, who, while telling himself that de Gaulle's thoughts were only and always for France, jotted in his private notebook an unflattering comparison between Napoleon's readiness to reward his brave soldiers and the General's apparent indifference to the men who had fought by his side.[94]

This Gaullian desire to be the sole incarnation of the spirit of the Resistance could provoke quarrels even among the most faithful. In 1956 General Larminat decided that from then on only representatives of the Free French Association would be allowed to lead the flame ceremony at the Arc de Triomphe on the 18th of June: All the other resistance associations that had up to then taken part in the rite would be excluded.[95] In the outcry produced by his letter, the president of the Association of Knights of the Cross of Lorraine protested energetically against this exclusion, recalling first of all that England had not been the only cradle of the Resistance, for many men and women had responded to the General's appeal "on French soil." Striking an attitude worthy of the General himself, he proudly asserted that he was "fighting a lone battle" and would continue "so long as there is breath in my body."[96]

The 18th of June spirit obviously still haunted the imagination of this old combatant—not only as an abstraction but in his day-to-day life. How far was this generally the case in the 1950s? The trend was certainly toward a certain fragmentation. To the perennial divide between Communists and Gaullists were added other grounds for disagreement within the resistance generation: notably, the war in Indo-China, experienced as a dreadful humiliation by the army; in 1954, at the ceremonies in Paris for the tenth anniversary of the Liberation, retired soldiers of the colonial army burst into tears.[97] Some officers laid the blame on General de Gaulle, whose silence was seen as a failure to support the army. Contemporary events also gave a new and definitely more ideological slant to the memory of the 18th of June. In an article published in Le Monde in 1957, Edmond Michelet declared that the "18th of June spirit" was defined by two refusals: one to recognize military defeat and the other to accept "totalitarianism"—a distinction that allowed the exclusion of Communists in France but determined the interpretation of events farther afield. Thus, for Michelet, the true heirs of the Resistance were not the nationalists of the Algerian National Liberation Front, inspired (he said) by a "racist frenzy analogous to that which Hitler tried to impose upon the world," but rather the anticommunist Hungarian rebels against Soviet domination in November 1956, "unshakeable opponents of foreign tyranny."[98]

The 18th of June also symbolized for the General's supporters the ideal of an evolution, a profound transformation of French society that the Resistance had tried to bring about but that had foundered among the failures of the Fourth Republic. For some of them, this ideal took on a frankly Bonapartist coloring, as with the supporter of the General who, frustrated by the regime's failure to act and its apparent inability to suppress the Algerian revolt, wrote, "The people are waiting for a leader who will wield the thunderbolt and galvanise them with a new 18th of June message, and who will be pitiless with the gravediggers of France who are clogging up Parliament."[99] For others, the ideal of the 18th of June struck a more republican note—like the call for a "pure and stern Republic" published in the *Courrier de la colère* by Michel Debré, soon to become de Gaulle's prime minister under the Fifth Republic, or in the "Spirit of the Resistance" movement which, starting in 1957, drew on the symbolism of the 18th of June to preach a "political, social and economic" revolution.[100] They did not restrict themselves to words: Gaullist supporters also took to the streets to contest and subvert official celebrations. In 1958, a few days before the General's return to power, during the 8th of May ceremonies, fourteen demonstrators were arrested in Paris for shouting "Long live de Gaulle" and handing out leaflets saying, "France has been sold out by the system. Power to de Gaulle!" along with copies of the *Courrier de la colère*. Among those arrested were students from Sciences Po and office and building workers.[101]

A perfect illustration of this abiding faith, but also of the tension, in the memory of the 18th of June between contemplation and action was the attitude of the inner circle of the General's followers, the Companions of the Liberation.[102] Closed in 1945, the Order was made up of just over 1,000 honorands and represented the elite of the Gaullist combatants during the war years. Most of them were still unconditional supporters. When questioned about the possibility of the General's returning to office, one of them stated: "Of course I am a supporter of Charles the

Great. It's a matter of gratitude and affection. When I think of him, I don't weigh reasons any more."[103] In May 1958, after a meeting in Paris, 223 Companions signed a petition to President Coty demanding de Gaulle's recall to power in the name of public safety.[104] This support for the Man of the 18th of June was based on the solidarity born of the action they had shared and also on a certain nostalgia for a "pure" period when moral and political choices had been clear. However, this solidarity did not rule out a certain diversity of feeling, which finds a fascinating echo in the responses to a circular sent out by Roger Barberot in March 1958. All the respondents, of course, still identified themselves as heirs of the resistance, but there was no consensus as to what the "memory of June 1940" signified. Some thought that "our only objective should be the return of the Man of the 18th of June as head of government";[105] they also agreed that this return should take place by purely legal means ("if de Gaulle did not play by the rules he would be nothing but an adventurer").[106] But others maintained the opposite: that legality was not an absolute value. Some even thought that the General's respect for the law was, in the present context, an obstacle to the country's recovery: "[De Gaulle] cannot open his mouth without talking about republican legality. We don't give a damn about republican legality, that's what has got us into this mess. We need a man to whom we can give a club and who will know how to use it."[107]

There also was no agreement about the role the Companions of the Liberation should play in public life. Some thought that they should simply dwell on the glories of the past: "When we come to talk about the present or the future, we cannot be unanimous any longer."[108] But others were chiefly concerned to transcend the "old soldier" side of the Order: "Let's leave the 14–18 veterans to their gatherings where the only thought is for the dead and the only talk is of pensions. We must not let our associations become middle-class and our gatherings turn into directors' meetings. Our purpose now must be to save the spirit of the 18th of June."[109] But how was this to be done? Here, too, the Companions were not necessarily all on the same page: Some thought that the General and he alone should be free to decide on action "as he thinks best,"[110] for the security of France. The Companions could and should be nothing but a supporting force. That was more or less what de Gaulle politely told a delegation that he received in March 1958.[111]

Others, like Pierre Finet, had a more lofty and more ambitiously republican conception of the "18th of June spirit"; this Companion of the Liberation gives a fine definition of it in a passage in which he draws on his personal experience of Free France in the Middle East: "The Free French are not like the general run of Gaullists—simply those who 'support General de Gaulle'—but are those who in June 1940, faced with the same crisis of conscience, resolved it in the same way as he did. Most of us in Lebanon and Syria did not hear the Appeal of the 18th of June. Each of us decided for himself to continue the struggle. The more personal our decision was, the more Free French we considered ourselves to be."[112] Buttressed by reason or carried away by emotion, firmly attached to legality or driven by authoritarian impulses, fascinated by the leader's charismatic power or inspired by a wholly individualistic concept of the autonomy of the subject, the "spirit of the 18th of June" was an ideal as rich in its sources of inspiration as in its diversity.[113]

The General's return to power in May 1958 brought a new lease on life for Gaullian political rituals. Commenting on the newly increased attendance at the 18th of June commemoration in Calais, the General's brother-in-law Jacques Vendroux noted, "It is curious to see many Calaisiens who previously did not trouble to commemorate this anniversary now rushing to be photographed in the front row of a capacity crowd."[114] This enthusiasm can be read as an attempt at reenergizing the ceremony, but its results were, to say the least, unpredictable. An example is the ceremony organized by Malraux at the beginning of September 1958 in Paris: Its ostensible aim was to present to the people the new design for a constitution, on which they would vote in a referendum, but the true object of the performance was to advertise the General's claims to republican legitimacy, which were vigorously contested by the Left. In fact, Malraux chose a highly symbolic place and date for the General's speech: the Place de la République on September 4, the anniversary of the fall of the Second Empire and its replacement by the "exiled Republic"[115] in 1870.

The contrast with what had happened in 1945 was not without irony. As we noted earlier, the General had then rejected the idea of too lavish a celebration of that anniversary so as not to appear hostage to a republican tradition overshadowed by the parliamentary spirit and the memory of the humiliating defeat of 1940. In 1958, however, de Gaulle chose to rely heavily on the symbolism of the 4th of September so as to attest to his republican bona fides. The anniversary therefore became a pretext for a celebration of his own values: "the sovereignty of the people, the appeal to liberty, the hope of justice"; against his detractors, he insisted particularly on the "legality" of his return to power: Its legitimacy would be confirmed by the French people.[116] With its U-turn from 1945, its improvised character (100 manual workers, chosen one is not quite sure how, were awarded the Legion of Honor), the pasteboard aspect of its decorations, and the violent counterdemonstrations that it provoked, this 4th of September ceremony was evidence of the uncertainties of Gaullian institutional memory in 1958. It also highlighted the profound traces left by the memory of the 1940–1944 years, to which the notion of a "Republic in exile" constituted an implicit tribute. Exile was a multifaceted metaphor in Gaullian rhetoric. It symbolized suffering and distance but also purity in the face of the mundane; the "crossing of the desert" in the 1950s had in this sense been a kind of exile.

It is precisely when political events are at their most disturbed that appeals to tradition are the most effective. Thus in these early years of the Fifth Republic, when the conflicts resulting from the Algerian War were at their most intense, the commemoration of the 18th of June found its place at the heart of the Gaullian commemorative project. The anniversary was a helpful means of marking the General's return to power by a distinctive national symbolism and of countering the Communist Party on its recognized memorial territory. The ritual could also serve to reaffirm the General's "resistancialist" legitimacy in the face of his ideological opponents, the supporters of French Algeria, many of whom also traced their ideological ancestry to the Resistance.[117] Already in 1958 the anniversary, which fell a month after the General's return to power, demonstrated the strong popular support for the celebration. De Gaulle was met on the Place de l'Etoile by a "delirious ovation" from a crowd estimated at 50,000, and found 10,000 people waiting for him later in the day inside the mont Valérien, with a further 5,000 massed at the entrance to the fort.[118] The following year the crowds were somewhat smaller, but nevertheless, between 6 and 8 P.M., the police estimated that more than 400,000 cars were stuck in a giant traffic jam, for this time the General had decided to visit the Hôtel de Ville as well. In his speech to the city councilors, he recalled the unforgettable memory of the summer of 1944: the Parisian uprising, the arrival of the Leclerc divisions, and the demonstrations of August 25 and 26. He ended by saluting, in the person of the Parisians, the "exemplary attitude of so many French men and women."[119]

The year 1960 was the high point of this mythification of the Gaullian memory of the Resistance with the inauguration of the Free France Memorial at the mont Valérien. This project was first conceived at the Liberation but had been shelved during the Fourth Republic; the decision to reactivate it was one of de Gaulle's first symbolic gestures on his return to power[120] and evidence of his wish to give the 18th of June a "new aspect."[121] This monument also marked a clean break with the 18th of June celebrations under the Fourth Republic, which were underpinned, as mentioned earlier, by the idea of a "continuity of national sacrifice." The architect of the project, Colonel Félix Brunau, was particularly well qualified to undertake it: Not only had he been one of the first people to conceive of the monument at the Liberation, and one of the General's most faithful (and most discreet) lieutenants during the "crossing of the desert," but he himself had been singled out by destiny: he was in fact born on the 18th of June.[122] In Brunau's scheme, the memory of the 18th of June was shifted in time; as the architect specified, the mont Valérien Memorial was designed to convey the scale of "that most sorrowful and most heroic page of our history which was written between 1939 and 1944 by Free France."[123] A clear sign of this redesign was that the sixteen high reliefs of the new monument would show only allegories of the Second World War. This new emphasis was echoed in the official invitations, sent out by the Order of the Liberation, which mentioned only the "18th of June ceremony";[124] there was no further mention of the Gaullian desire to unite symbolically, by means of the flame, "the heroes of both wars."[125]

Finally, to give a truly national basis to the anniversary of the 18th of June, the ceremony was broadcast in real time by French television with, beginning in 1959, a commentary by Michel Droit, one of the leading French journalists of the era, who went on to become the President's main interviewer during the 1960s.[126] De Gaulle also positively leaned on the prefects, who were officially informed that the government wished to make the 18th of June commemoration "as striking and solemn as possible" and that they should themselves make up any initiative that was wanting from the local associations should they fall short. As the circular from the Ministry of the Interior explained, "the departmental branches of the Free France Veterans will organise the celebrations, but I wish to give them all official support. If there is no FFV branch in your *département*, it will fall to you to organise the ceremonies, in consultation with local veterans' associations, particularly veterans of the Resistance. Your presence and that of the sub-prefects of your *département* at the principal ceremonies will attest to the Government's concern for the success of this anniversary."[127] With this government patronage in the country at large, the 18th of June became an official part of the State's memory under the Gaullian Republic.

It remained, however, to define more precisely the place of this anniversary in the full range of official rites. This was made all the more difficult by a disagreement that arose in 1959 between the Order of the Liberation, which traditionally organized the mont Valérien ceremonies,[128] and the Veterans Ministry, which was responsible for building the new Memorial. The first skirmishes took place in the spring of 1959, when Minister Raymond Triboulet tried to broaden that year's 18th of June ceremony to include the laying of the foundation stone of the new Memorial. He was rebuffed by the Order of the Liberation: "The mont Valérien ceremony is a complete and self-sufficient ritual."[129] Triboulet tried again in 1960, ahead of the inauguration of the Memorial. In a letter to General de Gaulle he observed that the organization of the 1959 ceremonies by the Order of the Liberation had been less than perfect and requested that in the future the government (that is to say, his ministry) should take charge of the 18th of June, "along the same lines as all the national patriotic ceremonies: the 11th of November, 8th of May and the national day commemorating the Deportations."[130] This petty turf war concealed an issue of considerable substance: was the 18th of June to become a true national anniversary? For the Order of the Liberation, which was trying to preserve the "private character" of the ceremonies and give them an atmosphere of "quiet meditation," the answer could only be negative.[131] De Gaulle immediately rallied to the view of his Companions.[132]

The last part of the game was played out in April 1961, when a meeting was convened at the Paris headquarters of the Order of the Liberation to define the future character of the 18th of June celebrations. In attendance, alongside the leadership of the Order, were representatives of the various ministries involved, other government bodies, and the Elysée itself. The discussion was lively, and those in favor of a radical revision of the Appeal ceremony pressed their case, notably in the person of Félix Brunau, who clearly voiced his opposition to the traditional concept of a "family" ceremony.[133] Now that the Memorial was in place, Brunau (and others) wanted to celebrate the 18th of June on a "grandiose" scale: There was talk of turning the ceremony into a mass demonstration (a figure of 30,000 participants was mentioned), a return to the popular Gaullism of the late 1940s, and a triple homage to de Gaulle in person, as Head of State and as incarnation of the Resistance.[134]

Speaking in the name of the General, the representative of the Elysée at the meeting vetoed this conception, which came across as excessively grandiloquent. De Gaulle in fact insisted that the ceremony be kept to "reasonable proportions."[135] There, as always, the General showed his preference for short and sober ritual practices. In a note dated June 23, 1961, de Gaulle stated that the 18th of June ceremony should be a "closing of ranks."[136] But this view also betrays a deeper sense that for him the 18th of June was above all a nostalgic anniversary: It was on these grounds that, from 1959 onward, de Gaulle would invite all Companions of the Liberation still living (more than half of them were, at the beginning of the Fifth Republic) to a reception at the Elysée. This gathering took place every June 18 in the morning, quietly and without any official protocol.[137] When he attended the mont Valérien ceremony, as of 1958, de Gaulle went not as the President of the Republic but as Grand Master of the Order of the Liberation and wore on his uniform only the insignia of Free France.[138]

This almost private, intimate spirit thus continued to mark the atmosphere of the 18th of June celebrations. De Gaulle was invariably received with "enthusiastic fervour"[139] by his loyal followers on his appearances at the mont Valérien, and for his entourage the ceremony was "moving as always."[140] In the first years of the Fifth Republic, many requests for invitations were sent by members of the public to the Chancellery of the Order or directly to the Elysée; among the latter were touching letters such as the one from Roger Weill, a Free French veteran living in Brazil and now in very poor health, who wrote to the General to ask for a pass to one of the official stands.[141] Others, such as the one from a Gaullist party activist from Enghien-les-Bains, wanted an invitation so as to be able to approach the General "calmly, without having to fight my way through the crowd." This writer added, "I remember the 4th of September [1958], when I stood for four hours and was really manhandled."[142] For some, this wish to get near to the General, even to touch him, was a real obsession[143]—like the opera singer who opened her heart to her idol: "How lucky are those who can get close to you! My greatest hope since the 18th of June 1940 has been that one day, perhaps, I shall have the immense privilege of shaking your hand, my dear General, and reaffirming all my loyalty to you."[144] Among the reasons given for requesting an invitation, no doubt the most original was the one put forward by a former female militant of the RPF years in the late 1940s, who asked the General to send her an invitation, "simply because I have a son born on that day, and I called him Philippe after your son, and I think that makes me even more French [sic]."[145]

But as the years passed, the words used by officials and the press to describe the event indicated a certain predictability, even a certain ossification; the reports speak of the day following the "normal pattern"[146] (a typical euphemism for an event where nothing really stood out), and one Paris newspaper even announced that the following day the "moving ceremony of the mont Valérien" would take place.[147] As for the classic republican rites, the collective feelings to be experienced were, so to speak, prescribed in advance. Observers could not help but note a waning of the public's enthusiasm. Warning signs of this receding tide from 1960 onward included lower attendance at the ceremony ("the crowd was much thinner in the enclosures," the police reported)[148] and a reduction in commemorative fervor. The year 1960 was, after all, the 20th anniversary of the Appeal, and on that occasion, following a suggestion of Félix Brunau's,[149] French state radio and television invited the population of Paris and the suburbs to leave flowers at their town halls for the mont Valérien Memorial from the afternoon of the 17th onward, which would then be taken to the Fort by the police the following morning.[150] The response was somewhat disappointing: from Paris, sixty-four wreaths spread over all twenty *arrondissements* and eighty-three from the twenty-five largest towns in the suburbs. The geographical origins of the bouquets tell us about the political segmentation of Gaullist official memory: The middle-class neighborhoods made a good effort, with thirteen bouquets from the 7th *arrondissement* and forty from Neuilly. But the working-class areas, especially those under Communist influence, remained impassive; there was not a single bunch from Saint-Denis or Ivry. As the police report summed it up afterward in measured terms: "Overall, this depositing of flowers only elicited a moderate attendance."[151]

Other more directly political factors helped to dampen the commemorative zeal in the 1960s. At the height of the Algerian War, especially in the final years between 1960 and 1962, as France prepared to grant independence to its colony while at the same time containing the terrorist campaign waged by the pro-French Algeria settler movement, the Organisation de l'Armée Secrète, the organizers of the ceremony lived in constant fear of an assassination attempt against de Gaulle. In 1961 a "suspect" wreath placed near the Arc de Triomphe was removed for examination by the municipal laboratory (in the end it was found that only good taste had been endangered: The flowers were plastic),[152] and a large number of plainclothes police were placed in the crowd at the mont Valérien, some with "hidden megaphones."[153] After being inflicted by the

General's supporters on their political opponents' commemorations, it was the turn of Gaullian rites to bear witness to counterdemonstrations. More than sixty people were held by the police in Paris at the time of the 18th of June 1958 celebrations[154] and almost twice as many on the 4th of September.[155] The General was booed and insulted as he traveled toward the mont Valérien and again at the unveiling of the Memorial in 1960, when one Bitschif, a railway engineer, shouted, "What a load of cobblers!" at the Memorial. When questioned by the police, he admitted that his intention had been to insult the Resistance veterans.[156] A few years later, Gaston Thibaut, an undertaker's clerk from Suresnes, was held for questioning near the mont Valérien where he had been seen "using a spatula to tear down the posters announcing General de Gaulle's visit": Obviously prepared for all eventualities, he was also carrying on his person a "rubber truncheon weighted with lead."[157] Such incidents also added drama to the 18th of June ceremonies in the provinces, especially during the first years of the Gaullian Republic. For example, in 1958 fistfights broke out in front of the PCF headquarters on the Cours Napoléon in Ajaccio; shots were fired, and the police had to use tear gas.[158]

However, in general terms, the 18th of June ceremonies really took off in the 1960s, working their way, with some help from the prefectures and boosted by the local Free French associations, into the official calendars of commemorations in the provinces (notably at Grenoble, Limoges, Lorient, Rennes, Strasbourg, Metz, Bordeaux, Lille, Lyon, Roubaix, Reims, Marseille, Tourcoing, and Libourne).[159] The celebration of the 18th of June at this time also became an international affair. In London, French Ambassador Geoffroy de Courcel (who had been the General's aide-de-camp during the Free France years) marked the day every year by laying a wreath at the Free French monument in the military cemetery at Brookwood in Surrey and then presiding at a ceremony before the plaque on the General's old headquarters in Carlton Gardens.[160] In Francophone Africa, the 18th of June was again marked by wreath-layings, notably in Tunis, Libreville, Yaoundé, Bangui, Tananarive, Brazzaville, and Algiers; the practice even spread to some English-speaking cities with historic Free French connections, such as Lagos. Thanks to de Gaulle's decolonization, the memory of 1940 could be wholeheartedly celebrated in the Third World. In 1966, Algerian president Boumedienne sent a telegram to General de Gaulle, declaring that the 18th of June Appeal was "a great moment in the history of France and in the struggle of all peoples and individuals for liberty."[161]

The only seriously sour note in relation to the 18th of June in France was struck by the ongoing divergence between Gaullists and Communists. The 1960s marked the apogee of the "memory battle" between the two forces, with the PCF trying both to play down the importance of the 18th of June and to establish a different date, July 10, when Maurice Thorez and Jacques Duclos (falsely) claimed to have launched an appeal to fight against the invader.[162] In this Gaullo–Communist conflict, the mont Valérien site was an essential symbolic stake—but it was far from being the only aspect of the split between them. Outside Paris, this struggle between the two camps that had been dominant during the Resistance was often carried on through their respective veterans' associations. Thus Roanne had to wait until 1964 for the two communist-influenced groups, the National Associations of Resistance Veterans and the National Patriotic Federation of Resistance Survivors of Deportation, to agree to take part in the 18th of June ceremony. But at the same time in many other towns, including Toulouse, some associations of veterans and war victims still refused to attend the official commemoration, while in Narbonne it was the representatives of the city council who would not agree to be associated with the ceremony.[163] More generally, a series of studies undertaken by the Institute for Contemporary History on the 8th of May celebration shows that commemoration of the Second World War was marked by important local divisions throughout the 1960s—and often later.[164]

For it was often difficult, in the provinces but in Paris too, to dissociate the celebration from a certain partisan spirit. In the 1960s, the mont Valérien ceremony was stewarded by the Civic Action Corps (SAC), a muscular volunteer association that did not represent (to put it mildly) the most ecumenical side of Gaullism.[165] In 1964 de Gaulle left the mont Valérien to cries of "Seven more years!"[166] and in 1968, in the course of a ceremony that took place only a few weeks after the student protests in May, cries of "Pompidou! Pompidou!" were heard. Ironically, the celebration of 1968, marked as it was by a spirit of partisan and vengeful Gaullism, was the only one to bring out the large crowds of yesteryear (estimated by the police at 15,000).[167] Security at the Elysée noted with alarm that 70,000 open invitations had been sent out and concluded apprehensively that "we must regard this as a public meeting which it will not be possible to control."[168]

On the 18th of June 1969, the Mont Valérien ceremony unfolded in a strange, almost surrealist atmosphere: General de Gaulle, having been defeated in the April referendum, had resigned from the presidency and was in Ireland on a private visit.[169] His presidential successor, Georges Pompidou, had just been elected but was not yet officially in office. He went to the mont Valérien, but only in his private capacity.[170] One farcical detail was that the organizing authorities, fearing the appearance of the interim President Alain Poher (a centrist who was hostile to Gaullism and who was detested by the Gaullists), instructed the police that if he did head out from Paris, he was to be given wrong directions for reaching the site.[171] The small crowd (only a quarter as large as the previous year), the obvious disappointment of many former resistants (many had not bothered to make the journey), and the curtailment of the ceremony (there was no visit to the crypt) were evidence of a general malaise. Jacques Foccart, de Gaulle's right-hand man at the Elysée, did try to find a formula that would be convincing, at least for himself: "It is obvious that the General is with us, absent in the flesh but so very present in the spirit";[172] but the syntax betrayed his unease. For many people, including one of the policemen present, the Appeal ceremony seemed to have lost its soul, since "nobody wanted to take General de Gaulle's place."[173]

That it should appear almost inconceivable that the anniversary of 1940 could be celebrated without the Gaullian presence shows the extent to which the Man of the 18th of June had left his imprint on this memorial rite—a personal stamp, made more significant by his unquestioned status as herald of the Resistance and finally given permanence by his many years as Head of State and founding father of the Fifth Republic. Thus one could note that even in its dimension as an individual tribute, the 18th of June rite had been marked by a certain syncretism. This hybrid character was accentuated by the many variations in the meaning of the anniversary over time: During the war, the 18th of June had been the symbol of refusal to accept the defeat of 1940, while between 1946 and the late 1950s, de Gaulle had tried to make it the symbol of the "Thirty Years' War" and the continuity of French national sacrifice across the two world wars. A determinedly martial and patriotic celebration to begin with, by the 1960s the 18th of June had begun to take on an increasingly irenic and poignant character, as the oldest members of the Resistance generation were beginning to die off. Having been a rite of opposition to the government of the Fourth Republic in the 1950s, its audience shrinking to the last of the faithful, with the stands sometimes half-full,[174] it became a State ceremony under the Fifth Republic, overseen by the local administrations and honored throughout France by the veterans' associations.

The mont Valérien rite was a collective celebration of the chief values of the Resistance but also, through the various and sometimes contradictory interpretations of what was meant by the "18th of June spirit," a reminder of the profoundly personal dimension of the "Resistancialist" ethic. Finally, after 1958, the 18th of June symbolized the Gaullian reconquest of power but also, recalling as it did the "Republic in exile" and the heroic purity of the resistance struggle, carried an implicit recognition of the fragility, the mediocrity even, of the present time.[175] For some Companions, this feeling that the 18th of June rite was losing its "sacred" character would obviously be accentuated after the death of the General.[176]

Across these variations with time, one could still observe several constants in the practice of the 18th of June commemorations. First, the particular, even unique, place that this political ritual held in the General's heart. In the 1960s, preparations for the anniversary began in the spring with a visit to the Elysée by the Grand Chancellor of the Order of the Liberation to receive "his instructions for the organisation and running of the ceremonies."[177] In 1965, in a private conversation at the Elysée with Jacques Foccart on the 25th anniversary of the Appeal, de Gaulle did begin by saying that he was "constantly" celebrating anniversaries but added, with typical Gaullian understatement, "this one is different."[178] The journalist Jean Mauriac recalls de Gaulle saying that he did not want to be "trapped" by the memory of the 18th of June, but his decision to be out of France for the anniversaries in 1969 and 1970 shows us how important the date remained for him until the end of his life. "If God spared him," he was planning to spend the day in China in 1971.[179] As he declared himself, in a message sent to the 18th of June Club in London in 1944, "The 18th of June was the day when our hearts were right in the face of reason! Some of us that day listened to our hearts. So they were the truly reasonable ones."[180]

At the same time, his attachment to the date did not suppress the Gaullian preference for short and simple ceremonies: Even under the Fifth Republic, the General's appearances at the mont Valérien never lasted more than forty minutes.[181] These two key qualities were also in evidence in most of his commemorative journeys. Thus, in April 1965, on the occasion of his inaugural visit to the Memorial of the Martyrs of Deportation on the Ile de la Cité, he went to pray silently in the crypt, having previously insisted that "his visit to that spot should be as simple in character as possible."[182] In the same year, for the 20th anniversary of Victory in Europe (VE) day, de Gaulle led a brief military ceremony at the Arc de Triomphe: He was back in the Elysée inside the hour.[183] At the time of the 50th anniversary of the armistice in November 1968, the General carefully studied the program of proposed celebrations handed to him by his secretariat and took out anything he thought overblown—for example, the idea of a "Son et Lumière" display in Paris on the night of the 10th.[184]

There was a similar continuity in the silence that the General observed in public.[185] This attitude, which by the early 1950s the Order of the Liberation was already considering a "tradition of grandeur and self-mastery,"[186] could be interpreted in various ways: as a dominating silence; a silence of spiritual communion; a silence of civic meditation inherited from wartime Gaullism, when the General encouraged the population to observe a minute's silence at national celebrations, a discreet way of flying the republican banner then crushed under the Nazi jackboot;[187] or even a silence in tribute to the unknown dead, those who vanished without glory or triumph, humiliated, tortured, deported, or murdered. The General's silence in these places in a sense expressed the vanity of social discourse in the face of individuals who had made their commitment and sacrificed themselves of their own accord, unsupported by conventions or other social constructs.[188] As Régis Debray has thoughtfully remarked, great myths function by withholding explanations: de Gaulle's silences were pure genius.[189] But at the Liberation, and especially after 1958, this habit of silence also became an instrument for the reification of memory. The Gaullian impenetrability made it easier to establish the legend of the Resistance—the unification of what Malraux called the "disorder of courage" into a single movement. The mythification of the 18th of June 1940 into a moment of national collective enthusiasm would make it possible to gloss over inconvenient facts like the initial stutters of Free France, the real enthusiasm of the French public for Marshal Pétain in the first years of the war, and—last but not least—the important Communist contribution to the liberation of the country. What better symbolic (and devilishly efficient) method could there have been to encroach on the territory of the "party that had 75,000 members shot" than to build an exclusively Gaullian Memorial on a site where the majority of men and women executed were Communists?

Let us note in passing that this difficulty in defining the true "meaning" of the 18th of June is a sign of a recurrent problem in French political culture: how to represent in official memory the founding act of a new political order. From the great Revolution and the 18th of *Brumaire* through December 2, 1851, and September 4, 1870, to May 1958, French regimes born of insurrectionary movements have always had difficulty in devising an image of themselves that would transcend the circumstances of their birth—a difficulty linked to immediate circumstances but also to the inherent fragility of the national consensus. De Gaulle was quite aware of this problem, and that no doubt partly explains why there was no serious effort at creating a new national festivity after his return to power in 1958. A General Commissariat for Commemorative Memorials was created in 1960, but it never really achieved effective institutional autonomy.[190] Apart from this, the only notable act of official memory of the Gaullian Republic was the transfer to the Pantheon of the remains of Jean Moulin, de Gaulle's representative among the French Resistance groups, who was captured and killed by the Nazis in 1943—a tragic symbol of all those anonymous heroes of the Resistance who fought for French freedom between 1940 and 1944.[191]

Looked at over time, what was the deepest sense of the political rite of the 18th of June, and what does it tell us about the construction of the Gaullian legend? The General always insisted that his own fundamental legitimacy stemmed from the Appeal of 1940, and for him this historical legitimacy obviously transcended all other procedures of political sanctification—even, one imagines, his direct election by universal suffrage in 1965. The General was often called a "Republican monarch," and in the crowd's desire at the 18th of June commemorations to see and to touch de Gaulle, or simply to catch his eye, there was certainly something that recalled the sacred aspect of monarchy before 1789. Seeing the populations of the Ardennes and of Champagne rushing toward the General in 1963 during an official visit to these localities, Alain Peyrefitte (a Minister in de Gaulle's government at the time) asked himself whether the French popular cult of de Gaulle represented an implicit return to a form of monarchist sentiment.[192] Is such a view borne out by our analysis of the rituals of the 18th of June?

Certainly there was a kingly element in the Gaullian "mystery," in the inability even of members of his inner circle to "read" him,[193] as well as in the Gaullian claim to be the incarnation of sovereignty, to—in his own words—"take responsibility for France." From the earliest years, the 18th of June ritual at the mont Valérien was designed to display the Gaullian charisma, notably with the General's striking arrival in an open car.[194] But as we have seen, de Gaulle always firmly opposed (at the Liberation, and still more in the early 1960s) the idea that the 18th of June ceremony should take on a truly monarchical character, either by attracting larger crowds, developing longer and more triumphalist ceremonies, or including grandiloquent speeches. In 1960 and again in 1965, at the time of important anniversaries of the 18th of June, the General rejected various proposals to organize more grandiose displays (including one suggestion by a former war veteran to strike and issue a gold medal bearing his portrait).[195] Whatever one may say about the areas of symbolic and substantive similarity between Gaullism and Bonapartism, political ceremonial was not one of them. There is nothing surprising in that, for while they shared a love of "greatness," each political tradition conceived it in very different ways. Napoleonic festivals were driven by a strident nationalism and a triumphalism that knew no bounds, while in 1944 and 1945 de Gaulle celebrated the return of the Republic in a patriotic rather than a nationalistic spirit and was careful to include Churchill and the other Allies in the victory celebrations. Returning to power in 1958, de Gaulle took an official part in the 8th of May commemorations, especially the 15th anniversary of Victory in 1960—but here too the tone was extremely restrained and the rites very short;[196] it was a date to be celebrated but, as he once said to his son-in-law, "without overdoing it."[197] More generally, the chief qualities of the mont Valérien rite were privacy, silent meditation, restraint, and humility, as well as its lay character, for the design of the ceremony did not include any overt sign of religious belief or practice. During the 1960s, as the General became visibly older, the theme of death also discreetly underlay the ceremony. It was sometimes whispered that the ninth (empty) tomb was being kept for his remains.[198]

In fact, de Gaulle himself had his own "18th of June spirit." Far from trying to set himself above those close to him, or to inspire any kind of monarchical deference, at the ceremonies de Gaulle set aside his grandeur to become once more, for a few minutes, an ordinary resistance member, on par with all his companions; as he had once said, "The 18th of June is a time when I look back on myself along with all the others."[199] If the 18th of June ceremony was not explicitly a memorial practice of republican inspiration, it looked strangely like one. And that is no doubt why, on the 18th of June 1970, as he was correcting his *Memoirs of Hope* in an isolated country house in the Sierra Blanca in Andalusia, the General—once more in exile—received a voluminous post on the day of the anniversary of the Appeal.[200] All these letters, notes, postcards, and telegrams expressed the emotional tribute of Frenchmen and Frenchwomen to a decidedly unusual private citizen.

CHAPTER 5

♔

Father of the Nation

I n March 1960, General de Gaulle received a letter from Mme Clergerie, headmistress of the Lycée Jean Dautet in La Rochelle. This fervent Gaullist began by expressing her joy at the prospect of a presidential visit to the Charentes, and then dived back into her memories:

> I have not forgotten your last visit to La Rochelle, on the 23rd of July 1948. On that day I had the great pleasure of being presented to you, and you were kind enough to sign a little photograph of you that I had secretly obtained during the siege of La Rochelle . . . Ever since the 18th of June 1940 you had been our only hope! The late Monsieur Moinard, then mayor of La Rochelle and formerly deported by the Germans, had told you how I put up your portrait in the hall of my school on the day of our liberation, and how I then had to struggle to keep it there, when a Communist town councillor tried to make me take it down when you founded the RPF.[1]

This missive shows the extent to which Charles de Gaulle, first president of a new republic, had remained in the eyes of his supporters a figure separate from the vicissitudes of day-to-day politics, and the incarnation (and inspiration) of a bedrock of fundamental values: patriotism, loyalty, hope, and determination. The photograph of the General, treasured like a holy icon by this schoolteacher and protected like a relic first against the occupier's injunction and then against Communist insult, is a fine illustration of the renewed fervor of the Gaullian cult at the dawn of the Fifth Republic. The letter shows, too, in its evocation of the magic date of his visit to La Rochelle in 1948, how profoundly a meeting with the General could mark the men and women who had experienced it. The Gaullian

legend was built over time from immense blocks of granite, briefly sur-
veyed in the preceding chapters: the titanic combat of the Resistance, the
epic narrative of the *Memoirs*, the solemn political rites of the postwar
years, and the first years of the Fifth Republic. But the same providentialist myth also took shape, on a different scale, among the scraps of individual recollections, carefully stowed away in the memories of tens of
thousands of anonymous individuals who had one day found themselves,
by chance or design, on the General's path. The Charentaise headmistress's letter is particularly emblematic from this point of view, for it fo-
cuses precisely on a key element of the Gaullian mythological repertoire:
the journey. From his wartime odysseys across the northern hemisphere,
to his travels across France at the Liberation and his unofficial movements during the "crossing of the desert," followed by his official journeys
in France and all around the world during the Fifth Republic, to say
nothing of his last travels after 1969—as with all political giants (again,
Napoleon inevitably comes to mind), there was always something rest-
less about de Gaulle, an arresting mixture of the figures of the pilgrim,
the explorer, and the commercial traveler.

Above all, this piece of preserved memory sent from the provinces
symbolized the intense epistolary relationship established between the
French and the General. Like many men of his generation, de Gaulle was
a keen letter-writer throughout his life, as is shown by the collection of
his letters published by his son, admiral Philippe de Gaulle.[2] Less well
known but equally fascinating is the considerable body of correspondence received by the General, starting in the Resistance years. This
mass of writing, which already astonished his secretary, Claude Mauriac, when de Gaulle first assumed public office at the Liberation, grew
further at the beginning of the RPF years and particularly in 1948 when
the movement organized a letter-writing campaign; several hundred
thousand letters were sent to the General at Colombey.[3] When the General returned to public life in 1958, some 100,000 messages of all kinds
were posted each year to the first president of the Fifth Republic, with
peaks at the times of exceptional events. For example, during the second
fortnight of April 1961, at the time of the Algiers putsch, de Gaulle
received no fewer than 22,000 letters (more than 1,400 a day); in April
1969, in the days immediately following his departure, the Elysée
counted more than 50,000.[4] These missives, from French correspondents but also from abroad, were first scanned by the president's secretariat at the Elysée, who then wrote analytical reports that were sent on

to the General. Now kept in the National Archives,[5] this correspondence often continued the long republican tradition of requests for interventions and favors,[6] but it could also take the form of critical commentary on important subjects of national and international politics, as well as raising smaller- scale issues: personal historical memories, everyday concerns, and local problems, such as the building of schools, roads, and bridges; the future of agriculture; and even the depopulation of rural France. These day-to-day reactions allow us better to appreciate the rhythm of the history of the Gaullian presidency as it was experienced by ordinary French men and women. It is striking also to note the small amount of correspondence generated by certain grand events in Paris: the reburial of Jean Moulin in the Pantheon, for example, or even the events of May 1968, compared with the veritable deluge provoked by some affairs that are now completely forgotten, like the question of veterans' pensions or the declarations of would-be independence by a Communist deputy from the island of La Réunion.

In fact, what these extraordinarily varied letters had in common was their authors' desire to share a kind of intimacy with de Gaulle: to involve him in their lives, their experiences, their hopes and fears, to tell him of their love for him—and sometimes their hatred. This epistolary fixation thus throws a fascinating light on the way in which representations of the General took final form during the first ten years of the Fifth Republic. For as his myth was taking off, thanks to his public actions in France and around the world and to the cumulative effect of time (one Swiss correspondent, writing in 1967, seemed to think that the General had been "at the helm for 27 years"),[7] de Gaulle was also becoming a more irenic figure: a protector of the nation, a figure of Christ-like holiness, a benevolent father. At the same time, a movement that is characteristic of the construction of political myths was in operation: First was the time of protest (often vehement, sometimes even violent, as at the time of the Algerian War in the early 1960s), followed by remorse and a sense of guilt, and finally, with the approach of death, the leader is seen as a martyr and a transcendent figure. This Gaullian dialectic thus culminated in the anthology of tributes to the General found in the public condolence books that were opened all across France and that in November 1970 put a final seal on his entry into legend.

As Resistance veteran Daniel Cordier recalls in his memoirs, the representation of the General as a father figure was already well established during the 1940–1944 era.[8] Accentuated by the passage of time, this paternal image constantly looms in the thoughts of the ordinary men and women who wrote to the General after his return to power in 1958. This identification was often meant literally: In June every year, de Gaulle would receive hundreds of Father's Day cards. Letters, telegrams, and cards also poured in on St. Charles's Day at the beginning of November and the General's birthday on November 22. Good wishes were also sent, though in smaller numbers, for the General and Madame de Gaulle's wedding anniversary. The Constitution of the Fifth Republic enshrined the president's role as "arbiter," but this function was obviously given a wide interpretation by the public. The General's intervention was constantly sought to settle strictly private conflicts; in his correspondence we find many letters concerned with divorces and the custody of children, or about family differences between generations. One young man asked de Gaulle to help him find new lodgings, since he no longer wished to live with his "tyrannical" mother.[9] The father of one large family (eleven children) asked the General to help him find a school for two of his offspring;[10] young girls sometimes asked his permission to marry.[11] Men of the younger generation often ended their letters by mentioning their "filial feelings" for de Gaulle[12]—feelings shared by the General's bodyguards, who among themselves referred to him as "Pops."[13] Pierre Lefranc, one of the most faithful members of the General's staff at the Elysée, asked his permission before marrying.[14]

Among the senders of greeting cards, the favorite date was June 18, a totemic anniversary, as we saw in the last chapter, symbolizing the General's historic legitimacy as well as the originality of the political tradition he created and his ability to "take responsibility for France." In the public mind, this date transcended all the "republican" political anniversaries. From this point of view there was an interesting divergence: The overwhelming majority of the greetings received by the President on July 14, France's national day, were official messages from foreign heads of state; for his fellow citizens, the General might now be president, but he was still the Man of the 18th of June. The anniversaries of the Appeal were also marked by a large number of letters sent from abroad by private individuals; thus at the time of the twenty-fifth anniversary in 1965, the president received greetings from the United States and from Britain (mostly from veterans), but also a considerable number from Germany and Italy.[15] Many of the letters from France contained expressions of gratitude, loyalty, and respect, sometimes approaching religious veneration—like the one from a woman from the town of Vanves, who wrote to the General, "Ever since I was fifteen, in 1940, you have been the focal point, the great joy and the great concern of my life; some experiences that we shared with you, at some 18th of June gatherings at the mont Valérien, were unique moments that I felt transcended my own tiny personal destiny."[16]

The General/Father was also an authority figure, and this aspect was never more important than in the early days of the Fifth Republic, when he was struggling with the Algerian problem, which kept him fully occupied during the first four years of his presidency. It was a crisis in this territory that brought de Gaulle back to power in May 1958, and initially the French settlers (backed by the local military) had high hopes that the General would support the continuation of French rule. However, the demand for self-determination by Algerians was too strong to be contained, and, after a negotiated settlement was reached between French and Algerian officials at Evian, a national referendum confirmed the territory's independence in 1962. Among the most memorable moments of the period was de Gaulle's journey to Algeria in June 1958, when he made his famously ambiguous statement: "Je vous ai compris!"—which could mean that he had understood French settlers but also that he had taken the measure of them. He also made an appearance on television in April 1961, when de Gaulle, in military uniform, lambasted the "handful of retired generals" who had attempted a military coup against him to prevent Algerian independence—after which the rebellion fizzled out.

The General's television appearances were always the subject of comment, mostly favorable, and this no doubt pleased him, since he always prepared his broadcasts carefully, even taking speech lessons at the Comédie-Française.[17] In his incarnation as Commander, de Gaulle was undoubtedly seen as a man of order, and many letters congratulated him on his action against the forces of subversion in France (communists) and in Algeria (the main organization fighting for self-determination, the Front de Libération Nationale). One correspondent even suggested that the Marseillaise should no longer be the national anthem, given its "too revolutionary" connotations, and should be replaced by an "Ode to de Gaulle" of his own composition, of which he sent a copy to the General (we shall spare the reader this effusion).[18] The General's regular appearance on television during the 1960s also produced a curious kind of familiarity: The viewing public[19] wrote to him to criticize the programs of the state television service. Subjects varied from the "trivialising" of the

Marseillaise to the "appalling" treatment of the news and even the over-exposure of the French singer and actress Line Renaud on Easter Monday 1960.[20]

The General/Father was a saving and protecting figure but a merciful one: hence a very large body of letters begging the president to exercise his right of reprieve. On average de Gaulle received almost 1,000 such requests every month during the early years of the Fifth Republic, almost all relating to criminal convictions. To these must be added several hundred requests for help addressed to Madame de Gaulle, whose active support for charity was well known. During presidential visits in France she would slip away to hospitals, hospices, and other charitable centers, where her appearances were much appreciated.[21] During the Algerian War, presidential pardon was avidly sought: In 1959, several thousand people wrote to ask him to order the freeing of conscientious objectors who refused to take up arms against Algerian nationalists.[22] At the height of the war, extremist supporters of French Algeria formed a terrorist organization, the Organisation de l'Armée Secrète (OAS), which resorted to armed struggle to prevent the territory's independence; it attempted to assassinate de Gaulle on several occasions. In April 1962, at the time of the trial of the OAS deputy leader General Edmond Jouhaud, after which he was condemned to death by the High Tribunal, de Gaulle again received 859 requests for a pardon—but also 571 letters demanding his execution.[23]

Another dimension of the paternal figure represented by de Gaulle was that of rebellion. To be sure, this questioning of the Father's authority found its most dramatic expression in May 1968, but the ground had been well prepared in advance, from the first years of the Fifth Republic. This spirit of rebellion was shown notably during the miners' strike of 1963, which had a considerable (if temporary) negative impact on the presidential image.[24] It sometimes took unexpected forms, as in the letter of August 1963, which attacked the General's family background: "You're just a Bavarian, a Frenchman by adoption," while a small but persistent minority accused him of selling out France to the Jews, with the help, said one, of the "Rothschild-Pompidou brain-trust."[25] But the two principal sources of protest were the exercise of presidential power and the Algerian War. From the moment of his return to power in 1958 (and largely because of the disturbing political and military circumstances under which he returned), the General's "authoritarianism" was roundly denounced by the republican Left. This tendency, always present in an undertone in his correspondence, reached its paroxysm in September and October 1962, when the (controversial) referendum on election to the presidency by universal suffrage was being organized. De Gaulle did receive messages of support, but many French men and women also expressed their alarm at such a concentration of power, which could easily be exploited by a cynical or unscrupulous successor. As one letter put it in more robust terms, "We don't want some 'bastard' coming in after you."[26] The most hostile shrieked about dictatorship: Dozens of letters compared him to Henri IV, Louis XIV, and (the supreme insult) Napoleon III.

These "political" protests were accompanied, particularly in 1961–1962, by a growing flood of letters about Algeria, expressing the whole range of national feeling, from enthusiasm through resigned acceptance to bitterness and cries of treason. Messages of support in general outnumbered objections: During the first fortnight of February 1960, de Gaulle received no fewer than 112,000 letters, cards, and telegrams, with the overwhelming majority (106,000) approving his Algerian policy "unreservedly."[27] But as the conflict reached its end, the two groups came more and more into balance, and during the first fortnight of August 1961, de Gaulle received 71 letters supporting and 71 opposing his policy[28] (the fall in the total number is easily explained—in August in France, holidays always come before political passions). In December 1961, more than 400 letters of insult were sent to the Elysée: Some of them came from the extreme Left (until the beginning of 1962, a number of letters accused him of being "in cahoots with the OAS"—this at a time when the General was the target of several attempts on his life and also received every week dozens of letters and OAS pamphlets, some of them threatening him with death).[29] When General Larminat, a distinguished Free French veteran, took his own life in July 1962 after being appointed chief judge of the Military Court of Justice, a disenchanted supporter wrote that de Gaulle should commit suicide too.[30] The General knew he was hated by a section of the population and took it philosophically: "There is one segment of Frenchmen, maybe one in five or ten, who will hate me until their dying day, for having turned them into debris of history. The Vichy people, the politicians of the Fourth Republic, the *piedsnoirs* [French settlers in Algeria][31] curse me, not so much for the harm I have done them as for the good I have done France by treating them harshly. Time is showing that they were wrong, and for that they will never forgive me."[32]

If the decolonization of Algeria was an end in itself, it was also a means of enabling France to resume her "rank" in Europe and in the world. The international aspect of the General's action was an important component of the Gaullian myth of "grandeur." As soon as the Algerian conflict was brought to an end, de Gaulle put the last touches on the Franco-German reconciliation, first by inviting Chancellor Adenauer to a state visit to France in July 1962, then following it by his own triumphal visit to Germany in September. Constantly invoking the friendship between the two peoples, and speaking in German on six occasions, de Gaulle was enthusiastically welcomed everywhere he went; 10,000 people came to see him in Bonn and 50,000 in Cologne and in Hamburg. His visit was ecstatically reported by *Der Spiegel*: "De Gaulle came to Germany as President of France: he leaves as Emperor of Europe."[33]

The show had begun. The German visit was the first of a series of grand diplomatic maneuvers (recognition of Communist China, rapprochement with the USSR, distancing of France from the integrated military command of NATO, criticism of the Vietnam War, vetoing Britain's entry to the Common Market), all with the object of demonstrating the "greatness" of France in the face of "Anglo-Saxon hegemony."[34] A fundamental element in this scheme was de Gaulle's constant international travels, from Mexico to Cambodia, via Poland, the USSR, and Quebec; these journeys confirmed the epic image of the General throughout the world. Malraux asked him one day why he was so popular in the farthest corners of Latin America; the General replied that he reminded them of Don Quixote, and added, "You know, my only international rival is Tintin! We're the little guys who don't let the big guys get the upper hand."[35] The feeling of pride restored was evident in the letters sent to the General at the Elysée. One correspondent celebrated the Gaullian success on the international stage in these terms: "Beyond our frontiers people have acclaimed you: they recognize in you the perfect guide for France and for Europe." Another letter, sent from Cambodia by a *lycée* teacher in October 1965, said the writer was "proud to represent France in the Far East" and added that "here they love France, as symbolised by you."[36] For many of his correspondents, de Gaulle personified not only the greatness of France but also her political and cultural influence. As a Dominican missionary wrote, returning from a journey across Africa and the three Americas, de Gaulle had restored the good name of France and above all her "moral, spiritual and, in a word, human prestige."[37] A totemic symbol of this representation of de

Gaulle as an all-powerful and irenic guide is a folder of twenty-odd drawings by a primary school class in the Rhône, illustrating the career of General de Gaulle and sent to the president by their teacher. Among these naïve depictions, two referred to foreign policy. One showed de Gaulle holding the peoples of the world by the hand, with the legend, "France has no enemies any more. The war leader has become a peace-maker." The other image showed de Gaulle standing in his car, greeting a foreign crowd in an official procession. The message was equally gallo-(and Gaullo-)centric: "In all the countries in the world people acclaim the First Frenchman."[38]

Popular acclamation was also the main object of presidential trips in metropolitan France. With these journeys, de Gaulle was continuing the tradition of presidential visits under the Third and Fourth Republics, with their strict protocol and "unanimist" stage management. But there were also distinctively Gaullian details: the promotion of a new political order (in this, de Gaulle was in the line of descent of Gambetta, who had carried out a series of journeys across France in the early to mid-1870s to win over provincial and rural populations to the republican cause); the unashamed presentation of a new incarnation of political power (here the General was picking up the thread of Louis-Napoleon's provincial travels in 1851–1852 at the moment of transition between the Republic and the Empire); and finally the desire to outplay his predecessors, both in form and in substance. For not only did he visit every *département* of metropolitan France during his first seven-year term of office, but he did so on a truly punishing schedule. The presidents of the Third and Fourth Republics stopped seven times on average on each journey; de Gaulle typically had thirty-eight engagements per journey—five times more than his predecessors. What was the point of this traveling frenzy? The General had no doubt: It was to accomplish, to make manifest through his person, a "striking demonstration of national sentiment."[39] One of the indices of his success was the popular mobilization he provoked: Crowds appeared—often in huge numbers—on the planned routes of his visits. Another important sign was the weight of local memories. Those who had seen de Gaulle, and above all those who had been presented to him or had fought their way through the sometimes indescribable crowds to shake his hand or to touch him, were to keep an unfading recollection of the encounter—often, this was one of the most vivid memories of their youth. One example among hundreds was the words written by Odette Duvivier of Douai, who, eleven years after she had seen de Gaulle, wrote this tribute to him on his death: "To the man who shook my hand when I was ten years old in 1959, when he passed through our town."[40]

These presidential visits were occasions for the projection of Gaullian myth and memory in metropolitan France but also gave rise to intense local controversies, with mayors desperately trying to have their commune placed on the presidential itinerary and councilors using de Gaulle's visit to try to secure a war decoration for their village. There were petty local conflicts between mayors and village schoolmasters, or mayors and priests, and protests and rebellions by various groups, from war veterans to nationalist groups campaigning for greater political and cultural autonomy from Paris, as during the General's visit to Brittany in early 1969.[41]

Behind all this activity and the appearance of sometimes sizable crowds that assembled to see the General pass, should we see another manifestation of the rise of Gaullian charisma, or was it rather, as a recent study of presidential travels in France suggests, an attempt by the authorities to "gift-wrap" local populations for the visiting dignitaries?[42] There is no doubt that the crowds did not appear by chance; the authorities did all they could to stir up and organize the enthusiasm of their fellow citizens, all the more so because it was often a question of countering the directives of the General's opponents. The PCF and the communist-led Confédération Générale du Travail, France's largest trade union, sometimes called on the local population to boycott the visit, as for example during the General's visit to the Michelin works at Cataroux (in the Auvergne) in June 1959. This attempt to spoil the Gaullian party was a failure: Almost all the workers turned out to welcome the president or even to cheer him. But the cries of "Vive de Gaulle!" had no doubt been warmly encouraged by the employers; de Gaulle's "success" with the workers was celebrated as a political triumph by the local political and administrative authorities.[43]

There was also a strong routine element in the ceremony rolled out on these occasions, from the gifts of "local produce" offered to the General (miners' lamps in the coal regions, pottery in Lorraine, game in the remote country districts) to the speeches by local dignitaries, which normally trotted out again the litany of accepted formulae for welcoming their distinguished visitor. When the president stopped in Dieue (Meuse) in June 1961, the town council declared itself proud "to welcome the Great Frenchman who for Twenty Years has been defending the Future of the Country," unanimously moving a "vote of confidence, of loyalty and gratitude to the leading figure of France."[44] The same expressions could no doubt have been used fifty or even 100 years earlier. In the president's speeches also, we find the usual understatements and discursive devices (among them the use of the third person to speak of himself). Whether he was in Pau, Grenoble, Lille, or Blénod-lès-Pont-à-Mousson, de Gaulle unfailingly stressed the patriotism and creativity of the local population, and (a recurring figure in Gaullian rhetoric) "read" in their presence their confidence in the destiny of the nation. It is not surprising, therefore, that the presidential mail should include (particularly during his first term of office) some letters highly critical of his provincial visits; particular exception was taken to the heavy security presence and the ineluctable schedule imposed by "Colonel de Bonneval's stop-watch."[45] There were protests against the organization of "waves of applause," something "contrary to the republican spirit,"[46] and the most daring (or the cheekiest) reminded him that Pétain too had been enthusiastically applauded by French crowds on his provincial tours.[47]

But despite the speed with which they were carried out and the pressures and various constraints to which they gave rise, these visits by the General to small towns and villages could also be the scene of intense collective emotion.[48] There was nothing contrived in the enthusiasm aroused by the General in most of the places he visited. One example was his visit to Alsace in November 1959. Despite the frostiness of the local centrist party, long-standing adversaries of the Gaullists, the General's appearances were greeted by sizable crowds—more than 10,000 at Guebwiller, more than 20,000 at Colmar, and more than 5,000 at Ribeauvillé. As the prefect noted, "Maybe more than the number of people present, what was truly exceptional was the wild enthusiasm of the crowd. In the villages on the General's route, the entire population was assembled at the point where he was to stop and the houses were deserted. For several kilometres on either side of the route, the villages were practically empty, everyone who could walk had gone to wait at the side of the road."[49] Such "naïve and touching scenes" as the official cortege passed through small villages were often reported by Parisian journalists covering the General's visits.[50] In these fleeting moments, the General became the focus of sometimes contradictory feelings—joy, respect, local pride, but also no doubt curiosity, as well as (in the most isolated areas) demands for support and help and a desire for individual recognition, symbolized by the crowd's frantic attempts to catch the Gaullian eye.

De Gaulle was a figure who personified authority, power, and fame— but also a certain vulnerability. In 1964, after he underwent a major operation, the president received many letters about his travels in France and abroad (the General had also undertaken a long journey around Latin America immediately after his operation). In these messages, admiration for his sense of duty and for his physical strength was mixed with expressions of concern about his health.[51] During the Algerian War, and the repeated attempts on the General's life, many correspondents begged him not to take unnecessary risks during his travels in the provinces and in particular to reduce his contact with the crowd. Let us note in this context that, according to police archives, his bodyguards found on individuals trying to get close to the General coshes, penknives, razor blades, and even syringes. These words of caution were repeated by the General's security entourage (and sometimes by the minister of the interior himself), but he rejected them with contempt. Warning letters continued to arrive, however, right up to the end of his first term of office. Some were particularly delightful, like the one sent by an inhabitant of Saint-Martin du Ré, on the island of Ré, to Madame de Gaulle in May 1963, just before the presidential visit to the department of the Charente, on France's southwestern coast. The writer began by noting that the island "hadn't done so badly during the occupation" and that some traders "missed the good times"; now, he continued, a new population from Algeria had settled on the island, and many of them were OAS sympathizers. If the General planned to visit the island, the letter suggested that a keen eye should be kept on those circles, and it gave not only a list of the names of potential plotters but also their usual meeting places and the registration numbers of their cars. A colorful detail, worthy of a French gangster movie screenplay, was that their leader drove a yellow Citroën DS and was known as "The Monocle."[52]

And what about de Gaulle himself in all this? The General's provincial journeys were occasions to display his benevolent paternalism. The president was often touched by his encounters with the various aspects of local life, such as the welcoming gestures of the authorities who received him in their towns and villages. A sign of this feeling was the way the president dispatched to Colombey various gifts made to him by the local authorities; such was the fate of a fifteenth-century statue of St. Michael slaying the dragon, which was given to him by the city of Rouen on the occasion of his visit there in 1963,[53] and of two young swans given to the General by the commune of Fontenay-le-Comte (Vendée), which were ceremonially rehomed in the Colombey grounds in July 1965.[54] De Gaulle could also be touched by the fates of thousands of individuals who introduced themselves to him during his official visits: old First World War comrades; members of Resistance networks or of the RPF, whom he often recognized immediately thanks to his extraordinary memory; even members of his extended family—but also anonymous men and women that he was meeting for the first time. Sometimes these unplanned encounters made such an impression that the General set his staff to find out more about them, as in the case of the twelve-year-old juvenile delinquent he met at Arles in 1961 and about whom he had his staff inquire the following year.[55]

On his provincial visits, the head of state—like all his predecessors and successors—was apprised of local problems and the communes' investment needs. But de Gaulle did not simply listen with half an ear to the notables' complaints: He sometimes intervened directly with the ministries concerned to get certain cases that had been delayed moving again, as with the church at the martyred village of Oradour-sur-Glane, the site of one of the most infamous Nazi atrocities against civilians on French soil in 1944 (which de Gaulle first visited in march 1945),[56] or with the Bailey bridge over the Meuse at Saint-Mihiel, which had been damaged during the war and where the General was able to speed up repairs.[57] Where a project or a region involved him directly, the president—in the purest tradition of royal munificence—took action and dug into his own pocket. On February 25, 1962, for the inauguration of the Cultural Centre at Colombey-les-Deux-Eglises, the General invited the whole population of the village to a "vin d'honneur"; the bill for champagne and cakes was paid by de Gaulle himself.[58] At other times, the sums he disbursed were considerable. After his visit to Champagne in 1963, for example, de Gaulle sent checks for a total of 28,000 francs to the mayors of Colombey-les-Deux-Eglises, Lavilleneuve-aux-Fresnes, Buchey, Juzennecourt, Argentolles, Harricourt, Pratz, Biernes, and Rizaucourt (Haute Marne) to help support the public works going on in these villages; not surprisingly, his own commune took the largest share, with a gift of 10,000 francs.[59]

But—and this is no doubt the least-known and most surprising aspect of the General's journeys across the Hexagon—Gaullian generosity was at its most notable in the religious sphere. Not only did he make sizable gifts (usually through the agency of Madame de Gaulle) to orphanages and hospices in the regions he visited, but he also sent a check to every church where he had been welcomed, either for their good works or for maintenance and repairs. He continued this practice from 1959 to 1969. Whether for the cathedrals of Poitiers, Lyon, or Lille or a humble parish like Coulange la Vineuse (Yonne), the ritual was the same: The presidential visit to the church was followed a few weeks later by a letter from the secretary-general of the General's presidential office and a check for a sum of between 500 and 1,000 francs, addressed to the priest who had welcomed de Gaulle; the recipient was asked to regard the gift as "personal and confidential."[60] When he traveled through the Nord region in 1966, de Gaulle took this religious concern to the point of sending a financial contribution of 2,000 francs to a priest he had never met who had fallen and hurt himself after saying mass at Ebblinghem in the place of Father de Gail, who had been preaching a sermon before the General at the time of his visit. Though there had been no direct connection between this accident and de Gaulle's visit, and against the advice of his entourage at the Elysée, the General insisted on carrying out this gesture of Christian charity.[61]

As he moved through his second term of office after his reelection as president in 1965 (which had not been as easy as he had expected, as he had to fight a runoff against his socialist opponent), the General's image in public opinion was developing in two directions. On the one hand, he was venerated, idolized even, by the large following he had already acquired and that celebrated in him a providential Father, personifying the private virtues of goodness, kindness, and generosity, and also the founder of a new political order—or, as one admirer put it, in terms that might have been used of the French revolutionary leader Robespierre, "the saviour and purifier of the Republic."[62] But on the other hand, as we have already seen, this paternal Gaullian figure was increasingly challenged—sometimes even in his own camp. As well as the wear and tear of power that it evidenced, this questioning of his authority had deep political causes (the Right won the parliamentary elections of 1967 only by the smallest of majorities [one seat]). These tremors would soon culminate in the earthquake of May 1968, which made Gaullian power tremble on its pedestal, not least because the challenge to the president came from such an unexpected source, that is, France's youth. At the height of the student protests in Paris, de Gaulle seemed isolated, out of touch, and overtaken by events, and there is no doubt that his authority suffered a serious blow, even though he managed to seize the political initiative and win an absolute majority of seats for the Gaullist party in the subsequent legislative elections of June 1968. This gloomy end to his presidency culminated in his defeat in the referendum of April 1969, which led to his resignation. It was not unlike the equally anticlimactic final years in power of other mythical figures, such as Napoleon at the end of his reign.

This weakening of the Gaullian image had its effects even on the General's foreign policy, which could sometimes produce serious disquiet in certain sections of national opinion. France's withdrawal from the integrated command of NATO in 1966, for example, occasioned a continuing wave of letters to the Elysée, most of them solidly hostile to the General's symbolic gesture. Many critics wrote from the regions of France that had been liberated by American troops; for example, a woman from Alsace wrote to the General, "Remember that without the American army Alsace would not have returned to France."[63] Responding to the General's violent criticisms of America's war in Vietnam, some correspondents from the United States did not hesitate to speak of a "stab in the back."[64] The General's anti-Americanism was meat and drink to cartoonists, who often exploited the theme of ingratitude. For example, a drawing by the Swiss cartoonist Jean Leffel shows de Gaulle turning his back on an American ship; on the deck stands a soldier who is calling out to the General, "Remember, if you're ever in trouble and need us again, the number is 14-18-39-45."[65]

Having said this, it is curious to note that some aspects of Gaullian policy toward the "Anglo-Saxons" could generate enthusiastic support in the very countries against which it was directed. Thus, de Gaulle's veto against British entry into the Common Market occasioned a lively correspondence from across the Channel. Far from expressing any displeasure, the overwhelming majority of these Britons congratulated de Gaulle on his position, and some begged him to shut the door of the European Economic Community on their country permanently.[66] During the summer of 1967, one Englishwoman traveled as far as the gates of Colombey to tell de Gaulle "not to give in," adding that England should not enter the Common Market "at any price."[67] It was thus, in his own lifetime, that the General began his long career as an icon of British Euro-skepticism. Much less positive, on the other hand, was the reaction to his press conference in November 1967, when the General criticized Israeli expansionism, castigating the aggressive behavior of "the chosen people, sure of themselves and dominant." Between November and the end of December 1967, de Gaulle received several hundred letters of protest from French Jews; some accused him of forgetting that "Jews were active members of the Resistance," whereas others, still angrier, accused him of anti-Semitism.[68] The episode had a lasting effect on the Jewish community in France, and some would never lose their feelings of resentment toward the General—so much so that in the middle of May 1968, de Gaulle received a letter driving home the point: "If France is damaged by these events, you should see in it the hand of God, punishing you for your anti-Israel policy."[69]

These clashing voices were suddenly silenced in April 1969 by the General's departure from politics after losing a referendum he had called on the issues of regionalism and the reorganization of the French upper legislative chamber, the Senate. This was the fifth referendum de Gaulle had called since returning to power in 1958, and on each of the previous occasions he had won decisively. This time, however, he was defeated by a small majority (10.9 million votes in favor and 12 million against). In the rise of the popular Gaullian legend, this 1969 exit, all at once sudden, brutal, and irreversible, had a major impact. De Gaulle's departure from public life was perfectly staged and executed, from the brief communiqué stating that he would no longer be exercising his presidential functions to the silence into which he retreated, saying to his entourage: "I will speak no more."[70] And when the General reappeared a few months later, he was, as Jean Mauriac says, "a man suddenly grown old, wrapped in a long ulster, walking with a stick on the sands of Ireland."[71] His aide-de-camp had the feeling that they were "almost banished."[72] And to bring out clearly this symbolism of shipwreck, one of the bedside books the General chose for his Celtic interlude was Napoleon's *Mémorial de Sainte-Hélène,*[73] that bible of political exiles. After April 1969, the General's close associates noted that the Man of the 18th of June was interested only in writing his *Memoirs* and seemed indifferent to French political events (Georges Pompidou's election to the presidency prompted the acid comment: "Now France will go on sliding towards mediocrity").[74] De Gaulle effectively withdrew from the world. Between his resignation from the presidency and his death in November 1970, he received only a handful of people at Colombey and did not attend any official or public ceremony—not even the funerals of longtime associates or men he intellectually admired, such as the writer François Mauriac. There had been a real "break" between the General and France.[75]

The emotional shock of the presidential resignation was expressed in the flood of mail sent to the Elysée and to Colombey immediately after the announcement of the General's departure. In these 50,000-odd letters we notice first of all (unsurprisingly) very many expressions of support, especially from Free French veterans, and of admiration for the political work carried out by the General, which one writer summed up in the expression "eleven years of greatness."[76] Another, age eighty-seven, went further back in time, saluting the General as "the greatest Frenchman since the Dreyfus Affair," while a third went so far as to recognize in him as "the greatest monarch that France has had in all her history."[77] Others went through the magnificent sequence of Gaullian successes, insisting on the decisive role of the man sent by providence: "In 1940 you gave France back her honour, then her independence, then her liberty. Since then, on more than one occasion, you and you alone have saved the country from the dangers that threatened her, disorder, enslavement, civil war, bankruptcy and misery. Your African policy has spared France innumerable unjust and ruinous wars. The French owe you everything: their national independence, their political freedoms, their institutions restored to health, their material prosperity, their economic advances. They owe it to you above all, and only to you, that France, ever since you have been leading her, has always been respected."[78]

Many also saluted the democratic principle shown by the president in leaving the political scene immediately after losing the referendum in 1969; some even wondered whether this Gaullian withdrawal "was not, in the end, for the 'heroic' statesman, the most dignified and also the most effective exit."[79] Another writer makes the same point in a different way: "The French have given you, as they did to Clemenceau, the only present they could give, and the only one worthy of you: ingratitude."[80] But the dominant note was astonishment, conveying first of all a strong sense of collective guilt. Evidence of this were the regrets of those (and many expressed such feelings) who had fought against or rejected Gaullian power from 1958 onward—like the communist mayor of Montfermeil, who stated at a lunch party, "The French made a big mistake in not holding on to General de Gaulle: He was a great man and a good man who will be impossible to replace, and we may pay dearly for our stupidity."[81] A *pied-noir* wrote that the General had made him weep with rage in 1962, when Algeria became independent, but that on the evening of April 27 he had wept again, this time with despair. He added that he had never been a Gaullist but that he now regretted it "bitterly."[82] Some confessed openly that they had been blind: "It took your leaving to make me understand how great your place was."[83] In others, their distress was expressed as a range of more personal feelings: love ("We love you," wrote one, "that is well known and will become better known"),[84] sorrow ("We are in mourning"),[85] anger and shame at "the ingratitude and decadence of the French,"[86] chagrin ("This time the French have burnt Joan of Arc"),[87] and disoriented grief, as with the retired miner who wrote that his friends and family had become used to seeing and hearing the General and that now he was gone "everything seems paralysed."[88] One woman experienced the General's departure as an event on a cosmic scale: "The sun is gone, Spring is fading and our hearts are sad."[89] Similarly, a letter from a group of schoolmistresses ends by saying that the Gaullian departure had "plunged the universe into astonishment."[90] Some came to doubt whether things could ever return to normal. A young university teacher from Paris asked, "Is it possible that, after this, life will move on towards what they call the future, when suddenly everything has changed, been put into question and become uncertain?"[91]

Many people wrote to the General to say that France had shown herself unworthy of him: "One does wonder whether the French people really deserve the great men that history puts in their way at tragic moments in time."[92] But others simply could not see the point of his gesture: One letter read simply, "Why?" It was suspected—rumors always spread quickly in France—that medical problems may have determined his retirement, leading one correspondent to write, "Please believe that if you are leaving for health reasons, I and my three sons are ready to provide you with whatever organ you may require, including the heart."[93] Some felt let down, like orphans (an expression often used), and experienced his departure as a distancing, even a severing of relations—while others clung to the belief that he might still stand in the presidential elections of June 1969[94] or even that he was plotting another "18th of June"; these optimists asked him to "tell us what we should do to carry on the fight."[95] Some, paradoxically, felt closer to him, as if his return to private life had miraculously abolished the distance between him and his fellow citizens. One woman wrote to him, "Tonight I feel like writing to you as a brother. At this moment, my whole being is one great sorrow, simple, like a family bereavement."[96]

Eighteen months after leaving the Elysée, de Gaulle passed away at Colombey. If his resignation in April 1969 had been experienced as a national catastrophe, his death on November 9, 1970, unleashed one of the most intense moments of collective emotion in twentieth-century French history. As often happens, it was an image that summed up the national grief most directly: Jacques Faizant's drawing in the *Figaro*, showing a giant oak uprooted, with a Marianne weeping over it. This moment of shared mourning sealed the General's mythical status once and for all in the national consciousness and imagination, erasing with a single stroke the difficult final years of the Great Man's reign. As Jean Daniel wrote in the *Nouvel Observateur*, de Gaulle's death had overturned a negative trend that began with his failure to be reelected in the first ballot of the presidential election of 1965: "Damaged in 1965, broken in May '68, killed off in April 1969, the Gaullian magic has returned to life, and in dazzling fashion."[97]

This crystallization of the legend had been partly occasioned by de Gaulle's own rejection in his will (dating from 1952) of any official ceremony in his honor. By this gesture—truly republican in its austerity—the General had wished to free himself from any link to the Fourth Republic; in the context of the late 1960s, leaving this provision unaltered showed de Gaulle's wish (shared by his family) not to have his name exploited by the clique around his former associate Georges Pompidou (with whom de Gaulle had fallen out since 1968). It was also a way of saying (once more) that de Gaulle did not belong to any institution, party, or group but to the whole nation—and to immortality.[98] One sign of this mythogenic elevation was the separation between official rite and private ceremony. A requiem mass was said at Notre Dame on the morning of November 12, with the representatives of "official" France and more than eighty foreign heads of state in attendance; the American delegation was led by President Nixon. But the body of the deceased was elsewhere. The true funeral rite was celebrated a few hours later, in private and as simply as possible, in the church of Colombey, attended by the General's family, the municipal council of the village, and (a vital distinction between "State" Gaullism and "historic" Gaullism) the Companions of the Liberation, and they alone. The body was laid to rest in the family tomb, where his daughter Anne was already lying. On the gravestone were carved only the words "Charles de Gaulle 1890–1970."

The coverage of the event by the local and national press, and the filming of the funeral at Colombey by French television, allowed millions of men and women in France to accompany the Man of the 18th of June on his last journey.[99] Evidence of this extraordinary collective fixation was the richly illustrated volume published by Julien Roux-Champion, describing in detail every moment of the ceremonies at Colombey.[100] But it was not simply a matter of passive wallowing in grief. As always in the history of popular Gaullism in France, national feeling also found expression in writing: first in the thousands of letters of condolence that were sent to Madame de Gaulle at Colombey and, most of all and in an even more remarkable manner, in the written messages that soon appeared in the public condolence books opened by city, town, and village councils everywhere in France. Kept in the Charles de Gaulle Foundation[101] and never hitherto cited, these documents bring to a resounding conclusion the remarkable cycle of epistolary contacts between the General and the nation. In their thousands of pages of personal messages, these volumes shed a fascinating light on collective representations of the figure of de Gaulle at the time of his death. Of course, many who went to sign the book did simply that, leaving only their name preceded by a word or two of conventional condolence, but a good many also left longer comments, sometimes quite detailed, giving their view of the Gaullian political heritage; some even addressed their messages directly to the General, as if to add a last word to the dialog they had carried on with him during his long public life.

The most striking aspect of this mass of tributes, apart from its sheer size, is the exceptional social mixture within the Gaullian cult: Among this mass of anonymous writers, we find civilians and war veterans (of both world wars), members of the working and middle classes, northerners and southerners, laypeople and religious, the young and the old—even the very old, like Madame Louis Prévost, aged over 100, who made her way to her town hall in Nevers to place a firm signature, with her date of birth, in the public condolence book.[102] The second element, almost as striking as the first, is the great number of messages that mention having seen or met the General on one of the presidential journeys of his first term of office—like the one from the woman who remembered having seen the General in her town in 1960 and who cast her condolences in this form: "From a young Castellane girl who remembers once kissing him."[103] Such formulae (very common in these registers) also show that the intimacy between the General and the public had now gone a stage further. This growing closeness had already begun, as we have seen, with the emergence of de Gaulle as a Father figure. But this Father was still somewhat distant and aloof; his death transformed him, almost from one day to the next, into someone familiar, a relative or close friend. Thus at Marseille and Aix-en-Provence there were many expressions of affection and tenderness for the departed—de Gaulle was mourned "like a friend."

A few went so far as to do something unthinkable when he was alive and address him by the familiar *tu* (instead of the more formal *vous*), as in "tu vivras toujours."[104]

Created in great measure by the psychological shock of the General's death, this note of intimacy surfaced again in the writing of men who had been close to him, sometimes decades before. In the crowd of venerable figures who went to their town halls to pay their final tribute, we may single out the veteran of Squadron 102 during the Great War who had fought again with the Free French forces and who wrote simply, "Goodbye Charles, old man."[105] Other messages came from an officer who had served with the Polish Army in 1920 under Captain de Gaulle,[106] Colonel de Gaulle's driver in 1939–1940,[107] and Adrien Locardel, the head of the Free French forces' garage in London in 1940–1945.[108]

Among the major themes that recur in these comments, we find an echo of the reactions following de Gaulle's resignation in 1969 but now expressed with even more intensity, including an overwhelming sense of remorse. This guilt was in a way the logical pendant to the violence, even hatred, that had been shown by de Gaulle's opponents at the beginning of the Fifth Republic—chiefly by those on the Left who had accused him of "fascism" but also by the *Algérie Française* supporters. By some writers this remorse was presented as collective guilt, with words (very frequently recurring) like "Forgive the ingratitude of the French,"[109] but there were others for whom the General's death had obviously been a personal shock—like the man who wrote de Gaulle begging him to "please forgive me."[110] This remorse was felt by all generations, from the Communist who blamed himself for his long refusal to recognize the General's historic achievements (resistance, liberation, decolonization)[111] to the opponent of the "authoritarian" political order of the Fifth Republic ("We disagreed about everything, but I have to respect him today"),[112] and even the repentant youthful militant of 1968 who expressed his distress in simple words in his local condolence book: "I was there in May '68: I was an idiot, a child rebelling against his father and his family, against the head of state and against France itself. With the passage of time I see that you were right as always."[113] One woman in Menton thought that the ingratitude of the French had caused the unhappy exile to Colombey to die of grief: "De Gaulle suffered a lot. They stopped him being President and I don't think he never [*sic*] got over it."[114]

We find here, in these sorrowful expressions of collective guilt, three great mythogenic waves: first, the search for reconciliation, as necessary as it is impossible, with the figure of the departed Father. Many of the letters of condolence sent to Madame de Gaulle by women mention the recent deaths of their own husbands or fathers, in parallel with that of the General; his totemic figure in some way symbolized the ideals and sufferings of his generation. As one correspondent from Lussac-les-Châteaux (Vienne) wrote, "De Gaulle like my father suffered in 14–18 so that men would not have to go to war again."[115] Suffering for one's neighbor—these admissions of guilt also marked the elevation and consecration of Charles the martyr. In their different ways, the rejection by the French of de Gaulle in 1969, followed by his interior exile and a death both holy and sublime, played the same galvanizing role for the Gaullian myth as Saint Helena had for the Emperor Napoleon between 1815 and 1821. Finally, this representation of a martyred general was also sustained and reinforced by strong religious feeling. Here, too, we can assume that the presidential journeys through France, and particularly the General's private and public charitable gestures, had profoundly moved the Catholic community. In an ode published a few days after the General's death, one believer even hinted at his future canonization, adding that it would be justified by the perfection of his life, his admirable teaching, his love of justice, and above all "the persecutions that he suffered."[116] Throughout France, mourning French men and women wrote in their municipal registers that de Gaulle had been "a great Christian";[117] it was also said of him that "God had sent him to save France."[118] Sometimes this presumption of sanctity was voiced explicitly, as by the fervently Catholic woman who expressed her confidence that from where he now was, de Gaulle would continue to "watch over the future of France."[119] In the same vein, the General was compared to a prophet, to Christ,[120] even to God himself.[121] Some took this ecumenical creativity so far as to devise a new Trinity: "Jesus Christ, de Gaulle and my husband," wrote a woman from Aix: "There you have the humble life of a Frenchwoman."[122]

Beside these private epitaphs, looking forward to the beatification of the new Saint Charles, the condolence books also abound with notes and observations on de Gaulle's historic significance and political legacy. There was a remarkable absence, however; in these tens of thousands of inscriptions, Algeria was very rarely mentioned. It is true that two former inhabitants of that territory, now based in Aix-en-Provence, took the trouble of going to their town hall to record their lasting resentment against de Gaulle ("Shit on him. Signed: two *pieds-noirs*").[123] But the overwhelming majority of these repatriated settlers—more than a million of them returned to France after 1962—did not take up their pens. It is difficult to know how to interpret this silence except by recalling two things. First, as we have already seen in this chapter, de Gaulle had no illusions about what the *pieds-noirs* thought of him, and second, this resounding silence at the time of the General's death perfectly echoes the erasure of memories that marked the end of the Algerian War in France. This collective "amnesia" represented, for those who had had to leave their Mediterranean homes forever, the sense of a great affliction that was never to receive public expression. One small, sad sign of the impossibility of speaking of this sorrow was the message left by an inhabitant of Douai that simply read, "1957 to 1960, Algiers"[124]—as if to show his inability to sum up the range of emotions that he felt when trying to recover the memory of those eventful and tragic years.

The particular place of the Algeria syndrome in French collective memory becomes even clearer when we contrast it with the expressions of reconciliation, gratitude, and admiration from other notable opponents of the General's policies. "I never agreed with you politically," wrote one left-winger from Menton, "but I always admired you; you brought France back to life and I thank you for it."[125] Unlike the refugees from Algeria, mourning in silence, many Communists came to pay an explicit tribute to de Gaulle in November 1970, "in memory of the shared struggle against the Nazi occupier"[126] or to salute "the politician who stood for the freedom of peoples to decide their own destiny."[127] At the other end of the political spectrum, old hatreds also died away, as with the inhabitant of Saint-Cannat who wrote, "Our resentment fades before the Great Man and the great Christian that he was."[128] Several old Vichyites also put in an appearance, like the former admirer of the Marshal, now a de Gaulle supporter, who wrote, "I held against you for a long time what you did to Pétain. . . ."[129]

Other historic memories also featured in the varied tributes to the Gaullian legacy. Remembering the nationalizations of the Liberation era, his support of workers, and attempts to promote greater "participation," a man from Marseille stated, with perhaps a slight touch of exaggeration, that in the end the General had been "the first real socialist,"[130] while a woman from Salon-de-Provence, remembering the General's 1944 decree granting French women the right to vote, also noted that de Gaulle had "given French women full citizenship."[131] Others tried to sum up the General's policies in abstract terms: "De Gaulle meant above all justice."[132] His bold and novel foreign policy was not forgotten, particularly by the man from Aubagne who celebrated the memory of the "French leader" who had constantly fought against "Yankee imperialism and Zionism."[133] But—and this is not really surprising—the historic success most often credited to the General was his essential role in the Resistance: De Gaulle had been "a great soldier who freed our country from the German yoke."[134] And so, in thousands of inscriptions, the Man of the 18th of June was thanked for his Appeal (which many claimed they had personally heard) and for having "saved" France. In many cases, a double gratitude was expressed, for having pulled the country back from the brink during the war and again in 1958; one person, obviously still traumatized by the events of May 1968, wrote, "Thank you for saving us three times from France [sic]."[135] Already the supreme figure of the liberator and savior, on his death de Gaulle became the emblem of the nation; a thought that persistently recurred in the tributes was that without the General's personal action, France would simply have been wiped off the map. He was "the one who kept us French"[136] and "the man without whom France would no longer exist";[137] another writer expressed his gratitude by addressing the deceased directly: "If we are still French we owe it to you."[138]

Crowning all these tributes, the General's death also prompted a series of popular reflections on the place that the Man of the 18th of June would now occupy in the pantheon of national historic figures. We know that de Gaulle himself had intended to undertake this task in a third volume of the *Memoirs of Hope,* which he did not have time to begin. As if to underline the symbiosis that now existed between the General and French collective feeling, ordinary citizens made their views on this question clear in their local condolence books, writing in some sense a spontaneous coda to the Gaullian project.

What is striking about their observations is first the variety of the historical analogies drawn: As the incarnation of greatness, de Gaulle is often compared to Julius Caesar, Joan of Arc, and Louis XIV;[139] sometimes he is placed at the culmination of a series of heroic figures, as by the inhabitant of Ajaccio who wrote, "De Gaulle has entered the realm of legend. In telling the history of our great country, we used to say: the France of Joan of Arc, Bayard, Mirabeau, Bonaparte . . . Now we shall also say: the France of de Gaulle."[140] These comparative tributes often still insist on de Gaulle's uniqueness. A parish priest from Châlons-sur-Marne declared, "In our Western world I can see only Julius Caesar and General de Gaulle who were at the same time great generals, great statesmen and excellent writers. But in other respects, and particularly in their deaths, what a difference!"[141] A man from Corrèze added, "General de Gaulle has often been compared to Joan of Arc, but Joan was a symbol which was exploited, while de Gaulle was a man who imposed himself on events."[142] All this meant that de Gaulle was not just the last avatar in a series but its culmination, the ideal type of the political icon: "France has had many Great Men: she has had only one Charles de Gaulle."[143] Another went further, "Homage to the greatest man of all time,"[144] while yet another explained, "De Gaulle is the greatest of all, for he was the only one who embodied all the four virtues: freedom, faith, greatness and peace."[145]

Final signs of this Gaullian consecration in the public and private imagination of the French were the frequency, length, and intensity of the comparisons made between the General and Napoleon Bonaparte. The two legends were similar in the speed of their growth among the people (the Napoleon myth was born in 1815, on the Emperor's departure for Saint Helena). At the same time, we can see in this the completion of a symphony left unfinished by events—for many of the letters sent to the General after his resignation in April 1969 were already making comparisons and contrasts between the destinies of the two great men. A quote from a letter from a history teacher from the town of Saint-Denis in the Indian Ocean island of La Réunion, affirmed that de Gaulle had miraculously brought together in his person "Bossuet, Chateaubriand, Richelieu and Bonaparte," before adding these well-chosen words, "but a Bonaparte who had the extraordinary merit of refusing for himself the Napoleonic mirage."[146] In the same vein was the composition sent to de Gaulle by a teacher at the International Lycée at St. Germain en Laye, which began by noting that, unlike the Napoleon of the Hundred Days, who ended his reign with the defeat at Waterloo, after his loss in the referendum de Gaulle had left power "like a hero." The text ended with these words: "He did not shine with the glory of the conqueror and legislator, like Caesar or Napoleon, but like them Charles de Gaulle deployed in the service of his statesman's genius an incomparable gift as an orator and a writer. Like these illustrious predecessors, he brought to such a point of excellence the various talents with which he had been endowed, that just one of them would have been enough to win him immortality."[147]

Such comparisons between de Gaulle and Napoleon were in the air in 1970 for another reason. The previous year had been the bicentenary of the Emperor's birth, which had made a strong impression on the public.

Some of the General's correspondents had not failed to make the connection, which had prompted on the one hand contrasts ("See how the two of you are treated in the same year, Napoleon celebrated and yourself repudiated")[148] but on the other hand direct comparisons between de Gaulle's exile in 1969 and the Emperor's banishment in 1815. As one woman wrote, "You will have been spared nothing, even the aura of misfortune that also surrounded Napoleon: it will only add to your glory."[149] The visit of the liner *France*, flagship of the national passenger fleet, to St. Helena prompted one correspondent to write, "A strange coincidence! Just as the 'France' is making a pilgrimage to St Helena, France is sending you in exile to Colombey. Napoleon's legend began on St Helena, yours is starting now."[150] Another letter added, "All great men have been left in the lurch, hated and then missed. It happened to Napoleon I the Great [*sic*]. Like him you will have had your two abdications, your victories and your defeats."[151] But the comparison between the General and the Emperor was also made in more positive terms: "Not since Napoleon had France known such respect, such prestige abroad and such stability at home."[152]

And what did de Gaulle himself think? The archives show that the General—despite what a simplistic reading of the relationship between Gaullism and Bonapartism might imply—had been keenly involved in the preparations for this Napoleonic commemoration. It was de Gaulle who, as early as July 1967, pronounced that it was for the State to organize the various ceremonies marking the bicentenary.[153] It was the president, once more, who chose Malraux to coordinate the preparations,[154] and de Gaulle again who settled the disagreement with Prince Napoleon about the make-up of the organizing committee, which for a moment had threatened to unravel the scheme.[155] And in February 1969, General de Gaulle replied favorably to Jacques Rueff, Chancellor of the Institut de France, who had asked him to a commemorative ceremony in honor of Napoleon planned for Tuesday June 24, saying, "I welcome this programme, and in response to the invitation you have sent me in the name of the central administrative commission of the Institut, I fully expect to attend the meeting of the 24th of June."[156] Last but not least, it was de Gaulle himself who approved the final program of national commemorations, while insisting on an additional ceremony at the Invalides to take place in September or October 1969, at which "the Head of State would make a speech in tribute to the person of Napoleon."[157]

This Gaullian speech was never delivered, since the president resigned in April 1969, but its spirit was in some sense echoed in the popular tributes to the General at the time of his death. Also, in a remarkable anticipation (and confirmation) of Malraux's remark, when he placed the basis of the Gaullian myth on his ability to personify transcendence and to capture the collective imagination,[158] there was a veritable outpouring of Napoleonic comparisons. From everywhere in France, de Gaulle was saluted as the continuer of Bonaparte's work; one recurring expression was "the Napoleon of the twentieth century."[159] Some confirmed this illustrious descent by adorning their tributes with Napoleonic metaphors: "The sun of Austerlitz will shine forever on you."[160] But often the comparison was made in simple terms, without embellishment: "The most illustrious Frenchman since Napoleon";[161] "First there was Napoleon and then de Gaulle";[162] "De Gaulle was the greatest since Napoleon: we will miss you";[163] "In homage to the man I consider to have been the greatest public man, after Bonaparte";[164] or even "To the most brilliant war leader and head of the French state since Napoleon."[165] In raising this virtual mausoleum to the departed warrior, some took the final step of crowning de Gaulle as "a greater soldier than Napoleon."[166] Hence this prophetic thought by an inhabitant of Saint-Valéry-en-Caux: "De Gaulle is dead, but his shadow will hover over France forever."[167]

CHAPTER 6

⌒⋁⌒

Pilgrimages to Colombey

Some weeks after the death of the General, one of his fervent admirers in Paris sent a letter to the prefect of the Haute-Marne. The letter began by expressing pleasure at the news that the former Place de l'Etoile in the French capital had been renamed Place Charles de Gaulle—a harbinger, according to him, of what was sure to happen in every part of France in the coming years. Then, looking toward the future, he observed that Colombey-les-Deux-Eglises would become, like Lourdes, "a place of pilgrimage." He added that the General's country home at Colombey, La Boisserie, would in due course become a museum, like Napoleon's former residence "la Malmaison." He concluded: "The church square will be called 'Place du Général Charles de Gaulle' and they will put up a statue to him there. Colombey will be on a railway line and hotels, cafés, blocks of flats and all kinds of businesses will be built there."[1]

This vision of Colombey transformed into a Mont-St. Michel of Gaullian memory, halfway between a sacred place of worship and a great tourist honeypot, was (happily) never realized. In any case it offered a striking contrast with the famous description at the end of the *War Memoirs*, in which de Gaulle drew an irenic picture of his "family seat" and the surrounding countryside as a haven of peace where the book had been written.[2] But if Malraux is to be believed, the General had somehow foreseen these changes to Colombey at the end of his life, making the comparison with Lourdes himself, while including in it a characteristic note of self-mockery. Describing the Cross of Lorraine that would stand high above the village, Malraux has him saying, "You'll be able to see it from miles around. But as there will be no-one to see it, it will be seen by no-one. It will rouse the rabbits to resistance."[3] In fact, Colombey was always an ambiguous symbol. For de Gaulle, the village represented the bucolic life, family privacy, solitude, and reflection and also a certain kind of retreat from the world.[4] A psychological and physical distance that sometimes gave the house a fortress-like quality, as during the Fourth Republic, when Colombey symbolized "the myth of isolation, of banishment, of silence"[5]—that was the brief experience of it that Paul Ramadier, president of the Council, had in 1947 when he came from Paris in person to inform the General that he would henceforth be denied military honors and was shown the door without further discussion. Even the General's close collaborators dreaded the "interminable journey" from Paris to Colombey, to that "distant, inconvenient house in that gloomy landscape, that indeterminate countryside under a lowering sky."[6]

Only Chancellor Konrad Adenauer, in the name of Franco-German reconciliation, was honored with an invitation to stay at La Boisserie in September 1958, but the exception only proved the rule. For Colombey was a cloister, a place for meditation and preparation for action; under the Fifth Republic, every one of de Gaulle's most important journeys and press conferences, every difficult presidential decision, was preceded by a stay in his village sanctuary.[7] Colombey was above all the symbol of one of the cardinal virtues in the Gaullian scheme of values: loyalty—an informal and respectful loyalty shown by the villagers, who saw de Gaulle at Mass on Sunday, at the polling station on election days, or at local anniversaries or feast days, and a strictly hierarchical loyalty, like that of the "companions" who had the rare honor of being invited to La Boisserie, or of the (very small) group who were permitted to talk de Gaulle there on the telephone.[8] Loyalty could be demonstrative and spectacular, like that of the air force pilots who showed their enthusiasm for de Gaulle's return to public life in May 1958 by repeatedly flying over La Boisserie and dipping their wings in salute.[9] But loyalty could also take the form of discretion, like that of the servants in the house, or the young medical students who were on call when the president was in residence and who used to sometimes watch American films on television with him on weekends,[10] or the police detachments who guarded the General's residence day and night and organized the protection of the estate and its surroundings, as far as the edge of the Forêt des Dhuits and the wood of La Montagne. During the Algerian War, such was the fear of an air attack that serious consideration was given to installing antiaircraft batteries in the woods near Colombey.[11]

Loyalty might also be colored by tender feelings, as when a young girl wrote to de Gaulle after his resignation in 1969; she imagined him walking in his garden at Colombey and wrote, "How I wish I could be a flower in your garden, so that when you picked it some of its perfume would stay on your fingers and soften your terrible sadness. . . ."[12] It might be an unrestrained, even outlandish kind of loyalty, as in those anonymous figures who turned up uninvited in the village at various times in the 1950s and 1960s and demanded to see the Great Man to share their gifts, their thoughts, or their grievances with him. Among these curious pilgrims, surely the strangest was the woman who was found several years in succession hanging around the gates of La Boisserie and telling anyone who would listen that she had come from Lourdes to fulfill Our Lady's instruction to her that she should bear General de Gaulle's child.[13] Loyalty expressed itself in tears when he passed away in November 1970 and his funeral showed France and the world his plain, unadorned grave. Clinging to the memory of the Great Man, thousands of men and women wrote to Madame de Gaulle in the years following the General's death.[14]

Strength and vulnerability, openness and isolation, mysticism and modernity, grandeur and sadness: In the General's lifetime, Colombey was already a place where contrasting images and emotions mingled, which largely reflected the contradictions of the Gaullian sensibility. In this chapter, based on the rich materials on Gaullian memory collected in the Charles de Gaulle Foundation between the early 1970s and the present day,[15] we explore how the village became the principal memory site of the Gaullian myth and how the legend sought to manage these contradictions during the decades following the death of the General.

As it was already a famous place, one the General had particularly loved and where he had asked to be buried next to his daughter Anne,[16] Colombey was the obvious location to give a territorial basis to the Gaullian myth after November 1970—all the more so as the Parisian rite of the mont Valérien immediately lost its mystique with the death of its totemic figure. Jacques Foccart, who now worked for President Pompidou, noted this development on the anniversary in 1971: "The ceremony was as sad an occasion as could be imagined. It was the first 18th of June since the General's death. Fewer people came, and those who were there had a bigger lump in their throats than usual. I'm astonished to see how quickly the whole thing is fading away."[17] But there was another, more complex reason for this decentralizing of a collective national memory that would usually be focused on Paris. Far from political passions, the village in the Haute-Marne was a perfect setting for the mythological ideal of a Gaullian figure, which would now belong "to France" rather than to any particular regime, group, or political party. The danger of a political exploitation of de Gaulle's memory appeared almost at once with the Place de l'Etoile affair, which caused a huge storm in Paris in the immediate aftermath of the General's death.[18]

Passed by the Paris city council, the roundabout's official renaming as Place Charles de Gaulle was received enthusiastically by the General's faithful supporters, as the beginning of this chapter shows. But it also provoked reactions of doubt, even criticism, among the public, in the intellectual community, and in the political arena. Gaullists and centrists disagreed about the appropriateness of the gesture, which seemed to contradict the General's own wishes expressed in his will. A Committee for the Defence of the Place de l'Etoile was founded by Paul Antier, a former minister, and it managed to collect more than 40,000 signatures.[19] On December 2, Antier went to Colombey, where he gave the commander of the guard post a personal letter for Madame de Gaulle, begging her to have the project canceled.[20] Finally the inauguration ceremony did take place on December 15, 1970, led by Prime Minister Jacques Chaban-Delmas, but the affair left a rather unimpressive memory. There was some booing, and a few hard-core demonstrators called out "Algérie française." Twenty-six people were arrested.[21] The extreme Right, which had been notable during the controversy for its bitterness against de Gaulle, tried on several occasions during the ensuing weeks to inscribe dissident slogans on the new street signs. One Parisian was stopped by the police at the corner of the Avenue de Friedland and the Avenue des Champs-Elysées while delivering himself of this lyrical outpouring: "De Gaulle, you poor bastard, to think that I voted for and believed in you, but you did so many bloody stupid things, we can't worship your name on a plaque, that's idolatry."[22] In the face of this antifestive spirit, the authorities could do nothing but send a strong detachment of police to protect the new street signs. Circulated by the Paris press, pictures of the General's name under police protection did not fail to provoke some acerbic comments in the newspapers.[23]

Far from Parisian sound and fury, Colombey therefore emerged from 1971 onward as the principal home of followers of the Gaullian cult, who converged there from all over France, either individually or in organized groups. Their travels were often overseen by para-Gaullist national or regional groups, like the National Association for Loyalty to General de Gaulle, created in 1971 by Pierre Lefranc, one of the president's former lieutenants,[24] or, in the Essonne, the Departmental Committee for General de Gaulle's Memory, founded, again in 1971, by Pierre Coulomb.[25] The veterans' associations were among the most active. In November 1971, for the first anniversary of the General's death, the Grand Chancellery of the Order of the Liberation organized a "Pilgrimage to Colombey" for the Companions of the Liberation, holders of the Resistance Medal and former members of the Resistance, as well as former deportees and their families. Organized with the help of the national railway company the SNCF and the army, the journey was charged 90 francs per person (a special rate), to include return tickets from the Gare de l'Est to Bar-le-Duc by special Pullman train, and from there to Colombey by bus, with a set meal on the return journey "with drink and coffee." The pilgrims' program had a pious simplicity: a visit to the General's grave, followed by a special mass in the village church.[26] This excursion became an annual fixture.

It was in this atmosphere of almost religious piety that the campaign to build a Cross of Lorraine at Colombey was launched. The monument was to be built at the top of La Montagne, the little hill to the west of the village. Under the auspices of the Ministry for Veterans, a Committee for the National Memorial to General de Gaulle was set up in Paris in March 1971, with offshoots in every department.[27] The national subscription list was opened on the magic date of the 18th of June by Claude Hettier de Boislambert, the Grand Chancellor of the Order of the Liberation, in a radio and television broadcast. In the name of the National Committee, he recalled that General de Gaulle himself had looked forward to the construction of such a cross on the hill after his death. To make quite clear the spirit in which the commemorative monument had been conceived, the Committee wished the cross to be unveiled on the 18th of June 1972 and hoped also that all French men and women, regardless of their means, would contribute something to the fund. Boislambert added that "the most modest contributions will be welcome—perhaps the most welcome."[28] The aim was therefore to give the relaunch of the Gaullian cult a truly national and popular impetus. The subsequent meetings of the National Committee and the departmental representatives brought out a second imperative, just as fundamental as the first: a need for cross-party appeal. Obviously the unfortunate effects of the Place de l'Etoile affair were still causing apprehension: "We must constantly bear in mind and demonstrate publicly the non-political character of the operation. No-one is to be excluded on political grounds. The General's family is absolutely insistent on this point."[29]

This wish expressed by the family of de Gaulle was not their only involvement in the process. Though playing no part on the political scene, the de Gaulle family had an important role at every stage of the memorial project. This was the beginning of a legitimating tradition that has not changed since 1970: From then on no significant public event could take place at Colombey without the family's overt or tacit approval. Thus it was the de Gaulle family who originally asked for the National Committee to meet under the auspices of the Ministry for Veterans (one way, no doubt, of keeping their distance from the "'usurper'" Pompidou); they who nominated its principal "Gaullian" members;[30] and they, too, who indicated what the precise appearance of the monument should be (notably the north–south orientation of the cross).[31] Even certain nominations to the departmental committees, like that of General Gabriel Bourgund in Haute-Marne, for example, came about as a result of Philippe de Gaulle's personal recommendation.[32] Last but not least, it was the de Gaulle family who put their seal on the final choice of the architects, Marc Nebinger and Michel Mosser, in November 1971.[33] Weighing a massive 1,500 tons and almost 45 meters high, their monumental Cross of Lorraine was designed to be seen from a distance of some 10 kilometers in every direction.[34] The national subscription raised 9 million francs, far more than the National Committee had dared hope for,[35] and in spite of all material and time constraints, the new memorial was inaugurated as planned by President Georges Pompidou on the 18th of June 1972.[36]

Was this clear and massive success a sign that the collective national feeling that had shown itself at the time of the General's death was still strong? The sum raised by subscription and the considerable involvement of the public in the project would seem to suggest so. But under the surface things were not quite so simple, as for example in the extreme coldness, "almost an affront," shown by Madame de Gaulle to Georges Pompidou on the day of the unveiling.[37] More fundamental disagreements emerged among various Gaullists, notably about the sheer size of the monument, and even whether it should have been built at all. Some anti-Pompidolian Gaullists were particularly angry about the presidential pardon recently given to the Vichy local militia leader and war criminal Paul Touvier and stayed away from the unveiling, going instead to the mont Valérien for the traditional 18th of June ceremony. Jacques

Foccart found some people "excessively heated."[38] The Free French Association chose to meet on that day at the Arc de Triomphe.[39] Jean Mauriac noted these disagreements in his diary: "As far as I am concerned, I don't think the General would ever have approved of this Cross at Colombey. But the poor dead never see their wishes respected. The General had made it clear enough, heaven knows, that he wanted no statues or monuments to him after his death."[40]

There were also disagreements on the political meaning to be given to the Colombey monument. All the representatives of the *départements* were, of course, unanimous in wanting to celebrate the memory of de Gaulle, but some of them wanted to make the monument into a tribute to the Resistance as well as to the General himself, for instance by placing inside it urns containing the ashes of resistance fighters or by naming the paths leading to it after the main currents of the Resistance.[41] None of these "republican" suggestions was carried out: In the minds of the Parisians who first conceived the memorial, and the General's family, the Colombey cross could only be a monument to the glory of the Man of the 18th of June. Another aspect of this gulf between Paris and the provinces was the considerable disparity in the sums raised by different *départements*, which seemed to show quite different levels of enthusiasm for the General's memory in different parts of France. At the head of the league table, as one might expect, were the traditionally Gaullist areas of the east, the Paris region, and the north: the Bas-Rhin (in first place, with 294,877 francs), followed by the Haute-Marne (188,975 F), the Marne (185,356 F), the Yvelines (179,753 F), the Alpes-Maritimes (170,729 F), the Hauts-de-Seine (168,717 F), the Nord (158,533 F), the Moselle (147,995 F), the Haut-Rhin (134,389 F), and, in tenth place, Corsica (128,251 F), the first French department to be liberated in October 1943, where the memory of the Resistance years was obviously still alive.[42]

At the other end of the scale, none of the seven *départements* at the bottom of the national classification managed to raise even the modest sum of 10,000 F. The Tarn-et-Garonne, bringing up the rear, offered the derisory total of 2,730 F. In general, the most reluctant *départements* were either rural (the majority in the bottom quarter of the list) or politically left-leaning. For many of those who had paid sincere tribute to the Man of the 18th of June in November 1970, hostility to "cesarism" seemed still to constitute a cultural and political stumbling block; these reservations were no doubt exacerbated by the gigantic character of the proposed monument. Another complicating factor is that public bodies were allowed to contribute to the subscription on the same basis as individuals. This decision caused the resignation of Jean-Marcel Jeanneney from the National Committee. Like many Gaullists, the General's former minister believed that only individual subscriptions should be allowed, so that the monument would truly be the product of a collective effort by the "people of France."[43] When we realize, for example, that the Conseil Général (departmental council) of the Haute-Marne voted to contribute 50,000 F to the subscription (more than a quarter of the entire sum raised by the *département*), despite several councilors expressing their doubts about the planned monument,[44] then it becomes clear that the involvement of local authorities skewed the subscription list to some extent, while also discreetly politicizing it—for it was most often the Prefect who masterminded the whole operation. But what could be more Gaullian, in the end, than these contradictions between an apolitical ideal and an effective politicization and between the appeal to popular mobilization and the de facto control by central power?

In spite of these hitches, the fact remains that hundreds of thousands of French men and women answered the appeal and did their best to give the subscription the biggest possible impact. Among them were a great many small contributors—like the veteran Félix Féry, who was keen to be one of the first to send his modest offering (a 10-franc note) to the Ministry of Veterans, at the beginning of April 1971, even before the subscription was officially open. With his (long) letter he sent a song lyric dedicated to General de Gaulle. The refrain might have been carved on the monument at Colombey: "I'll be back, I'm de Gaulle/The man who won't go away./In spite of this war's ups and downs/We'll win again someday."[45]

The authorities had estimated that more than 40,000 people would come to Colombey for the unveiling of the memorial in June 1971. The fact that this was an overestimate (only about 25,000 came) was not, as it turned out, a bad omen for the village's new monument. On the contrary, the ensuing decade marked in many respects the golden age of Colombey as a memory site. The General's village was to become a place of commemoration and recollection, a space for political differentiation and source of legitimacy, and, last but not least, the point of convergence of a vibrant popular cult. At the same time, the site acquired an additional place of pilgrimage: After Madame de Gaulle's death, La Boisserie (exactly as the General's Parisian admirer had predicted in 1970) opened its doors to the public at the end of 1979. However, here too, as with the memorial in 1972 (and the Place de l'Etoile in 1970), the organizers made rather heavy weather of the opening ceremony. Initially planned for November 9,[46] the date of the General's death (calendar fetishism was definitely a key part of the Gaullian myth), it was later postponed until December 17. On that gray, wet Monday morning only a handful of people attended the opening; there were more journalists and photographers than visitors. Having fought their way through the crowd of reporters, the first visitors to enter were a couple of pensioners from Picardy, Mr and Mrs Tetelin, who had traveled from Amiens. They said as they left, "We'll come back when it's quieter." Some of these first visitors did, however, find at La Boisserie what they had been looking for: an echo of the Great Man's presence. "In its very simplicity," one of them declared, "this house breathes all the greatness of the General's soul."[47]

Between 1972 and 1980, this search for the spirit of the Man of the 18th of June brought an impressive number of pilgrims to Colombey.[48] The record year was 1972, when it is estimated that the site received 740,000 visitors: a figure never equaled subsequently and all the more surprising since the memorial was inaugurated only in mid-June. Between 1973 and 1976, the annual total varied between 400,000 and 700,000, then numbers began to fall off, to as low as 200,000 in 1979, before rising again in 1980 thanks to the opening of La Boisserie: 250,000 people visited the General's house in its first year of opening.[49] Summer months were the busiest—particularly August, when, as in 1976, more than 4,000 people might arrive at the house on a single day (7,000 on August 1 alone).[50] This veritable human tide made Colombey the most-visited village in the Haute-Marne and drove one local newspaper to conclude that "General de Gaulle may be dead, but he is still alive in the thoughts of thousands of people."[51] It is true that not all of these visitors were pilgrims in the strict sense of the term; some were there by chance, and there were also school parties. The village was also included on classic tourist itineraries, particularly those to Verdun, which allowed a single bus tour to revive both Gaullist and Petainist memories. According to the estimates of Christian Paul, the manager at La Boisserie, foreigners made up about 10 percent of the visitors (led by Dutch, Belgian, and Swiss, followed by German and British). The French visitors' regional origins corresponded closely to the distribution of public donations to the Colombey memorial: Most numerous were visitors from the *départements* of the east (especially from Alsace), followed by those of the Paris region and the north.[52]

Who were these visitors, and in what frame of mind did they visit Colombey? There were, obviously, Gaullists of every stripe; during the first years some of them even walked there, as if to a religious gathering, and explicitly demanded to be called "pilgrims,"[53] while others preferred to describe themselves as "loyal friends."[54] Among notable individual visitors, a constant succession of French "celebrities" passed through the village at one time or another to meditate on the General's tomb—or, in the case of the French diva Mireille Mathieu, to sing her latest song (the title was, not unpredictably, "De Gaulle").[55] From de Gaulle's old comrade General Jacques Massu (who arrived in June 1971 on horseback) to the radical barrister Jacques Vergès, these figures spanned the whole ideological spectrum and usually left again without making any comment, leaving it to journalists and local law-enforcement officials to interpret their visit.[56]

Especially during the immediate aftermath of de Gaulle's death, there were also some eccentric groups who turned up at Colombey, like the so-called Centre for Free Republicans, founded in November 1971, which came to lay a wreath at the memorial soon after its unveiling and even made a solemn appeal to Admiral Philippe de Gaulle to "take in his hand the destinies of France." This movement, no more republican than it was freedom-loving, was in fact a front for a gang whose leaders had criminal records for theft, embezzlement, and drug trafficking.[57] A regular stream of visitors from abroad also came to Colombey to pay tribute to de Gaulle's foreign policy, among them the ambassador of the Soviet Union, missing the good old days of Gaullian anti-Americanism, and Prince Norodom Sihanouk, recalling nostalgically the General's support for Cambodian independence, reaffirmed on the occasion of de Gaulle's famous visit to Phnom Penh in 1966.[58]

Among these assiduous pilgrims, the hard-core group was made up of veterans—old soldiers of the Great War, holders of the Resistance Medal, members of the Free French Association, Companions of the Liberation—and members of the various para-Gaullist associations in Paris and the provinces. The evening before the inauguration of the memorial, a group of veterans from the Haute-Marne, 1,000 strong, received the holy flame brought from the mont Valérien and watched over it until midnight. In their cult of de Gaulle, these faithful followers were primarily celebrating the memory of the Resistance chief and Liberator of the nation. Typically, they honored the General's memory in their own districts on the 18th of June and then went to Colombey for the anniversary of his death in November. Some of the most active groups were those of the Paris region, particularly the Essonne,[59] and those from the Isère.[60] But, as always in France, commemoration of the past did not rule out present-day political concerns. Some veterans were heavily involved in Gaullist political activism, and they did not hesitate to use the Great Man's memory for openly partisan ends. Thus, on his return from Colombey in November 1979, Roger Crespin, Honorary President of the Free French Association of the Marne, declared that France "was living through an incredible degradation of political standards" under the presidency of Valéry Giscard d'Estaing, an independent centrist who had been elected in 1974 and was engaged in an increasingly acrimonious political struggle with his Gaullist coalition partners. So that there should be no misunderstanding, he added, "Today's France is one which de Gaulle would not recognize. This situation cannot go on. The country is waiting for a fightback."[61]

Such language is a token of the aggressiveness, as well as the political fragmentation, of Gaullism in the 1970s, especially after the founding of the neo-Gaullist Rassemblement pour la République (RPR) by Jacques Chirac in 1976, whose primary objective was to enable a Gaullist to recapture the French presidency.[62] From then until the presidential elections of 1981, Colombey became the chief symbolic battleground of a double conflict: on the one hand, the submerged warfare that the Gaullists were waging against each other, and on the other, the intense rivalry between the centrist Giscardians and the neo-Gaullist Chiraquians. The split between these two groups was such that government Gaullists like Alain Peyrefitte often made a separate visit to the village on Gaullian anniversaries.[63] Other historic figures, like Michel Debré, de Gaulle's first prime minister under the Fifth Republic, made their own arrangements; thus, for the 18th of June 1978, the General's former prime minister made a speech about "national independence" at Champcourt, a village seven kilometers from Colombey.[64] It was politely conveyed to the Giscardians that their coming to the village would not be appropriate: Giscard's prime minister Raymond Barre chose not to take part in the ceremonies of November 1977,[65] and the president himself, who apparently tried to have himself invited to La Boisserie in November 1980, was rebuffed.[66] This was not poor Giscard's first such humiliation. Already in November 1975, when he had gone to Colombey for the anniversary of the General's death, he had been received with shouts of "traitor"—obviously his appeal to vote "no" in the 1969 referendum had not been forgotten.[67]

In this heavy, byzantine climate, anyone's actions would be picked over and too much would often be read into them. The president of the Republic's absence from the mont Valérien ceremony on June 18, 1975, which produced a violent reaction among Gaullist members of parliament,[68] is a case in point, as was Madame de Gaulle's refusal to come to Paris to open an exhibition in honor of the General. Even though it was to be held at the City Hall, this move was seen by some as a deliberate slight to the president of the Republic and a gesture of support by the de Gaulle family to the mayor of Paris, Jacques Chirac.[69] On the other hand, when the president of the RPR organized a march of 40,000 pilgrims to Colombey in June 1980, at a time when the president was doing his very best to use the fortieth anniversary of the Appeal to pull the Gaullian mantle toward himself (even going so far as to claim, rather implausibly, that he and his family had personally heard de Gaulle's broadcast of June 18, 1940), there was little room for doubt. Colombey was now not only a Gaullist private domain but a memory site that had become highly politicized.[70]

But even if these conflicts sometimes became intense, the reflections in Colombey of these national political battles did not hide its real essence. For the General's village saw a flourishing popular cult grow up from the 1970s onward. A revealing sign of this galloping Gaullomania was the sale of pictures, which began in the first weeks following the death of the Great Man. Several people were indeed charged with fraud for trying to beat off the competition by claiming that the profits from their pictures would go to Madame de Gaulle's charities.[71] This scheme showed the unscrupulousness of its devisers but also testified to the immediate entry of the Gaullian myth into the pantheon of legends—for were not such swindles the contemporary version of the objects "owned by the Emperor Napoleon" that were sold in the Palais-Royal after his exile, or the miraculous colored liquids long touted by street sellers at Lourdes?

At first the local authorities tried to control the sale of Gaullian images and even the taking of photographs of the General's tomb, which was in theory forbidden. But these ambitions could not long withstand the tidal wave of worship, backed as it was by ineluctable commercial logic. Very soon, in fact, Colombey became the capital of a vast bric-a-brac industry, where a whole range of objects was on sale, all honoring the Great Man. Visitors and pilgrims could of course buy postcards and stamps, some of which were issued to mark key Gaullian dates; thus in 1977, for the fifth anniversary of the building of the memorial at Colombey, a stamp featuring the monument was issued.[72] However, in this all-out fetishism, the Gaullian image was also applied to barometers, frying pans, bottles, guitar-shaped ashtrays, T-shirts, beach bags, plates, snow globes, mustard pots, and lighters; key rings even came in three models, one "de luxe." The Cross of Lorraine emblem was greedily recycled, particularly on mugs, chocolates, mini-*képis* filled with caramels, boxes of Camembert, and patriotic prunes in brandy.[73] Some of these souvenirs revived traditions of the great popular political cults of the nineteenth century, and particularly the Napoleon cult, notably the busts of the General in wood, plaster, or bronze; the penknives with the General's picture on them; the Man of the 18th of June tobacco box; the chips of stone from the Colombey Monument; or the heart that opened up to show a miniature General inside.[74] Interviewed by *Paris-Match* in 1972, a manufacturer of Gaullian souvenirs confirmed just how lucrative the trade was; he had already sold 5,000 bronze busts, 100,000 bottle openers, and 500,000 pens bearing the image of the founder of the Fifth Republic.[75]

If the villagers and local councilors were sometimes exasperated by these objects—in a letter of January 1973, Madame de Gaulle herself mentioned the "ghastly objects that are being sold in Colombey"[76]—they certainly made a contribution to the local, national, and even global economies, since some were made in Germany, Spain, Greece, and even China and Japan—a pleasing posthumous vindication of de Gaulle's belief in the virtues of a multipolar world. The almost idolatrous fervor of some pilgrims to Colombey, especially during the first ten years after the General's death, could also be read in other signs—particularly the messages written on the wreaths and plaques left on the votive cross in the cemetery.[77] One veteran described himself as "the last of the Emperor's *grognards*"—another nod toward the shared Gaullo-Napoleonic memory—and had come from the mont Saint Jean to leave at the foot of the cemetery cross a large red and gold heart that opened to display nine small hearts bearing the names of the Walloon towns and villages where the General was most admired. This man and the group he had come with slept out that night at the foot of the memorial.[78] The piety of others could be read in the individual or collective efforts they had made to get to Colombey; for example, one sports club from Lorraine had insisted on walking the 130 kilometers to Colombey,[79] while a female veteran of the Free French forces, an ardent admirer of the General, had taken a taxi from Bordeaux to come and pay her respects to her hero.[80]

In some cases the Colombey cult took on an explicitly religious character, as with the woman from Auxerre suffering from a generalized cancer who insisted on being carried inside La Boisserie,[81] or the handicapped resistance veteran Ernest Jaggy, known as Boby, who made the journey from Lourdes to Colombey by tricycle.[82] This Gaullomania reached epic proportions in 1980 when Admiral Philippe de Gaulle noticed, just a few months after the public opening of La Boisserie, that visitors had removed a considerable amount of the gravel from the drive.[83] This habit of taking away relics of the path trodden by the Great Man drove the prefect of the Haute-Marne to request a stronger security detail.[84] The cult of the Man of the 18th of June was obviously growing in strength: Ten years after the street signs named after him in Paris, it was now his gravel at Colombey that needed police protection.

Monuments to great men have always attracted hatred, which after all is only the other face of adoration—think of the Communards tearing down the Colonne Vendôme in 1871. The Gaullian memory sites were no exception to the rule. Already on the day before the inauguration of the memorial in June 1972, the mayor of Colombey had received a letter saying that the stone would soon be blown up and the mayor with it.[85] In November 1976, after several similar threats, a Paris newspaper wrote that the General's tomb had been defaced.[86] The story was not carried by the national or local press at the time, but several years later a retired policeman confirmed it to a leading Parisian paper.[87] The same policeman added that in 1979 the letters forming the inscription "To General de Gaulle" had been torn off the base of the memorial; this, if true, would provide a more credible explanation for the prefect's request for reinforcements in early 1980. A few years later, an anonymous telephone call threatened to blow up La Boisserie, forcing it to be temporarily evacuated. But even here, we note that the threat was uttered two days before the 18th of June: The homage that vice pays to virtue, and a convincing proof, if it were needed, that the Gaullian calendar was now imprinted in the imagination even of his most bitter opponents.[88]

The 1980s were marked by subtle but far-reaching changes in the place occupied by Colombey in the Gaullian myth and, more broadly, in the General's place in the French national imagination. One clear sign of this change was the steady decline across the decade in the number of visitors. The correspondent of *Le Monde* who traveled to the village in December 1982 even reported that it no longer seemed an active site of memory;

only those who had "kept the faith" now regularly traveled to Colombey.[89] One such still-faithful pilgrim, Michel Cordier, put the matter more straightforwardly: "Since General de Gaulle died, I've been in the village on the 18th of June and even then found it almost deserted. I know that loyalty, admiration and gratitude are a matter of feeling and inner attitude, but there are limits . . . Nowadays in too many places the sense of the epic has been lost."[90]

Even if these words had an element of exaggeration, official statistics for the 1980s unquestionably show an ebbing of the "human tide"[91] that had washed over Colombey in the previous decade. To recognize this trend, one needs only look at the figures for the month of August, usually the busiest. Having fallen to 38,643 in August 1979, the number of visitors rose considerably in August 1980, when 63,753 people filed past the General's desk. The opening of La Boisserie to the public was responsible for this growth, if not in interest at least in curiosity. But the improvement was short-lived. From 1981 the figures began to fall once more: 28,412 in 1982; 27,761 in 1983; then an average of around 20,000 until 1991.[92] Colombey had not, it is true, become the desert that Michel Cordier had feared, but numbers had fallen dramatically from the extraordinary crowds of the 1970s. How can we explain this decline? First, the veterans had gradually disappeared, as had a whole generation that could remember two wars (especially the Great War) and who had comprised the majority of Colombey pilgrims. At the same time, as with any commemorative monument, its novelty faded with time—particularly as, after the opening of La Boisserie, there was no further attempt to renew the site.

On the contrary, the village seemed to settle into a somewhat sclerotic memorial posture, betrayed in the first place by its increasing political exploitation by the neo-Gaullists. It is true they no longer enjoyed a complete monopoly of the site. At the time of his presidential campaign in 1988, the centrist Raymond Barre made a brief but widely reported visit to the Colombey memorial; this was his fourth visit since 1976, thus establishing his Gaullian (as opposed to Gaullist) credentials.[93] But the site was soon reclaimed by the RPR, all the more greedily since, having been heavily defeated in two successive presidential elections, they had had little else to chew on in the 1980s. In this context of political gloom, even of radical self-doubt, Colombey became a last resort of "paleogaullism," a place where the elites of the RPR came to regroup, declaring their unity,[94] their faith in the restorative virtues of opposition,[95] and above all their unconditional loyalty to the General's inheritance, symbolized in 1986 by the legitimizing presence of his son Admiral Philippe de Gaulle, newly elected to the Senate.[96]

This representation of Colombey as a legendary stronghold was reinforced by local and national press coverage. Apart from the traditional anniversaries of the 18th of June and the 9th of November, the ritual visits by deportees and veterans,[97] and the occasional appearances of this or that minor Gaullist party official,[98] Colombey was mentioned rarely, and some articles bore a suspicious resemblance to the same ones published the previous year. Even the variations on this pattern fell within the accepted parameters of repetition. Thus in 1984 a journalist on *Le Figaro* looked up Yves Consigny, who was still living on the neighboring farm by La Boisserie; he had been one of the twelve young men who had carried de Gaulle's coffin from the church to the cemetery in 1970.[99] There was more harking back in 1987, when the Tour de France passed through Colombey, seventeen years after de Gaulle had gone out to see it.[100] In the same year Jacques Chirac, prime minister in the first "cohabitation," visited La Boisserie with the German Chancellor Helmut Kohl, almost three decades after Konrad Adenauer's visit. He used the occasion—another nod to history—to confer the Legion of Honour on the mayor of the village, Jean Raullet, an RPR supporter who had held the office since the 1960s.[101]

Probably the decisive factor in the sclerosis of Colombey in the 1980s was the triumph of the Left in the presidential and parliamentary elections. It is surely not mere chance that the year 1981 marked a considerable further fall in the number of pilgrimages to the Haute-Marne. The new tenant of the Elysée, François Mitterrand, who identified strongly with provincial France, managed in some degree to redirect public attention to new memory sites, like Verdun, where he symbolically held the hand of Chancellor Kohl in 1984, or simply his own favored locations, like his hometown of Jarnac, his municipal power base at Chateau-Chinon, his summer home at Latché, or even the rocky hill of Solutré, which he climbed in ritual fashion every summer, with a strong media presence. Mitterrand, whose envious fascination with the Gaullian heritage was well known,[102] even had displayed at Chateau-Chinon a selection of the gifts he had received since his election as president of the Republic: The obvious parallel with Colombey did not pass unnoticed.[103] Mitterrand's compulsion to imitate de Gaulle was such that on his own death, the former Socialist president had exactly the same procedure followed as at de Gaulle's: Two funerals were organized, one public at Notre-Dame, and the other private in the church at Jarnac.[104]

But alas for him, and no doubt for the General's village, Mitterrand was never able to make a place for himself in the symbolic scheme of Colombey. A revealing early sign of this failure came in November 1981, when the presidential wreath, solemnly laid on the General's grave by the head of François Mitterrand's military staff, was removed after the Companions of the Liberation protested (with a sense of humor as splendid as it was unintentional) against the "politicizing" of the Gaullian burial site.[105] This "war of wreaths" culminated in the following year with an attempt by the Friends of General de Gaulle association to encourage Mitterrand to go to Colombey in person.[106] As soon as news of this reached Paris, the Charles de Gaulle Institute, that ever-vigilant guardian of orthodoxy, delivered itself of a very dry communiqué, stressing that the association in question had "no links" with the Institute and that it had acted "on its own personal initiative."[107] In other words, the new president was persona non grata at Colombey. He took the hint and never set foot there.[108] Even at the mont Valérien, where he went every year for the 18th of June commemoration, the president had several awkward moments with the Gaullists; several Companions of the Liberation looked away so as not to have to salute him as he passed.[109] The wreath from Mitterrand, which adorned the tomb of Marshal Pétain every year from 1984 onward, no doubt had something to do with their decision.

The coming to power of the Left in France was something more than just a political alternation, however. The election of Mitterrand also reflected—and with hindsight one might almost say particularly symbolized—profound cultural changes in French society, first set in motion in May 1968, continuing under the presidency of Valéry Giscard d'Estaing, and brought to completion by the socialist generation that established itself in power after 1981. Though these changes had only scattered and sometimes contradictory effects on the memory and representations of General de Gaulle, their cumulative effects were undoubtedly positive in somehow allowing the Gaullian myth to survive the drying up of the well at Colombey by turning to other sources.

The first key aspect of this cultural change was the removal of the sacred aura surrounding the General's image and name. When the satirical weekly *Hara-Kiri* marked the General's death with the cover headline "One Dead in Colombey Dance-Hall Tragedy," the magazine was banned. A certain wind of change had blown over the national press in the 1970s, but the Man of the 18th of June was still spoken of in respectful if not reverential terms.[110] A small sign of change was the fact that the papers reported the opening of a discotheque at Colombey at the end of 1979. By sheer chance, the Barn opened its doors exactly at the time of Madame de Gaulle's death; it was a nine-day wonder, and some papers even reported a strip-tease session on the day of her funeral.[111] But we can take the real measure of change in attitudes by reading an article that appeared in *Libération* in November 1981, shortly before the traditional commemoration of the anniversary of the General's death. For here all the commonplaces were turned on their heads, starting with the title: "Suicidal Pedro and Crazy Anne-Marie of Colombey." Combining the stories of Pedro, a thirty-two-year-old who had just taken his own life, and Anne-Marie, a disturbed woman of *pied-noir* origin known (these were the 1970s) as the "village loony," they deconstructed the Colombey myth, describing villagers stuck in routine, like the old woman who had walked the same route every day for forty-two years; policemen standing "stiff as posts"; sad, gaping tourists (Anne-Marie was quoted as saying, "You're all bloody idiots, buying your little boxes of de Gaulle"). The underlying message was joyfully subversive: Colombey was a madhouse where (homage to Foucault) only the "loony" was sane and normal people were all potentially certifiable—like their "providential man," shut up in his big house: "General de Gaulle never went out. All his walks were around the garden of the property."[112]

At exactly the same time, the popular television documentary series *Les Dossiers de l'Ecran* devoted a program to General de Gaulle. The highlight of the evening was a series of home movies shot by his son, Admiral de Gaulle, a privileged witness to the life of the Great Man. Although its intention was to bolster the legend, this choice of an intimate, family setting was not far from the spirit of the *Libération* article. For it did not show de Gaulle as a sacred and heroic figure but as a "Colombey man," pushing his grandson in his pram and eating "creamed Pompidou" at Sunday lunch.[113] In this context, La Boisserie became the focus of a new representation of the General as a middle-class man in his Sunday best, as a man (almost) like the rest, or so his former interviewer, the academician Michel Droit, maintained: "General de Gaulle distant, unfeeling, inhuman? Only those who never knew him could describe or imagine him in that way! Only those who had never seen him at Colombey!"[114] In a long interview published in three installments in the *Haute-Marne Libérée* a few weeks later, Admiral de Gaulle took his inside story further, describing family life at Colombey and discussing for the first time Madame de Gaulle's role in relation to the General.[115] This "privatizing" of the Gaullian figure, as seen through La Boisserie, culminated in the interview the Admiral gave to *Figaro-Magazine* on April 20, 1983. Shortly to become part of the RPR bloc in the Senate, the General's son gave up all attempts at discretion: He angrily denounced the Socialist government for its incompetence and partisan spirit and even went as far as to describe himself as a victim of "fiscal racism." Outraged at having had to pay the new Tax on Large Fortunes from 1981 onward, the Admiral even threatened to part with La Boisserie.[116]

In the context of the subject here—the transformation of the Gaullian myth in the 1980s—the article had contradictory effects. On the one hand, it accentuated the demystification of the Gaullian image, notably by revealing a son who was more than a little materialistic and who seemed almost unaware of the symbolic value of La Boisserie in public consciousness. The satirical weekly *Canard Enchaîné*, which never missed an opportunity to make fun of the man it had styled, as early as 1972, the "rear-admiral of the washtub for family dirty linen," gave its article the title "Sosthène's 20th of April Appeal."[117] This mockery, and the circumstances that had prompted it, showed that the Gaullian myth was already losing some of its sacred aura. The readers' column to *Figaro-Magazine* made some similar points; several letters sharply criticized the Admiral's stance, complaining particularly about the "absurd and inappropriate" financial details he had seen fit to reveal. Others took the opportunity to settle old scores with Gaullism on such varied subjects as the Liberation, the postwar purges, and the General's departure from power in 1969. Yet a majority of correspondents did support de Gaulle's son and above all argued with some indignation that La Boisserie must continue to belong to the nation; several letters raised the idea of a public subscription to buy it, while others suggested that it be listed as an historical monument.[118] The excitement even reached Colombey, and the correspondent of *Les Dernières Nouvelles d'Alsace* went to the village to sound out the population. The postman's reply was the most revealing, as it seemed to suggest a certain element of confusion in the Gaullian memory: "The house must stay in the family. La Boisserie should never have been opened to the public, it isn't a museum."[119]

With his proverbial good sense, the postman had put his finger on one of the fundamental contradictions in modern celebrity culture: the tension between keeping the sacred mystique around a heroic figure and making him familiar by revealing the thousands of little personal details that marked his existence. In the France of the 1980s, the first de Gaulle had gradually been tucked away in the cupboard of "paleogaullism," but the second model was in full flush. The collective search for a new intimacy with de Gaulle was served in the literary sphere by the publication of memoirs of former members of the Gaullian inner circle. General de Boissieu, de Gaulle's son-in-law, thus described family life at Colombey, dwelling on such scenes as the Man of the 18th of June umpiring tennis matches between Boissieu and de Gaulle's brother-in-law Jacques Vendroux; de Gaulle obviously took seriously his responsibilities as arbiter under Article V of the Constitution of the Fifth Republic.[120] In 1990 Robert Lassus's fine work, *Madame de Gaulle's Husband,* an affectionate and sometimes surprising portrayal of the General, was full of examples of de Gaulle's wit and delightful anecdotes about his private life, stressing above all his attachment to his family;[121] this intimate vision was completed some years later by the story of Honorine, the General's cook.[122]

The power of de Gaulle's new myth was shown above all in the order of signs, by a prodigious multiplication of his symbolic presence. For de Gaulle's image no longer appeared only on the classic items of commemorative bric-a-brac, like stamps and coins:[123] It was also brought up to date. A fine example is its adaptation to the needs of advertising. In 1985, Radio Monte Carlo ran a campaign around the slogan "French people don't only listen to radio stations in Paris"; it was illustrated by a famous image of General de Gaulle speaking through a microphone marked "BBC."[124] For the fortieth anniversary of the DS model car, which coincided with the twenty-fifth anniversary of the General's death, Citroën devised a TV advertisement restaging the assassination attempt at the Petit-Clamart in 1962, in which the Gaullian DS had been machine-gunned but de Gaulle had emerged unhurt. A fine cue for the classic punch line: "You couldn't imagine all the things a Citroen can do for you."[125]

This privatization of Gaullian memory, in the strong sense of the term, was also shown in the public's growing readiness to buy Gaullian objects of all kinds. There were those who avidly collected Gaullian knickknacks, like the retired policeman Claude Beauvais, who began assembling his personal collection of souvenirs in November 1970; twenty-five years later, his haul comprised several thousand items, including popular art objects, newspapers, stamps, and books.[126] Some collected only publications concerning the General, like Alain Gournac, senator for the Yvelines, whose library—closed off behind a reinforced door—included in 1999 no fewer than 574 works on the Man of the 18th of June, some of them very rare.[127] Memorial associations were still being formed, such as Ecouen Together in Gratitude to General de Gaulle, founded by Jacques Chemeton. With sixty or so members, the association organized meetings and exhibitions of books about the General and other Gaullian objects: posters, photographs, and other writings.[128] On a more rarefied level came collectors of objects that had belonged to the Great Man. As early as 1979 the State had stepped in to preserve works of art and historic souvenirs belonging to the General, which the Admiral was threatening to send off to auction.[129] A sign that his celebrity was growing at all levels of international society was that the General was also becoming a favorite of the auction houses. In 1984 Sotheby's sold the first draft of his May 8, 1945, victory speech for 99,704 francs; the buyer was American.[130] Two years later, one of the original posters bearing the text of the 18th of June Appeal was sold at the Hôtel Drouot for 122,000 francs,[131] and in 1987 nine letters written by the General to General Giraud in 1943 made 250,000 francs in Hamburg. De Gaulle would have been particularly proud that on that day his writings were sold for more than the manuscript of a Wagner libretto.[132]

In June 1982 La Boisserie proudly put on display, in a glass case specially built for it next to the caretaker's house, the Citroën 15 CV, which the General had owned during the "crossing of the desert." Left with his faithful chauffeur Fontenil, after 1958 it was used by de Gaulle only to be driven to the mont Valérien ceremony every 18th of June.[133] But for the local press, the car was chiefly a reminder of how the General had liked to be driven through the nearby countryside; he had used the car for day trips to Vittel or Langres, during which he liked to hold forth about his surroundings; they even found a nephew of the Great Man who declared that "it was an education to be in the car with him."[134] Others were not to be outdone: A year later, when the first visitors arrived at the new Charles de Gaulle Museum in his birthplace in Lille, they discovered the DS in which the president and Madame de Gaulle had been riding when the attempt was made on his life at the Petit-Clamart. What finer symbol could there be of the General's ability to outwit destiny?[135] Also, inside the new museum were an array of objects to satisfy the most ardent fetishist: his sword from Saint-Cyr, the family tree showing his Irish and German forebears (MacCartans and Kolbs), and above all the cradle in which he had slept as a baby, his christening robe, and a copy of his birth certificate.[136] The sight of this last relic aroused considerable enthusiasm but also some temptation, for when the departmental archives asked the local high court to provide them with the original register in which the birth of little Charles was recorded, they discovered that the document had vanished.[137]

As a metaphor of the Gaullian spirit, Colombey made its definitive entry into legend in November 1970. As the unchanging symbol of the Great Man, the village became the true foundation of the Gaullian myth.[138] One association of Resistance members even suggested that it should henceforth be called "Colombey-le-Général."[139] De Gaulle's Haute-Marne retreat also became the model of a place that managed to keep its authentic rustic character and avoid the commercial excesses foreseen by the admirer of de Gaulle that was quoted at the beginning of this chapter. So in 1996, when tens of thousands of people started turning up at Jarnac to visit François Mitterrand's grave, the mayor, Maurice Voiron, immediately headed for Colombey to meet his counterpart Jean Raullet and learn from his "twenty-five years' experience."[140]

That experience had not always been easy, for the General's totemic village was always marked by a certain ambiguity. Lost in the farthest Haute-Marne, it had the unusual fate of hosting, in the same location, several symbolic sites of different orders. First the place of residence of the Great Man and of his carefully guarded family privacy, on his death it became his burial place and then the site of the monument to his glory, before the opening of La Boisserie added a new memorial dimension at the end of the 1970s. Despite the relative falling off in the number of visitors (and of the proportion of them who were "pilgrims" in the original sense), their absolute number continued to be highly respectable; more than 100,000 of them were still visiting yearly at the end of the 1990s (of whom some 40,000 visited La Boisserie).[141] And everything suggests that even in the twenty-first century he will not be forgotten—particularly as a new Gaullian memorial (a large educational museum) opened its doors to the public at Colombey in 2008.[142] The General's village retreat has also become the privileged site for the activities of a newly created association, the Amicale Gaulliste de la Haute-Marne. Under the dynamic and youthful leadership of its president, Paul Fournié (who was not yet born the year de Gaulle died), it organizes public lectures, film projections, and commemorative events, joining the Colombey villagers in the traditional procession to the Lorraine Cross on the evening of the 18th of June. The Amicale has also innovated by establishing a new ritual: a family picnic at Colombey. Held on the afternoon of the 18th of June, it has become a well-attended and popular event, drawing participants of all ages and social groups from across the region.

Colombey's ambiguity is creative, then—but not without its accompanying tensions, even contradictions, notably between the political neutrality desired by the General and his family for this place of meditation and the fundamentalism that sometimes underlay neo-Gaullist memorial demonstrations. Still more worrying were the divisions between the General's political heirs, which were expressed ever more openly during the declining years of Gaullism. For if Jacques Chirac's election in 1995 revived the flame of Colombey (the new president came to collect his thoughts there before entering on his duties, returning for the 18th of June and for the anniversary of the General's death),[143] Colombey became most obviously the scene of Punch-and-Judy battles for legitimacy among the various branches of the Gaullist family. Between Chirac and Balladur, RPR and RPF, Gaullist party and Institut Charles de Gaulle, followed in due course by the Villepinistes and the Sarkozystes, the conflicts were so byzantine that de Gaulle himself would have had difficulty in unraveling them. It is no doubt for this reason that the de Gaulle family in 1999 requested an end to the annual pilgrimages by the Gaullist deputies and senators.[144] It is true that many of them no longer came and that the original fervor of this rite had largely faded. Winston Churchill had once said, "I have carried many a cross since 1940, but none heavier than the Cross of Lorraine." Many of de Gaulle's political heirs could have echoed the thought.

But these internal quarrels did not seriously dent the Gaullian myth, which continued to grow in the form of a search for a deeper symbolic and memorial intimacy with the Man of the 18th of June. This intimacy was prefigured immediately after his death by the multiplication of Gaullian keepsakes and the reproduction of the General's image on various cult objects, which recalled the apogee of the Napoleon legend in the nineteenth century. Taken up again and amplified from the 1980s onward in a wave of new appropriations and representations, the General's image was marked both by a certain demystification and a greater objectification: Perfectly adapted to the requirements of celebrity, de Gaulle was eminently marketable. Paradoxically, at the same time, the rise in skepticism about politics among the French only reinforced the impact of

Colombey as a shining example of an ideal built on the values of sobriety and disinterested service. The connection did not come about by chance, for the village was the perfect incarnation of Gaullian syncretism, one of the most remarkable political and cultural phenomena of the twentieth century.

What, in fact, could be more syncretistic than the intertwining of memories at the mourning site of Colombey? As Maurice Agulhon very justly observes, the ambiguity of de Gaulle's choices allowed the General to reaffirm his transcendence of the division between Left and Right.[145] The division between religion and *laïcité* too, one might add, with on one hand the enormous Cross of Lorraine, a Christian symbol of "Crucifixion and Resurrection,"[146] and on the other the Gaullian grave itself in its naked simplicity. The General's village is almost a memorial microcosm, offering echoes of all the national commemorative sites and practices. Recalling the republican Pantheon in the simplicity of its inscriptions, the site also resembles the Invalides in the gigantic scale of its commemorative stone, Lourdes by the initial fervor of its pilgrimages, the Colonne Vendôme by the military cult sustained by several generations of veterans, and finally Mouilleron-en-Pareds by its austerity and rural isolation. The unchanging emblem of *la France profonde*, Colombey is also, thanks to the remarkable gesture of de Gaulle in September 1958, the symbolic site of Franco-German reconciliation—as shown by the choice of the village for the meeting between Nicolas Sarkozy and Angela Merkel in October 2008. Finally, and perhaps most of all, Colombey remains a place of absence, marking the real break that occurred with the Great Man's death. As Sarkozy said on that day: "In the end, Gaullism is a story that began with General de Gaulle and came to an end with him."[147]

CHAPTER 7

✣

The Consecration of an Icon

I t was in the last decade of the twentieth century that General de Gaulle took his final step to the summit of Olympus, moving from the status of a great historical figure to that of a political myth. Detaching himself from the world here below, the Man of the 18th of June entered into legend, becoming the supreme personification of the body politic and the nation and an emblematic figure in France and around the world. Memorial stones in his honor appeared in various loci of Gaullian memory, notably in Calais, in front of the church where he married Yvonne Vendroux.[1] Statues were erected too, as in London, at 4 Carlton Gardens, from where he had launched the epic struggle of Free France,[2] and farther afield, in Quebec, Warsaw, Bucharest, and Moscow, where he had made memorable visits. As a sign of his unquestioned fame, a plaque was even placed on the building in Baku where he had stayed in 1944 on his way to meet Stalin, and, despite the clearly expressed wishes of the Great Man, a large bronze statue was erected in his honor in Paris, on the Champs-Elysées, a few dozen yards from that of his old comrade Winston Churchill, who had arrived there some years earlier next to the avenue that bears his name.[3] In this case at least, the symbolism was faithful to history: The statues of the prime minister and the French leader are looking in opposite directions, and the Frenchman seems to be sauntering away from the Briton with long strides.[4]

This Gaullian sense of superiority was fully justified. For, adding to the dominant position that he already occupied at the beginning of the 1970s,[5] the General was now soaring in public opinion. For example, in

1988, a survey in the *Journal du Dimanche* placed him at the very top, with 30 percent of the historical figures most admired by the French, well ahead of Napoleon (22 percent).[6] Two years later, on the centenary of the General's birth, a survey in *Le Monde* confirmed the tendency: De Gaulle was now a majestic figure, enjoying a true "veneration" among the French public of all political allegiances. The figures speak for themselves: 84 percent of respondents thought that the General's actions had been "very positive" or "quite positive," with overwhelming majorities among supporters of the Gaullist party, the centrists, and the Socialists, and even among three-quarters of the extreme Right National Front sympathizers and two-thirds of Communists.[7] Almost all aspects of de Gaulle's political actions were acclaimed: The approval indices[8] were 82 percent for the 18th of June appeal, 69 percent for his role in the Resistance, 85 percent for the presidential election by universal suffrage, and even 62 percent for his decision to resign in 1969 after the "no" vote in the referendum. The General also had a good measure of support for Algerian independence (46 percent), even though a relative majority held it against him that he had "turned his back on the *pieds-noirs*."[9]

At the same time, judgments were measured. De Gaulle was still seen as essentially a man of the Right and not as a figure transcending ideological divisions (as he had always wished to consider himself). Also, he was admired much more as a national Liberator than as a founding Father: Only 15 percent of respondents celebrated in him the architect of a Fifth Republic, which was accepted rather than embraced. Just as the cult of Napoleon did not necessarily imply a celebration of the Empire, the Gaullian legend separated the wheat from the chaff and the Great Man from the institutions he had created. But if judgment was reserved on these points, and on some others (notably May 1968, de Gaulle's real nadir), the General was absolved from all the grave charges brought against him by his opponents over the years. Clear proof that his myth was now working at its strongest was that all the anti-Gaullisms—whether from the Right (the Vichy and French Algeria tradition), the center (in the name of Liberal and Atlanticist values), or the Left (hostile to his "personal power" and to capitalism)—had now lost ground in public opinion.[10] To put the same point in the positive, the core ideological values of Gaullism—the defense of the nation, the idea of a strong State, the need for a presidential incarnation of the Republic, and an independent voice for French diplomacy in Europe and the world—had become part of the fabric of national political culture. De Gaulle was also given the benefit of the doubt on some of the more dubious episodes of his political life. Thus an absolute majority of respondents rejected the idea that the General had staged a coup d'état to return to power in 1958: The old specter of Bonapartism had been laid to rest. Public opinion also threw out the idea that de Gaulle had been anti-European or (worse still) hostile to democracy. Furthermore, and a final tribute to Gaullian universalism, was that a large majority believed that "Gaullism" was no longer a line of political demarcation but a heritage belonging to all French people. In short, fifty years after his 18th of June Appeal, de Gaulle had become the incarnation of exemplary virtue.[11]

This consecration must first be seen as the culmination of a long process of insertion of the Gaullian myth into public space. This entry of the General into the everyday imagination of the French is symbolized by the attaching of the Gaullian name to streets and roads, which had begun, as we showed in chapter 2, at the Liberation. Today, according to a survey carried out by the Institut Charles de Gaulle, more than 3,600 communes—that is, one in ten of all of France—has one or more public thoroughfares named after de Gaulle, which makes him the unquestioned national champion in this field, far ahead of his nearest competitors, Leclerc, Jaurès, Clemenceau, Gambetta, Joan of Arc, and Jean Moulin.[12] The chronology of these namings is particularly interesting. The first wave (some 20 percent) came in 1944–1945, in the heady years of the Liberation. Between 1946 and 1970 there was a reduction in pace (11 percent), then a real explosion between 1970 and the end of 1990, when almost 60 percent of the communes that have them created a Gaullian thoroughfare.[13] In other words, it was during the two decades following his death that the General, thanks to his breakthrough in municipal nomenclature, completed his symbolic conquest of France.

What ideas, values, and memories were being particularly honored in these expressions of community gratitude to the General's memory? Certain variations can be traced in this Gaullian geometry. Especially between November 1970 and November 1971, the period of most frequent inaugurations, it was above all the figure of the Liberator that was celebrated. In Alsace, a land of great Gaullian fervor, this was the case in cities like Strasbourg but also in much smaller places like Vendenheim in the Bas-Rhin, with a population of 5,000, where the municipal council met as early as November 17, 1970, and unanimously accepted the mayor's proposal to give one of the main streets in the locality the name of

General de Gaulle, "saviour of France and a Great Frenchman, Liberator of his Country."[14] References to the Fifth Republic were few and understated, as at Colmar, where it was simply recalled that de Gaulle had "twice saved France."[15] Avoiding subjects that might give offense, councils chose instead to recall the glorious memory of local visits by the General; at Altkirch (Haut-Rhin), for example, when it was time to vote on naming a new street for the Great Departed, the deputy mayor proudly noted that his town had had three visits from de Gaulle, "the first time just a few days after the Liberation."[16] In local memory, de Gaulle often appeared as a protector of Alsace; when they were voting to create a General de Gaulle square, the town council of Bischwiller (Bas-Rhin) celebrated the statesman who had always shown "an image of nobility, courage and greatness" but also noted that the tribute was being made to "the military leader who, by his personal decision in January 1945, had protected Alsace from being once more attacked by the enemy."[17] Enthusiasm was such as literally to erase the memory of other liberators: In Ribeauvillé, the new Place du Général de Gaulle supplanted the old Place des Américains.[18]

The cult of memory was an end in itself but also an important means of civic education. For many local authorities, the figure of the General was a means of transmitting key moral values. Thus at Ammerschwihr (Haut-Rhin), speaking at the inauguration of the new Place du Général de Gaulle before a large and enthusiastic if sometimes pensive crowd, the mayor reminded them that the Liberator had visited their town, then in ruins, on the first of August 1945; he hoped that the younger generations would be inspired by his example and defend the values of liberty, courage, and self-sacrifice. The ceremony, organized for the evening of July 13 and attended by the town band and a detachment of firemen from Colmar, concluded with a fine torchlight procession and had an eminently republican character, combining entertainment, fraternity, and pedagogy.[19] The symbolism did not end there: Ammerschwihr's new square would later become the place where the commune organized all its official celebrations and military parades.[20] Here, as in hundreds of French communes that had given his name to their main squares, General de Gaulle became the emblem of republican civic life, not only on the anniversary of the 18th of June but also during other ceremonies of local or national significance.

This Gaullian exemplarity was reinforced by the action of memorial associations that were particularly active during the 1970s and 1980s and often prompted the creation of de Gaulle thoroughfares by launching campaigns and writing to mayors and local councilors. These latter—to show their responsiveness to associative initiatives—often recognized these democratic pressures in their deliberations. For example, when the town council of Auch (Gers) voted to create a new rue Général de Gaulle in May 1990, it underlined that it was acting "following requests from various associations."[21] Sometimes such requests became pressing, as at Rennes, where the council's decision to rename the Champ de Mars as Esplanade du Général de Gaulle was taken at the end of November 1970, a few weeks after the Great Man's death. As the mayor himself admitted, the council had received "a great many letters" on this subject, including one on the very day of the meeting from the president of the Resistance Co-ordination Committee, which brought together all the local veterans' and resistance members' groups.[22] Another sign of the importance that was given to such groups was seen at the inauguration ceremonies, where places were often set aside for veterans' associations. At Le Bouscat in 1990, the new Avenue de la Libération-Charles de Gaulle was officially named on the 18th of June anniversary; the council even organized a drive-past of vintage military vehicles in honor of the old soldiers and in the presence of the American and British consuls.[23]

These commemorative initiatives did not always please everyone, as in the case of the Cross of Lorraine erected at Rueil-Malmaison, on the outskirts of Paris, a fairly crude replica of the monument at Colombey set up on a roundabout with, in the foreground, a glorious No Entry sign.[24] And if it was good at making itself heard, the associative movement did not always speak with one voice. One of the questions often debated was apropos of the renaming of streets and squares Charles de Gaulle or General de Gaulle. Despite the example of Le Bouscat (which had a Gaullist mayor), councils with a Gaullist or centrist majority and the Gaullist-inclined veterans' associations tended to insist on the military title, while left-leaning associations and councilors preferred the simple name. Behind this lexical distinction were often purely local issues but also national political traditions. For Gaullists "the General" was both the accepted way of referring to the Great Man and also the symbol of his authority, while the civilian name recalled that the French Left has never been fond of soldiers (the heritage of Bonapartism again) and that in honoring de Gaulle it was chiefly trying to salute the political—and above all the collective—actions of the Man of the 18th of June. Thus when the city of Nîmes—which had a left-wing majority on the council and a Communist mayor—decided to create an Esplanade Charles de Gaulle in January 1980, it was a result of proposals emanating from the local committee of the Association Nationale des Anciens Combattants de la Résistance (ANACR). This group had clearly indicated that in its view the idea was to honor "the memory of the man who, during the occupation, was the recognized chief of all the resistance organizations."[25]

Gaullian exemplarity did not therefore exclude certain political—and even party-political—intentions. If one listens carefully, one can clearly hear these undertones in the records of council meetings, especially when they concern the naming of the new thoroughfare, as we have seen, and also its location. These debates could sometimes become heated, even dramatic, particularly when the extreme Right joined the fray. At Bron (Rhône), for example, as the creation of an Avenue Général de Gaulle was being debated (it was later approved unanimously), a cozy exchange between left- and right-wing councilors about the historic importance of General de Gaulle was rudely interrupted by the representative of the Centre National des Indépendants et Paysans (an extreme right-wing movement). This gentleman said he would vote for the proposal to honor the Man of the 18th of June but tried to create trouble by asking for another avenue to be named after Marshal Pétain (the traditional stalking horse of the French nationalist Right). To make matters worse, he also reminded the (Socialist) mayor that while de Gaulle was toiling away for French liberation, François Mitterrand was hand-in-glove with Vichy, before later falling victim, at the Observatoire, to an attack that he had himself organized (this was one of the major political scandals of the Fourth Republic).[26] It is clear that the object here was less to celebrate Gaullian virtue than to use the Great Man to recall that his Socialist successor had worked to a less than heroic code.

On the Left, the post–de Gaulle period was marked by a greater willingness to accept the celebration of the General's memory by the naming of public thoroughfares. Thus in the Camargue, in the little town of Le Grau du Roi, it was the Socialist mayor Jean Bastide who first proposed a Quai Général de Gaulle, on November 14, 1970.[27] There were, it is true, some initial hesitations. At Chaumont (Haute-Marne), a stone's throw from Colombey, the local Socialists supported the creation of a Place du Général de Gaulle in 1972. But they insisted that the date of the 18th of June 1940 should be added, arguing that "We cannot agree to celebrate the politician against whom we always fought."[28] These chronological quibbles became somewhat less frequent with the passage of time and particularly (as we shall see later) after the election of François Mitterrand to the presidency in 1981. On the Communist side, however, the volte-face was more rapid and more spectacular. Ten years after the poet Louis Aragon's violent diatribe, in which he compared de Gaulle to Louis Napoleon and Mussolini,[29] the French Communist Party (PCF) started naming de Gaulle thoroughfares in the areas it controlled, as at Vénissieux, where the Liberator joined Lenin, Nelson Mandela, and former PCF leader Maurice Thorez in the pantheon of benefactors to humanity. The mayor stated that they were honoring not only the resistance hero but "the man who had always fought for France's national independence."[30] One is struck by the way the tribute is made to two different de Gaulles, quite separate in time: the resistance chief, but also the architect of the foreign policy of the 1960s. Certain Communist councils, it is true, diluted their homage to the General by honoring other historical figures at the same time; thus in January 1978, the council of Vaulx en Velin inaugurated a Charles de Gaulle Avenue but also a Jean Jaurès School, a François Mauriac Square, a Jacques Duclos Esplanade, a Missak Manouchian Garden, and—something that would no doubt have provoked a chuckle from the General—an Edouard Herriot Hostel.[31]

But de Gaulle's exemplarity was undeniable even for the PCF: It stemmed in part from the sheer strength of the Gaullian character (as one Communist Party member said, "You have to give it to him—he was a hell of a guy")[32] but also from the desire to embarrass the Giscard government, which had had the unfortunate idea of discontinuing May 8 as a public holiday in 1975. Also part of this Communist attempt to make use of the figure of the General was de Gaulle's ability to personify a certain conception of national sovereignty. At the inauguration of the rue Charles de Gaulle at Grigny (Rhône) in May 1979, the Communist mayor went so far as to quote a long section of the General's press conference in 1962, when he declared that there could be "no other Europe than the Europe of nation states, except in myths, fictions and pageantry."[33] The approach of the June 1979 elections (the first European elections by universal suffrage) was therefore not wholly unrelated to the Communists' sudden enthusiasm for de Gaulle's patriotic virtues.

The PCF was not alone in this respect: In that summer of 1979, the other main political groupings also rivaled each other in neo-Gaullist zeal. A cartoon in the French weekly *L'Express* showed the four main party leaders in the European election campaign, Jacques Chirac, Simone Weil, François Mitterrand, and Georges Marchais, each desperately clinging to some part of the General's empty coat. The caption prophetically summed up the ecumenism to come: "We're All Gaullists Now."[34]

These manifestations of Gaullian exemplarity reached their highest point in 1990, a triply commemorative year as the centenary of the General's birth, the fiftieth anniversary of the Appeal, and the twentieth anniversary of the Great Man's death. One hundred sixty-nine de Gaulle thoroughfares were inaugurated in that auspicious year, almost 10 percent of all such namings since the Liberation. The scale of the tributes was such that even the most irrational anti-Gaullists briefly returned to the limelight. In Paris, the Pétain-Verdun Association returned to the attack and tried, with the help of two pieces of cardboard, to rename the Place du Général de Gaulle as the Place du Maréchal Pétain,[35] while in a few provincial and suburban towns (including Villemomble, Gournay-sur-Marne, Noisy-le-Grand, and Le Raincy in Seine-Saint-Denis), Gaullian monuments were defaced.[36] In a stranger vein—the extreme Right definitely works in a mysterious way—plaques commemorating the 18th of June that had been ceremonially added in 1990 to the war memorials of eight little towns in the Haute-Saône were mysteriously stolen in June 1991.[37]

But these ups and downs, and the few scuffles between supporters of the Right and Left at the unveilings of plaques (notably at Brignoles in the Var, where "an incident" led Socialist and Communist councilors to withdraw from the ceremony),[38] did not overshadow the essential direction of events. One could even say that, while the gradual designation of de Gaulle thoroughfares had laid the symbolic foundations of Gaullian exemplarity in the Hexagon, the 1990 anniversary established it on truly solid ground. "De Gaulle Year," as it was commonly called, was marked by a whole range of tributes, all designed to bring out the Plutarchian character of the General. It began with a cartoon by Jacques Faizant in the *Figaro* on the first of January, showing a giant de Gaulle coming in through a door held open by Marianne, the feminine allegorical representation of the Republic, while a tiny Mitterrand scowls in the background.[39] We can measure the unprecedented memorializing fervor by the number of invitations to commemorations received by Admiral de Gaulle in the year 1990 alone: 1,659.[40] Recognition came first from the highest sources, such as a plaque reproducing the 18th of June Appeal unveiled under the Arc de Triomphe by President Mitterrand himself—a significant gesture from a man who in the early 1960s had written a celebrated pamphlet denouncing Gaullian rule as a "permanent coup d'état."[41]

In Lille, the Socialist city council met in November in the presence of three ministers of the Rocard government and a selection of historic Gaullists (including the aforesaid Admiral) to unveil an abstract sculpture by Eugène Dodeigne in honor of the General. The mayor and former Socialist prime minister, Pierre Mauroy, paid a fulsome tribute to the "genuine republican"[42]—just if belated redress for the then Lille mayor Augustin Laurent's refusal to receive de Gaulle at the Town Hall during his official presidential visit to the northern city in 1966. An even bolder example of historical revisionism was Philippe Séguin's choice of the year 1990 for the publication of his remarkable book *Louis Napoleon the Great*, in which he is at pains to point out the "many resemblances" between the thought of Napoleon III and that of Charles de Gaulle.[43]

Everywhere in France visual tributes to de Gaulle were memorable, often touching the heart and sometimes the palate: The chocolate-maker Michel Cluizel created two souvenir boxes, the smaller containing thirty squares of chocolate bearing the General's portrait and the larger, thirty small bars tracing the great moments of his life; every mouthful contained "72% cocoa solids."[44] In a more epic register, Chirac's city council in Paris organized a great water festival on the Seine for the evening of the 18th of June, with more than 2,000 performers and gigantic scenery (including an enormous mock radio set planted on the Place de la Concorde); a giant image of the General was projected onto the façade of the City Hall. Some Gaullist mayors went a little far, like Robert-André Vivien, who had a 45-by-23-meter fresco of the General drawn in front of his town hall at Saint-Mandé, allowing him to boast that his commune had "the biggest de Gaulle in France."[45] The 1990 anniversary was also a bonanza for painters and draftsmen like Daniel Hugot, who took advantage of the exhibition of stamps in honor of the General at Colombey to place before the public his collection of envelopes, cards, and writing paper decorated with Gaullian themes.[46] Sculptors too were rubbing their hands; from everywhere in France came commissions for monuments to the memory of the Great Man: busts, like that of Georges Oudot at Sèvres (Hauts-de-Seine),[47] or abstract works, like the one by Bernard Hanin at Mennecy (Essonne), who produced three blocks of concrete to symbolize the General's life, his works, and the 18th of June Appeal.[48] Many Gaullian monuments were in the form of the Cross of Lorraine, as at Biarritz or Cannes.[49] Somewhat more exotic was the portrait of the General in mosaic produced by the Metz artist Jeannine Schrepfer.[50] And what could be more symbolic of the General's exemplarity than the creation of an "image d'Epinal" in his honor? The celebrated print design marked the 1990 anniversary by producing a sheet of the various episodes in the Great Man's life, superimposed, of course, on a Cross of Lorraine.[51]

One of the notable features of the 1990 anniversary, in terms of the heroic projection of the Gaullian figure throughout the country, was the emphasis placed on youth. The vocal and instrumental group Ici Londres recorded a rap version of the 18th of June Appeal.[52] An illustrated book on de Gaulle with text by Jacques Marseille[53] appeared in the Hachette *Histoire Juniors* collection, while Perrin offered a *De Gaulle Told to Children* by Henri Amouroux.[54] In several towns, among them Rouen and Beaune, there were exhibitions of the work of the caricaturist Jacques Faizant, including his best cartoons of the General.[55] In liaison with the Ministry of Education, an essay competition was organized in senior and junior high schools on the theme "General de Gaulle, leader of Free France and the Resistance."[56] Throughout France, school students set to work to bring to life the history and memories of the years 1940–1944; at Colombey, the secondary pupils went further and organized an exhibition on Adenauer's visit to the village in 1958, collecting from the older inhabitants their accounts of the atmosphere at the time, and more generally, their memories of the Great Man.[57] The most original demonstration took place at Monthélie (Côte d'Or), where the mayor organized a special commemorative ceremony in March 1990 attended by the classes of six- and seven-year-olds, in which he symbolically connected the bicentenary of the Revolution and the fiftieth anniversary of the 18th of June Appeal by planting a tree of liberty (a silver lime). In his speech, addressed particularly to the young, he traced the history of revolutionary emblems, before reminding them that trees of liberty had been planted in France in 1830, 1848, and also in 1944, after the Liberation; the 1990 tree was thus intended to symbolize, through de Gaulle, the continuing republican fight for liberty.[58]

Charles de Gaulle: disciple of the French Revolution. It was inevitable that the closeness in time of the anniversaries of 1789 and 1990 should revive the Revolutionary image of the General, which had made its first dramatic appearance in French political culture during the Resistance and Liberation years. But this symbolic assimilation was not simply the result of a random commemorative clash, for the year 1990 also marked a new historical approach to the Gaullian phenomenon. A few months after the mayor's speech at Monthélie, the question of a Revolutionary legacy in de Gaulle's thought and actions was treated in depth by the historian Claire Andrieu at the huge international conference organized in November 1990 by the Institut Charles de Gaulle.[59]

This meeting, which brought together more than 1,000 French and foreign visitors, people drawn from the university world and the world of politics and high-ranking civil servants, was one of the most influential commemorations of the de Gaulle Year. The conference, whose proceedings were published in eight volumes,[60] was doubly symbolic—first, as evidence of the unquestionable salience of the de Gaulle myth twenty years after his death, not only in France but across the world. Indeed the official participants came from sixty different countries, and the universal significance of the Gaullian phenomenon was discussed from every possible angle: the impact of de Gaulle's foreign policy and approach to decolonization, perceptions of the General throughout the world (from French-speaking Quebec to Turkey and Latin America), as well as his worldwide cultural and intellectual influence. The desire for completeness was such that there was even a paper on quotations from General de Gaulle in the writings of the Albanian leader Enver Hoxha. It is true that at the end of the twentieth century, the force of the Gaullian example was prodigious, not only in its extent but also in its variety. Posthumously awarded the medal of the First of September Revolution by Colonel Gaddafi in 1989 (in the company of Che Guevara, Martin Luther King, Mao Ze-Dong, Nasser, and Tito),[61] the General was honored some years later at Carlton Gardens, as we recalled at the beginning of this chapter, by the English monarchy, when the Queen Mother paid tribute to him as "a great Frenchman and a great patriot."[62] For other monarchs who had lost their thrones he symbolized the hope of a restoration, as for the unfortunate Simeon II, exiled from his former kingdom of Bulgaria since the 1950s, who liked to compare his retreat in Madrid to Colombey-les-deux-Eglises.[63] But de Gaulle was also the supreme example of sheer willpower, of resistance to enslavement, of a refusal to lie down and die: Those were the values personified by the Great Man for many revolutionary movements and notably for Yasser Arafat, the historic leader and president of the Palestine Liberation Organization. Abu Ammar, as he was affectionately known by his people, was never seen without a gold Cross of Lorraine pendant hanging around his neck; this talisman had been sent to him by General de Gaulle in 1970.[64]

As well as reflecting the wide dissemination and astonishing plasticity of the Gaullian myth throughout the world, the 1990 conference underlined the pivotal role of the Institut Charles de Gaulle.[65] Entrusted by the Great Man himself to its first director, Pierre Lefranc, this institution, founded in 1971, was both the faithful and demanding guardian of Gaullian memory and a place of debate and discussion from different viewpoints about the history of Gaullism. During its first twenty-five years of existence, the Institut organized more than 500 lectures and published some 100 issues of the journal *Espoir*; it thus gave a real impetus to the development of historical research on the General.[66] At the same time, its institutional presence could not but influence the directions taken by Gaullian historiography in France. For despite the undeniable successes of such research, and the advancement of our knowledge of the man and the period (particularly through the contributions of the "great eye-witnesses"), the fact that it had to be carried out under the auspices of such an organization had the effect of introducing a subtle normative bias. The Institut's output typically stressed the General's exemplarity, not least through its tendency to rely heavily on oral sources, which were already predisposed by their very nature to view de Gaulle as a wholly exceptional figure. This "in-house" historiography of the Man of the 18th of June was always marked by a fervid search for closeness, a wish to recover the private essence of the Great Man through his conversations and confidences: a virtuous circle that could only reinforce the sense of his otherness. This personalization of the General was accentuated by the fact that the end of the twentieth century and the beginning of the new millennium marked the glorious twilight of the "great witnesses," who fired off the last salvo of memoirs of the Gaullian epic.

One of the most edifying examples of this literary genre was *C'Etait de Gaulle* by Alain Peyrefitte, a former minister of de Gaulle in the 1960s, whose three volumes appeared in the late twentieth century.[67] Starting (as Claude Mauriac had done) from notes made during his private conversations with de Gaulle, Peyrefitte drew a fascinating portrait of the General through his confidences and remarks he made to his ministers and staff. One could sum up this work by saying it is a private portrait of the public man: It is full of details about the Gaullian entourage (notably Pompidou, whose witticisms appear throughout the book), about the General's pragmatism, about how his feelings could be read from his face (it turned pink when he was annoyed), about how little he liked living at the Elysée, and a thousand other things. The work destroyed certain myths, sometimes deliberately—as when Peyrefitte showed that the decision to have the president elected by universal suffrage in 1962 had been long and carefully thought out and was not (as legend had it) an immediate reaction to the Petit-Clamart assassination attempt.[68] But the demystification was often involuntary: When we see the General humiliated at the Ecole Normale Supérieure,[69] losing his way in a cabinet meeting,[70] or telling his minister of the interior to open fire on the students during the events of May 1968,[71] we realize to what extent everyday problems could encroach on the sublime. We also discover that the Great Man was not always respectful of his entourage—and even then, Peyrefitte admitted that he had excised certain wounding remarks about some of them. The Gaullian word was revealed in all its richness, with striking sayings and remarkable historical evocations—but also some brutal choices of words, as when, noting the huge Arab population by then living in France, he foresaw a "Colombey-les-deux-Mosquées."[72] Although Peyrefitte repeatedly insisted on de Gaulle's attachment to Algerian independence, and to decolonization in general, he also quoted highly skeptical Gaullian remarks about the "natives'" readiness for self-government;[73] such passages certainly deal a heavy blow to the myth of a "Third World-ist" de Gaulle.

In spite of these few discordant notes, the idea of Gaullian providentialism was undoubtedly reinforced by Peyrefitte's book. It was strengthened first of all by the remarkable equanimity of the General's observations of French political life and foreign policy, as reconstructed by Peyrefitte, which seemed to show that all the informal thoughts and even offhand remarks of the Great Man had the stamp of genius on them. It was strengthened too by the repeated presentation of the General as a prophetic figure, endowed with foresight about his own destiny (Peyrefitte managed to dig up a radio broadcast by the General in May 1940, which he seems to have been the only Frenchman to hear and which already sketches out the main lines of his June Appeal),[74] but also about the direction the world was taking. Like a clairvoyant, the prophet-General foretold in his conversations with Peyrefitte in the 1960s the resistance of European nation-states to attempts to impose federalism, the fall of Soviet-style communism, and even the reunification of Germany.[75] Above all, the book allowed one to measure the truly crushing effect the president had on those around him. While the genius of Las Cases, the narrator of the *Mémorial de Sainte-Hélène*, had transformed the Emperor into a Messiah for republican ideas and a tragically human and intimate figure, Peyrefitte constantly returned to metaphors of monarchy to accentuate de Gaulle's grandeur. Did he not have the General say, "The government has no substance without me"?[76] A kingly remark with which his prime minister could only agree: "I am just a reflection of de Gaulle."[77] And what are we to think of the relationship between the General and the author himself, if not that the latter was not only subordinate to the General but completely overshadowed by him and subject to his will? This is clearly shown by the scene that concludes the work, in which Peyrefitte describes his refusal to step inside the church at Colombey on the occasion of the funeral service in November 1970 on the grounds that the General had asked that this last rite should be attended only by his family, the villagers of Colombey, and the Companions of the Liberation. There is something sad, even tragic, in the "I am not worthy" uttered by Peyrefitte at that moment and his deliberate decision to exclude himself from the funeral of the leader he had served so loyally through the first decade of the Fifth Republic.[78]

At the same time that one of the greatest figures of the Right was setting the founder of the Fifth Republic on a pedestal as an Olympian figure—so highly placed as to be almost removed from the common run of men[79]—the French Left was rediscovering de Gaulle and, one could almost say, "its various de Gaulles." In 1990 the Communists celebrated the Man of the 18th of June but without any sycophancy; Fernand Grenier, who had been the Party's emissary to the General in London and then in Algiers, lent his voice to recall the decisive part the Communists had played in the overthrow of Vichy and the struggle against American designs on France.[80]

At the Institut conference in 1990, various figures from the French Left came to pay their tributes, while explaining their attitudes to the General's memory. This was a historical reappraisal from which the General emerged with considerably increased credit, if not totally whitewashed. All these speakers recognized de Gaulle's great political successes, especially in the Resistance, in the decolonization period, and in maintaining France's "rank" in the world. The journalist Jean Lacouture, whose biography of the General had been a considerable success with the reading public, traced the history of his own "long march" toward de Gaulle, which he summarized as a movement from "the condition of a reluctant citizen to that of a writer overcome by certain obvious truths."[81] In a double-edged tribute, the Trotskyist Alain Krivine saluted de Gaulle's ability to defend the interests of the bourgeoisie "sometimes against itself."[82] The historian Michel Winock even admitted having become a "posthumous Gaullist," converted not so much by Gaullian politics as by the style of the public man and his restoration of that "certain idea of France": "So long as de Gaulle was alive, we had the impression, as French people, of no longer being mediocre."[83] But beyond these attestations, there was still a real division between de Gaulle and the Left, summed up in the notion that de Gaulle had after all been a man of the Right and of "big capital," and above all in the unchanging mistrust of Gaullian providentialism. The former Resistant Claude Bourdet represented this position with talent and conviction: As a "great witness" and a Companion of the Liberation, he still refused to take part in the Gaullist rituals of the 1960s (notably the mont Valérien ceremonies), while never renouncing the memory of the "common struggle";[84] it was in this spirit (and in his capacity as a Companion) that he attended the funeral at Colombey in November 1970. Twenty years later, his judgment remained unshakable: "De Gaulle's main belief was in the absolute rightness of his own views on all subjects, and he had little regard for the opinions and behaviour of the rest of humanity."[85] Michel Winock put things less brutally, and perhaps more justly, when he concluded his essay with these words: "I wonder whether de Gaulle, in 1940 and later, was not simply standing in for the great people that we have ceased to be"[86]—an uncanny echo of de Gaulle's own formula in the *War Memoirs* about having to "take responsibility for France."[87]

The question of the Great Man therefore continued to be a stumbling block for the Left in its approach to memory and culture, and even in a political sense. It is true that from the presidential elections of 1981 onward, the Gaullian republic had ceased to be a complete bugbear. The idea of the "permanent coup d'état," so brilliantly defended by Mitterrand's polemical pen in the early years of the Fifth Republic, was quietly laid to rest. The new edition of the work in 1993 served only to draw attention to the author's shortcomings, during his presidential mandates, in the realms of liberty and public morals.[88] There were, however, some attempts to draw comparisons between the Father of the Fifth Republic and his Socialist successor; thus, Pierre de Boisdeffre noticed that both men had been "lovers of trees."[89] In the same private register, Frédéric Mitterrand, the president's nephew, trawled through his childhood memories to recall his double attachment, in the 1960s, to the General and to "Uncle François."[90] And in his fine essay on the "adventures of Mitterrandism," the journalist Jean Daniel tried valiantly to bring the two men together in a common anticapitalist heritage: "tradition and Christianity."[91]

Carried away by enthusiasm, Henri Lerner even tried to describe Mitterrand, after his acceptance of the institutions of the Fifth Republic, as "the de Gaulle of the Left."[92] The most ambitious exercise was attempted by the journalist Alain Duhamel, in a book published when Mitterrand was at the acme of his glory. Both figures of rebellion and talented writers, each with a visceral attachment to the land and an ambitious idea of France's place in the world—were not de Gaulle and Mitterrand "strangely similar"?[93] This was a gross error of judgment, as was rapidly shown by the Socialist president's disastrous last years in power and above all by the revelation of his far-Right sympathies and compromising associations with Vichy.[94] As often happens in France, memories were used not so much to understand the past as to draw even clearer demarcation lines in the present. Mitterrand's disgrace served only to throw a brighter light on the greatness of the General who, it was remembered, had said in 1945, "My only dialogue with Vichy has been an exchange of gunfire."[95] It was the philosopher André Glucksmann who had the final word: "There had to be François Mitterrand before we could rediscover de Gaulle."[96]

The gaping void created by the collapse of Mitterrandian socialism led to a more radical reconsideration, through the exemplary figure of de Gaulle, of the political culture of the Left. The work that launched this wholly new genre was the philosopher and former revolutionary activist Régis Debray's *A demain de Gaulle*.[97] Published in 1990 and deriving directly from the Institut conference, it was first received as an expression of the disillusion of left-wing intellectuals faced with the broken mirror of Socialism in France and the bloody failure of Soviet-style communism throughout the world. It is true that Debray, an early ally of Mitterrand and part of his staff at the beginning of his first term of office, made no secret of his disenchantment with the later political and moral backslidings of his old comrades at the Elysée.[98] But the book was much more interesting than a simple settling of scores. Faced with a left-wing pantheon "filled with skeletons,"[99] Debray was doubly original in trying to find in de Gaulle not only an exemplary historic figure but also a model for the future. The General thus became, at the hands of the former comrade of Fidel Castro and Che Guevara, "the first man of the twenty-first century."[100] To justify this miraculous metamorphosis, Debray "opened his eyes" to de Gaulle's legacy, restructuring the General as an epic and mythical figure by means of a series of comparisons with Napoleon, which showed that the two heroes had the same mythological structure in their relations with the Left—had not both first been admired as liberators, then hated as despots, and then, in a third, posthumous phase, praised to the skies and transformed into figures of legend?[101]

The parallel was undeniable and was a sign of the way in which the year 1990 marked a turning point in French political culture, as well as the cyclical (not to say circular) character of left-wing political thought. For the case of de Gaulle raised a troubling political question: Why this recurring blindness of the Left in the face of Great Men? Debray rightly noted that it was partly a problem related to the egalitarian instincts of the Left, for whom only the people were the real bearers of sovereignty.[102] It was also partly a reflection of the Left's inevitable mistrust of exceptional characters, especially if they came from the military: "We have to recognize great men and at the same time refuse to follow them."[103] Debray felt this very tension in the face of de Gaulle, who for him represented "the unattainable absolute."[104] But the deepest reason for this block was the Left's failure to define a true ethic of power. The practice of the great men of the Left in France—Gambetta, Jaurès, Clemenceau—was at best unfitted to present times and at worst useless as a coherent foundation for action. Léon Blum, the impotent Socialist leader of the Popular Front in 1936, and Mitterrand had been tragic examples of this failure.[105]

For Debray, the renewal of the Left therefore required the discovery of a new ethic of power, and it is here that the work went furthest in its revisionism, for it presented de Gaulle as the sole valid example of such a State ethic—first by the step he took in June 1940, in the name of a certain idea of patriotism, but above all in his unerring determination to put the nation at the center of his political commitment. In passing, Debray skewered his political family's chronic inability to understand the profound meaning of de Gaulle's idea of nationhood. It was not, as they had too often insisted, an arrogant and domineering nationalism but on the contrary an open idea, quite opposed to any form of ethnic exclusion, and constituting a "symbolic" third way between the universalism of the Enlightenment and the xenophobic and authoritarian nationalist tradition of the monarchist Charles Maurras, the intellectual inspiration of the Vichy regime.[106] It was precisely his ability to personify and promote this syncretistic idea of the nation in France and in the world that made the General the symbol of modernity. De Gaulle thus became, as refashioned by Debray, the very emblem of republican moral exemplarity and a prodigious disciple of the tradition of 1789.[107]

Debray continued his reflection on the failure of Mitterrandism (and on Gaullian exemplarity) in Loués soient nos seigneurs, which he concludes with these words: "Someone like de Gaulle takes things by the roots, someone like Mitterrand by the leaves."[108] His revisionist approach marks the beginning of a series of reappropriations of the figure of de Gaulle by the French Left. Among politicians, a neo-Gaullian sensibility began to reappear, notably in the socialist Jean-Pierre Chevènement's robust, martial brand of socialism,[109] which celebrated strong republican virtues and a centralized State leading the battle against economic and cultural "sectional interests." Hostile to the unbridled capitalism supposedly incarnated in the "Anglo-Saxon model," this new form of Gaullism derived from the General chiefly in its intransigent defense of the "nation," threatened as much by the siren calls of European federalism as by the vulture's claws of Anglo-American cultural imperialism.[110] As the presidential election of 2002 approached, Jean-Pierre Chevènement received the support of many historic figures of Gaullism, including Etienne Burin de Roziers, Roger Barberot, François Flohic, Raymond Triboulet, and Pierre Lefranc.[111] This neo-Gaullist sensibility also found favor among nationalist intellectuals like Max Gallo, a socialist who later converted to Sarkozyism, whose novelized biography of the General represented a certain left-wing indulgence toward the Great Man.[112] In quite another register, some left-wing intellectuals now stressed the democratic exemplarity of de Gaulle, like the journalist Jacques Julliard, who ended his pamphlet *La Reine du Monde* by paying homage to "great political educators" like Churchill, Gandhi, and de Gaulle, whose chief virtue had been to resist being carried away by short-term and self-regarding considerations. The General thus became the icon of a sort of democratic Stoicism: "A democratic leader cannot have as his whole programme the wish to be understood, and far less to be loved. But he brings the people round to want what is in their best interests. Gratitude can only come, if it ever does, at the end of his life or after his death"[113]—a fine saying that underlines the distinctive element in the Left's cult of great men, but it does raise a troubling question: If our support of a leader is founded on neither reason nor on sentiment, in what sense does politics differ from faith?

The most incisive representation on the Left of General de Gaulle as a republican hero was delivered by the historian Maurice Agulhon in a work published in 2000.[114] This meeting between the greatest historian of republican symbolism and the most complete incarnation of contemporary political exemplarity did not disappoint. The chief reason was that the book was the product of Agulhon's political reflection over several decades on Gaullian history and memory. Describing his first visit to

Colombey in 1978, the author stresses the impression made on him by the contrast between the arrogantly gigantic scale of the memorial and the human modesty of the inscription on it, complemented by the Christian humility of the General's grave in the cemetery. Hence his feeling, from the beginning, that de Gaulle was "an infinitely more complex"[115] man than left-wing anti-Bonapartist tradition would have it—a tradition to which Agulhon himself belonged and that typically presented the General as the usual perfidious soldier. He found the same complexity in Gaullian symbolism and historical imagination, which was syncretistic even in his private quarters at La Boisserie. De Gaulle might have turned his back on the republican allegorical tradition represented by Marianne (who had been promptly replaced by the Cross of Lorraine), but in his home the General displayed not a statuette or bust of Napoleon but a fine painting of the soldiers of Year II, presented to him by his old comrade Gaston Palewski—compelling evidence of his attachment to the republican tradition.[116] If Agulhon ended his book with an affirmation of de Gaulle's exemplarity—"even at the level of morals"[117]—it was not so much because of his personal political choices as his ability to be a "mythmaker," thanks to his thoughtful balancing of old traditions against new values: inflexibility and sense of opportunity, the great Nation and decolonization, social order and the enfranchisement of women, royalist sentiment and republican reason. De Gaulle thus became, under Agulhon's pen, the heir of the great republican tradition of the later nineteenth century.

De Gaulle was therefore triumphant as the new millennium approached. An exemplary figure in republican nomenclature, he was honored by local communities as well as by the State, by associations and intellectuals, by the whole political class, whether Right or Left, and by the overwhelming majority of public opinion. The personification of virtue, his integrity, and his moral probity were all the more admired for the contrast they provided with the failings of a political class—including the heirs of de Gaulle—whose behavior increasingly enraged the French.

In these depressing times, the Gaullian myth remained almost indecently healthy: a buoyancy that allowed it, with the supreme audacity of great legends, to appeal to conflicting impulsions. Already, at the beginning of the 1990s, the dissident Gaullist Philippe Séguin had invoked the General's memory to justify his fierce opposition to the Maastricht Treaty: de Gaulle had wanted France to be part of Europe but "standing on its own feet."[118] Following this, the Man of the 18th of June had once more personified rebellion and the spirit of subversion, as in Georges-Marc Benamou's book, in which de Gaulle symbolized the refusal to be cowed by conformism in all its shapes.[119] On the other hand, for those who were disoriented by the fast-moving pace of modern times, the General represented something to hold on to, the source of a certain nostalgia for the past. The Man of the 18th of June thus appeared as the guarantor of tradition, even of a certain conservatism; one of his great-grandsons (named Charles, as it happens) conceived the strange idea of joining the extreme right-wing National Front. To the disgust of his family, the black sheep figured in second place on the Lepenist list for the European elections in 1999.[120] It is true that the General was at the same time the icon of Euroskepticism, a doctrine successfully embraced by the neo-Gaullist RPF movement list at the same elections. In the autumn of the same year, Alain Decaux and Alain Peyrefitte's play *The Man Who Said No* was lavishly produced to great popular acclaim at the Palais des Congrès with Robert Hossein as director. A special performance brought together the elite of political and fashionable Paris and the last great survivors of the Gaullian epic, like General de Boissieu.[121]

Behind its literal meaning, the figurative sense of the title revealed a France that was tired and anxious. What symbol could have been more comforting, at a time when the political wing of Gaullism was being laid to rest amid general indifference,[122] than the image of the Father returned to life? The greatest mythogenic work of the new millennium, which in a sense marked the apotheosis of Gaullian exemplarity, was the book of interviews published by Admiral Philippe de Gaulle, *De Gaulle Mon Père*.[123] This key testimony was the work of a son who in late middle age resembled his father to an almost troubling degree and who had published his own (little-noticed) memoirs some years before.[124] Recounting the whole life of the Great Man, from his earliest years to his last moments, the book was a huge popular success, selling almost a million copies.[125] This "de Gaulle mania"[126] surprised commentators and made the General's son into a television star; he made a much-noted appearance in October 2003 on Michel Drucker's Sunday-night show. Reviews of the book were very positive overall, from the popular to the highbrow press: *Le Figaro* saluted the "miracle" of a book that was "as rich in events, in changes of fortune and in characters as a swashbuckling romance."[127] *Le Monde* saw in the Admiral's success a "triumph" for de Gaulle, particularly in his moral and financial "exemplarity": "De Gaulle symbolises the honest man, the leader of integrity who respects the common good."[128] *L'Express* was pleased by the humanization of the Gaullian figure,[129] and the *Nouvel Observateur*, in the person of Jean Daniel, noted that the book brought home the extent to which de Gaulle had been the "passion" of men of his generation.[130]

The Admiral's work offered a host of interesting details (about his father's love of football as a boy and his admiration for Jean-Baptiste Clément, the composer of *Le temps des cerises*) and also a considerable number of original elements, but above all it reinforced the "golden legend" in several fundamental respects, first in its ultra-Gaullian presentation of the General's determination and strength of character. Proud, solitary (with no close friends, not even Malraux),[131] ambitious, unfathomable, and cold,[132] the public man seemed to have only one passion: France. As the journalist Philippe Alexandre noted in *France-Soir*, "the Admiral does not admit to the smallest human weakness in his father."[133] It is true that the Gaullian quality most often referred to was pride, a consciousness in de Gaulle of his own superiority, which dictated his conduct and led him to refuse all decorations and honors.[134] The story as told by the son also echoed all the chief elements of the Gaullian political myth, notably the minimizing of the Communist role during the Resistance[135] and highlighting the (completely fanciful) notion that the General had no hand in the military putsch in Algeria that contributed to his return to power in May 1958.[136] The Admiral also contested certain interpretations of Gaullian history, including a number of accounts given by former colleagues of the General's that he considered mistaken, notably those of de Gaulle's former private secretary Claude Guy[137] and General Massu, whose judgment that de Gaulle had "lost it" in 1968 was vigorously denied.[138]

All of this was par for the course. But the real mythogenic force of the book lay in two other directions. First, and following on from Peyrefitte's approach, *De Gaulle Mon Père* offered a singularly monarchical reading of Gaullian history. While firmly rejecting the conservative nationalism of Maurras, the figure drawn by the Admiral "had no love for the Revolution nor for revolutionaries" and "thought monarchy preferable in theory."[139] Upsetting the received idea that de Gaulle was hostile to the Napoleonic tradition, the Admiral stressed that "Bonaparte, and therefore Napoleon, was the character in history who had certainly attracted his attention most";[140] he recalled that de Gaulle had always shown a great interest in the history of Bonapartist empires and that he considered Napoleon III's regime "more republican than monarchist, in spite of appearances."[141] This admiration for hybrid forms of neo-monarchy was carried into the economic and social spheres, where de Gaulle's attempt to find a third way between capitalism and socialism (notably for his great reforms of 1945–1946) had been inspired by Colbertian dirigisme.[142] The high point of this monarchical (re)reading of the Gaullian epic was the description of August 26, 1944, in Paris, the day of the famous march down the Champs-Elysées and as far as Notre Dame. Why Notre Dame, in fact? De Gaulle's reply, as reported by his son, was edifying: "In the time of the monarchy, this was done after every victory. When the King won the war, he went to thank God. We go to Notre-Dame because God is the master of everything. And today he ruled in our favour."[143] In this Christ-like representation, the Appeal of the 18th of June became the result of the divine will and the General God's, chosen messenger, to carry it out.

This passage also exemplifies the second, and even more fundamental, mythogenic quality of the Admiral's book: the portrait he draws of the General's home life. These were not just the scraps of information that had been provided by this or that staffer, or a brother-in-law or son-in-law who had been part of the inner circle at one time or another, but a life-size portrait of the private man, drawn by the one person who had shared the General's life longer than any other: his son—a son under his spell but whom (reading between the lines) he had sometimes wounded, who could provide limitless information about the General's private life. One of the most memorable themes of the work, in its private aspect, is the emphasis placed on the General as a Christian. From the Catholic education he received[144] to the simplicity of his funeral arrangements,[145] de Gaulle appeared as a profoundly religious figure, who readily admitted to his son that his Christian belief had inspired his vision of the world, particularly his compassion for underdeveloped countries.[146] According to the Admiral, his father's Christianity was of a solid, traditional kind: De Gaulle had paid no attention to the siren calls of left-wing Catholicism: "Jesus Christ was never a revolutionary."[147] More generally, *De Gaulle Mon Père* opened wide the doors of the family home, giving detailed pictures of the General's private life at various historic moments (notably during his "exile")[148] and especially at Colombey, where de Gaulle was fiercely protective of his privacy, his "peace and quiet."[149] The Admiral described (both fondly and discreetly) the "model couple"[150] of Charles and Yvonne. In fact, the strongest characteristic of this intimate portrait was its exemplarity: Unlike the great monarchs with their lax sexual mores, his father had been a faultless husband,[151] and when he closed the door of his study, the General, devoted to his family's happiness, became once more "an always attentive paterfamilias."[152]

In the chorus of praise that greeted the Admiral's work, a few sour notes were sounded. The "Saint's Life" side of the work was noticed and often derided.[153] This critique also prompted a resurgence of the left-wing tradition of anti-Gaullian irreverence, as for example in François Reynaert's article for the *Nouvel Observateur*, in which he raged against "the pathetic de Gaulle worship of today, the ghastly habit of wrapping a cloak of nostalgia around the reality of the General's France, those dreadful sixties, like one long Sunday after Mass in the provinces, the stifling reign of a fake-modern bourgeoisie that was still stuck in its corsets of convention."[154] Right-wing anti-Gaullism also resurfaced in the person of Jacques le Groignec, president of the Association for the Defence of Marshal Pétain's Memory, which published a virulent pamphlet against the Admiral's work.[155] Descendants of several figures mentioned in the book took issue with some of the Admiral's statements. In an article that caused a great stir, the journalist Jean Mauriac corrected several errors of fact and interpretation concerning his father, the writer François Mauriac, and Claude Mauriac (de Gaulle's former private secretary), indications in his eyes of "the resentment that General de Gaulle's son has always felt towards my family."[156] Wishing to protect his grandfather's memory, the grandson of General Giraud, de Gaulle's one-time rival during the Second World War, went so far as to put together a *Reply to Admiral de Gaulle*, in which nine specialists defended a series of figures who had been "slandered" (including Jean Monnet, one of the architects of European unity), while questioning the Admiral's overall reading of the events of 1940–1944.[157]

The most interesting reaction, for it raised a truly fundamental problem, was that of the General's biographers who, in a special issue of the journal *Le Débat*, reacted vigorously to the Admiral. Jean Lacouture questioned the slanted presentation of Blum, Mendès-France, François Mauriac, and Malraux,[158] while Eric Roussel criticized the "strange truths" asserted and repeated throughout the work and the contemptuous tone adopted toward historians.[159] In his presentation of these two texts, the historian Pierre Nora expressed regret that the work had "Marshalised" de Gaulle and that, where the General was concerned, memory (subjective and often biased) risked supplanting history.[160] But was not this a striking confirmation of the continuing power of that "backward-looking creation of illusions"[161] that was so characteristic of Gaullism, whose workings had already been brilliantly analyzed by Nora himself in his *Realms of Memory*?

But nostalgia was not the only notable aspect of the success of the General's son's book. By lifting the veil on his father's private life, the Admiral was also reflecting the change in perspective brought about by the new millennium, as a result of which the General had become—or more accurately, was beginning to become—a true subject for artistic creation. Maybe we shall say one day, with hindsight, that *De Gaulle Mon Père* was the first great work of historical fiction with the General as its subject. It is true that the few competitors for the title had been frankly mediocre. In 1990, just before the anniversary of the General's death, TF1 (the largest privately owned terrestrial television station in France) had shown a film called *I, General de Gaulle* based on an original scenario by William Faulkner,[162] adapted by Bertrand Poirot-Delpech. But despite this posthumous collaboration between a Nobel Prize winner and an academician, and the realistic incarnation of de Gaulle by the actor Henri Serre, the film was slaughtered by the critics and rightly so, for it offered nothing but a series of commonplaces about France and the De Gaulle character, a cigarette constantly hanging from his lip, and lacked all dramatic depth.[163] The de Gaulle family had in any case made clear its objection in principle to any fictional representation of the General on the screen.[164]

Filmmakers had long felt themselves bound by such self-constraint. An example is one of the great classics of French cinema, Jean-Pierre Melville's adaptation of Joseph Kessel's novel *The Army of Shadows*. In the scene set in London where the resistance chief receives his decoration from the General's hands—inspired no doubt by the account in the *War Memoirs* of Jean Moulin being decorated in Hampstead—one very brief shot (just long enough to recognize him) has de Gaulle facing the camera, then the Great Man turns his back to the lens. In the 1990s various films were planned, including one starring Gérard Depardieu as the Man of the 18th of June (which would certainly not have been dull), but none came to fruition. General de Gaulle did appear as a character in a few semidocumentaries, including one on Jean Moulin made in 2003, with Jacques Boudet in the Gaullian role, and a reconstruction of the Petit-Clamart assassination attempt in 2005.[165] For a real dramatic incarnation of the Great Man on the screen, we had to wait until March 2006, when the public television station France-2 showed *Le Grand Charles*, a film made for the small screen by Bernard Stora, with Bernard Farcy in the role of the General. In the press coverage of this event, *Le Parisien* had the most revealing headline: "France-2 dares to bring 'le grand Charles' back to life."[166] A taboo had indeed been broken, and this time the critical reaction was much more positive, for the General was no longer portrayed in stereotypical fashion. Instead there was a real attempt to show the character in all his complexity—and even, in the treatment of the "crossing of the desert," in his darker and more vulnerable aspects.[167] In accordance with the French propensity to remember their heroes chiefly at the time of historic anniversaries, it was the de Gaulle of 1968 who next inspired artistic creators around the time of the fortieth anniversary of the May events. Evidence of this was Jean-Louis Benoit's play *De Gaulle in May,* which showed a de Gaulle out of his depth;[168] we should note too Hervé Bentégeat's novel *The Flight to Baden,* which tried to reconstruct the Great Man's "most secret thoughts" during his flying visit to General Massu.[169] This novel inspired the film *Goodbye de Gaulle,* shown on the cable television station Canal Plus in April 2009, with Pierre Vernier in the role of a disillusioned, sleep-deprived General who admitted that modern France was quite beyond him.

These are only the first of such Gaullian representations: The General still awaits his Abel Gance, and, unlike Napoleon, for a long time de Gaulle hardly seemed to appeal to novelists as a subject for fiction.[170] Following his death, there were a few modest attempts, of which no doubt the most amusing was Jacques Kermoal's *Procès en canonisation de Charles de Gaulle,* in which reports of miraculous cures at Colombey—particularly of a blind man who recovered his sight after touching the Great Man's *kepi*—led to a national campaign that ends with the beatification of the General.[171] After this apotheosis, little more was offered to the reading public apart from Maurice Cury's *De Gaulle est mort,* in which the General's passing was merely the background to a rather obscure detective story.[172] Again, the Great Man appears only as "the one who screwed the *pieds-noirs*" in *Le Petit Gaulliste* by Alain Lorne, the story of a little boy from Colombey-les-deux-Eglises whose parents go to work as volunteers in the newly independent Algeria.[173] Here too the millennium seems to have marked a new departure. Five novels in particular presented a very different de Gaulle: *L'Etre et le géant,* by Bernard Fauconnier, which describes a meeting between the philosopher Jean-Paul Sartre and the General in Ireland in 1969 in which the two men recognize the similarities between them, even in their failures;[174] *Nom de code La Murène* by

Jean-Christophe Notin, a gripping detective story that reveals that it was de Gaulle himself who had Jean Moulin betrayed, seeing him as a potential rival;[175] *68, mon amour* by Daniel Picouly, a wild fantasy in which the Great de Gaulle salivates at the thought of eating his homemade stew and craves for things like a child;[176] *Pauvre de Gaulle!*, a fanciful, caustic anti-biography by Stéphane Zagdanski that tries to pulverize the Gaullian colossus of clay "after half a century of French stupidity";[177] and finally *Le retour du Général* by Benoît Duteurtre, which sees de Gaulle awaken from hibernation fifty years after his "death" and return to power to save France from the perils of globalization.[178]

These constructions of an imaginary private life for the Great Man, coming—not by chance—at the same time as the discovery of his real private life, thanks to the Admiral's book, surely offer the final proof that the figure of de Gaulle has become unshakably implanted in French consciousness. From the late 1950s, de Gaulle has inspired the adventures of Astérix, one of the most popular French comic strips in the world, which portrays a plucky little fighter from ancien Gaul who resists Roman occupation and whose pugnaciousness, perspicacity, and fight for universal values captures the essence of France's self-image in the Gaullian era.[179] Appearing in person this time, the General stars as the tragicomic hero of Jean-Yves Ferri's quirky strip-cartoon album *De Gaulle at the Seaside*. In this affectionate parody, we find an almost resigned General washed up on the Breton coast among the bathers in the summer of 1956, at the height of his "crossing of the desert," recounting his days of glory, launching an appeal to find a lost beach ball, dictating his memoirs to his faithful assistant Le Bornec, and meeting up in the hotel bar with the old lion, the inevitable Winston Churchill, who finds the words to sum up their shared sense of loss: "No more heroes like *nous*, Charles."[180]

CONCLUSION

✕

The Last Great Frenchman

As we saw at the beginning of this book, the fortieth anniversary of the General's death, and the seventieth of the Appeal of the 18th of June, were celebrated with great official pomp (including a special commemorative visit of President Sarkozy to London) and a rich harvest of publications.[1] The popular consecration of Charles de Gaulle is complete: He is a real statue of the Commander, his myth having been nationalized, universalized, and privatized. Indeed de Gaulle is now a cultural institution in his own right and perhaps the most accomplished example of the national hero the French have ever seen. What a distance has been traveled since the emergence of the unknown officer amid the storms of the years 1940–1944. But we must recognize today that the prediction made by de Gaulle to Jean de Lipkowski—"the French have had enough of de Gaulle in 1969, but wait and see how the myth will have grown in thirty years' time"[2]—has certainly come true. Note the prophetic genius of the cartoonist Louis Mitelberg (better known as Tim), a Free French veteran and a clear-sighted but always sympathetic observer of the General, who drew him for *L'Express* in 1960 as (in succession) Marx, Lenin, Stalin, Abraham Lincoln, and Major Thompson before concluding, "The whole of humanity, from the Stone Age to eternity, is divided into two great camps: left-wing Gaullists and right-wing Gaullists."[3]

The Gaullian legend was the last French providentialist cult; such was the charisma of the Man of the 18th of June that he could win people over and entrance them—that becomes clear from his correspondence and the testimonies of surviving Free French veterans[4]—by his simple presence, by the mere fact of his existence. The Gaullian myth was also the last great French secular religion, holding its ground for a long time against the erosion and finally the crumbling of national commemorations.[5] This cult of the General was marked with fervor by thousands of men and women, following the patterns of the royalist, republican, and Napoleonic traditions: a transcendental celebration, as expressed by the follower who saw in the General "shining light, self-evident rightness and imperious necessity."[6] His was a public and ostentatious cult, expressed in official visits and memorial rites. As one man wrote to him, "I stood very close to you at Verdun, at the mont Valérien and at the 14th of July parades, and that proximity had an electrifying effect on me."[7] But the myth was also a matter of quiet, private memory, cultivated around a treasured letter from the General, a visit to his birthplace at Lille, a flag flown from the balcony one 18th of June, a souvenir brought home from Colombey, or simply a yellowing photograph of the Great Man on the wall of the living room.

In the years following the General's death, one of the most striking characteristics of his legend was its plasticity. In November 1975, on the fifth anniversary of his death, a documentary was shown on French television. Made by Claude Santelli, *The One and Only Charles* put to some famous intellectuals of the time the fundamental question: What were the foundations of the Gaullian myth? What was fascinating was the variety of the speakers' responses. For Claude Bourdet, de Gaulle had succeeded because of his ability to adapt to very different milieux, particularly at the time of the Resistance, when he had, as Bourdet put it, "learnt the Republic's values as he went along." Malraux's answer was essentially the same: He presented de Gaulle as a kind of brilliant synthesis of Joan of Arc, Napoleon, and Saint-Just. For Maurice Clavel the General became a myth because of his power to win people over: "He was the man I loved most in all the world." And for Jules Roy, de Gaulle was the rebel, the nonconformist, but also the savior, "the man France was expecting." Yet for Jean Daniel, the General was remarkable precisely because he never did what was expected of him. The documentary gave striking examples of de Gaulle's iconic status throughout the world; perhaps the most extraordinary was the encounter, in a remote corner of India, of a French filmmaker with some Marxist guerrillas. When they realized that they were in the presence of a Frenchman, these jungle fighters reacted by breaking cover and shouting in unison a tribute to the General's famous anti-imperialist speech of 1966: "De Gaulle–Phnom Penh!"[8]

Certainly the myth has evolved over time. With the deaths of the generations of the two world wars, the Gaullian years have come more and more to belong to history rather than lived experience: We are reaching the time of the "last witnesses."[9] In any case, the memory of the war is manifestly no longer part of the national commemorative system. Since 2006, the 18th of June has been declared a "national day of commemoration of General de Gaulle's historic appeal to refuse defeat and continue the fight against the enemy," but the very verbosity of the description seems to confirm the fading of collective memory. A few years ago, who would have felt the need to explain the significance of the date? At the same time, the pilgrimage to Colombey no longer has the sense of mourning today that it had in the years immediately following the death of the Great Man. Besides, as we have already seen, de Gaulle, probably because of the lack of great feats of arms in his own past (and also because of his genuine personal modesty), never let himself be presented as a military hero; that role in the Gaullian legend was always played by Leclerc, the glorious liberator of Paris. And what better example could there be of the complexity of the Man of the 18th of June than the difficulty of pinning him down, and the different views of him held by some of his closest collaborators? Knight of a religious order, regal monarch, proclaimer of parliamentary rationalism, herald of a stakeholder society, the General was dressed in a fine range of costumes by his disciples—to say nothing of his global image, which even today covers a prodigious range of roles, from the liberator of oppressed peoples and fighter against American imperialism to the incarnation of the nation-state and paternalism, or even, as seen by the post-Communist strongman Vladimir Putin, the martial symbol of a highly authoritarian democracy.[10]

These changes and varied representations have hardly affected the essential point: The General is still in the firmament, majestically occupying his position as France's most respected historic figure. He is on par with the great iconic figures who are celebrated as liberators and nation-builders across the world: the American Founding Fathers, Simon Bolivar in Hispanic America, Kemal Ataturk in Turkey, and Mahatma Gandhi in India. One might add, borrowing a formula from Sartre, that he has become the impassable horizon of French political mythology. For de Gaulle is the only great national mythical figure who not only had a sense of history but was himself moving in the direction of history. His judgment on the great questions of his day (the continuation of the war after 1940, the need to unify the Resistance, the weakness of party government under the Fourth

Republic, the institution of a new presidential Republic and decolonization) was proved right by posterity. This is part of the reason his legend has
completely occupied the political imaginative space of the French: de
Gaulle's was the voice of a prophet. Nothing competes with the General's
personal image, his worldview, or his take on the recent past—on Vichy,
the Resistance, the Algerian War, the institutions of the Fifth Republic,
Europe, or even globalization—the views of the French (with some small
modifications) are still essentially his. Take the case of Vichy: The French
now know much more about those dark years of their history thanks to the
work of recent historians, but they still refuse to modify their view of
Pétain's regime and even more to reduce the absolute distance separating
it from the Republic. Despite occasional attempts (notably toward the
end of Mitterrand's presidency) to admit Vichy at least to purgatory, it
remains, in the national demonology, the complete example of moral de-
pravity in the political realm. How can we not attribute responsibility for
this to the man who—to his honor—first personified the refusal to, as a
former Free French combatant once charmingly put it, "see France become
a railway carriage hitched to another power's locomotive"?[11]

Another measure of the General's supremacy is that the fiercest forms
of anti-Gaullism have all collapsed or at least are in a state of advanced de-
crepitude. The founding Father of the Fifth Republic is now rarely criticized; in a striking reversal, it is his reputation as the initiator of resistance
in France that is now sometimes questioned, usually by followers of Pétain-
ism or French Algeria.[12] Thus, on June 18, 2011, the inauguration of a new
statue of the General in Nice provoked a public protest of around 100 supporters of Algérie Française—a symbolic acknowledgment of their defeat,
as their systematic attempts to block the project failed.[13] The General even
has the pleasure of seeing yesterday's opponents of his policies defend them
vigorously against their questioning by his successors of today. France's
return to the integrated military command of NATO in 2009 was vigorously opposed in neo-Gaullist circles, particularly by the former prime
minister Dominique de Villepin as well as several former advisers to the
General.[14] But the protests of these old faithfuls were joined, and even amplified, by the Socialists and centrists, the very same parties who had
denounced de Gaulle's decision in 1966 in the name of the Atlantic alliance.
We thus find François Bayrou, chief defender of liberalism in France and
heir to the tradition of centrism, protesting that this decision by President
Sarkozy "tore from our hands the standard of independence which we had
proudly borne since de Gaulle offered us this risk and this opportunity."[15]

Never had the General been so admired as he is today. He represents all the four figures of the political hero once described by Raoul Girardet:[16] the great captain, the prophet, the legislator, and the sage (in more or less chronological order, we may add—a good summary of de Gaulle's life). At the same time, this man so hated by "washed-up politicians" has never been so instrumentalized by them. Whenever it is a question of defining some great political, social, or moral question, whether it is the defense of the public sector, the preservation of the nation-state, or the sense of the common good, he is almost instinctively called into service as an example. Some of these (re)appropriations are quite remarkable. At a time when the economic and financial crisis is reviving a certain populist anti-capitalism on the Left, the General has been recruited by the Communist Party—the same party that once bitterly condemned him as the principal agent of "State monopoly capitalism"—as a symbol of the fight against financial greed. But never mind: In spring 2009, a PCF leaflet in my Parisian neighborhood reminded us that French bosses collaborated with the Nazi occupiers, but justice was done by the Great Legislator: "At the Liberation, de Gaulle threw Louis Renault into jail."[17]

How can we explain this symbolic plebiscite in favor of de Gaulle, and what does it tell us about French collective sensibility at the beginning of a new millennium? First, it underscores a certain tendency to turn the political past into folklore. In a country where "memory" has become a positive national obsession, the figure of the General could not fail to be the focus for every kind of fetishism. The de Gaulle museum in Lille is probably the most complete example of this transformation of memory into "heritage." This fine townhouse was occupied by little Charles's grandparents on his mother's side, and the visitor can even admire his birth chamber (dressed with appropriate period furniture); the General thus becomes a "Legend of the North."[18] To this heritage approach is added a certain tendency to cultural reification, as in the new Mémorial Charles de Gaulle at Colombey, which houses a very "country"-themed exhibition on the Great Man's life, also designed to be an introduction (it is subsidized by the departmental council) to all the "tourist attractions of the Haute-Marne."[19] The proliferation of "De Gaulle" thoroughfares in France is also a sign of the same instrumentalization of his memory. Ever-faster urbanization has seen the creation of many new streets and roads that had to be named; General de Gaulle's name was therefore adopted along with dozens, even hundreds, of others belonging to national celebrities. For example at Orthez, in the Pyrénées-Atlantiques, the creation of a new rue de

Gaulle in 1974 was accompanied, in the same bumper year, by the naming of 124 other public thoroughfares.[20] That being said, this introduction of de Gaulle into everyday memory is still light-years away from China's "red tourism," which has seen throngs of visitors rush to pay homage to Mao's glory at the Shaosan museum, which contains some 1,000 relics of the Great Helmsman.[21] Even among democratic icons, de Gaulle is left standing by the South African leader Nelson Mandela, whose foundation receives an average of ten requests a week for his image to be used throughout the world. Mandela's name has been given to buildings, streets, and public squares in more than thirty countries; in his native South Africa, there are innumerable Mandela Streets, and the Liberator has also lent his name to a bridge, a stadium, a theater, and even a bay. There is also an impressive range of Mandela trinkets: clothes, dolls, coins, caps, and mugs. A local company even tried to sell a line of Viagra-style pills with the Mandela trademark.[22]

If de Gaulle has escaped—for the time being—these extremes of commercial appropriation, his cultural reification has nonetheless been helped along by the State, which has always claimed a stake in collective memory in France. If they have not been in the foreground of action, public institutions have always played a discreet and effective part in the rise of the Gaullian cult, in particular since the General's death. From the building of the memorial at Colombey until the recent transformation of the 18th of June into a day of national celebration, the State has involved itself significantly in the General's virtual entry into the Pantheon—and not only the Gaullist state. At the end of the 1970s the Giscard government provided funds to safeguard the objects held at the General's country home in Colombey, and in 1990 (in its own interests as much as those of the nation), the Socialist Left then in power insisted on celebrating as splendidly as possible the centenary of the Great Man's birth; it was then that the text of the 18th of June Appeal was inscribed on the Arc de Triomphe and that a sizable public subsidy (50 million francs) was paid to the Charles de Gaulle Foundation. If we add to this the State's financial support for the Foundation's work in preserving the General's memory—particularly the creation of the memorial at the Invalides, which could never have been completed without the continuing commitment of President Jacques Chirac[23]—it becomes clear that the General's posthumous fame is underpinned by solid institutional support. Finally, because of the watchful approach of Admiral Philippe de Gaulle—the last guardian of the temple—General de Gaulle's official archives for the years 1940–1944 were not opened to the public until 2004, leaving the mythogenic narrative of the *War Memoirs* as sole master of the field. Thanks to all these forms of support, the Gaullian legend was able not only to thrive but also (to put it in Barthesian terms) to turn the Gaullian narrative from a historical contingency into a natural phenomenon.[24]

These contributions of the State to the takeoff of the Gaullian myth must be noted, but they were not decisive; and they should above all not skew our interpretation through overreliance on the notions of propaganda or coercive power. Such concepts are shown to be misleading by the mass of evidence, drawn from across time and space, that we have brought together in this work. These elements bear witness both to the real popular fervor behind the Gaullian myth and to its creativity—and this allows us also to dispose of the notion of "social conformity,"[25] a barely updated version of the old, contemptuous stereotype of the French people as always manipulated and incapable of free choice. Such notions are not only reductive; they neglect the rebellious, even subversive side of the Gaullian myth. The General was no doubt the incarnation of order and the authority principle but also of insubordination, or at any rate of the courage to say "no" to the unacceptable. Let us finally add, to bury once and for all the classic explanation of political myth as the product of propaganda, that the Gaullian legend really took off at the moment when the Gaullists were no longer in power and that it never held such fascination for the collective consciousness as it does today, when Gaullism is utterly finished as a party political force. From this point of view, as from many others, the parallel with the Napoleonic legend in the nineteenth century is compelling: Both demonstrate the relative independence of political imagination from political structures and institutions.

Let us return for a moment to the relationship between the two myths: the Napoleonic and the Gaullian, which has been one of the recurring themes of this work. It is clear that the connection between de Gaulle and Napoleon (and still more so between Gaullism and Bonapartism) deserves better than bald assertions, either that de Gaulle did not like Napoleon, or that Gaullism was, or was not, the heir to Bonapartism. Reality, as always, proves to be more complex and more subtle. In 1927 the young Captain de Gaulle attended the first showing of Abel Gance's monumental film *Bonaparte* at the Opéra[26] and, filled with enthusiasm, came home and wrote *The Torch*, a play about Captain Coignet, who accompanied Bonaparte on all his military expeditions and became one of the most passionate proponents of the Napoleonic myth.[27] Youthful folly? During the last years of his presidency, de Gaulle was still so far from being hostile to the Emperor that he himself insisted—the archives are crystal clear on this point—that the Ministry of Culture should organize the commemoration of his bicentenary in 1969. The speech on Napoleon that the General was not able to pronounce at the Invalides was in some measure replaced after his death by the public tributes expressed in letters and national condolence books, in which Gaullian greatness was often compared to that of the Emperor. That allows us to set the record straight, and it is important to do so, not only to establish the historical truth but because the General's legend is now sometimes so sanitized—particularly on the Left—that all the sharp corners of the Gaullian heritage have been rubbed off. Having once dismissed him as a mere imitator of the worst tropes of Bonapartism, the Left is now inclined to pass over in silence his authoritarian tendencies and even his military background.

What, then, are we to think of the relation between the two myths? From a historical distance, we can observe the significant overlaps between the legends of the two men. They were both obsessed by their own singularity (Napoleon would have been happy to say of himself, as de Gaulle did, "I had no predecessor and I shall have no successor");[28] both tried to overcome the divisions of 1789, while holding on to its gains—indeed they spoke of it in almost identical ways (Napoleon aimed to "bring the Revolution to a close," while de Gaulle wanted to "close the parenthesis opened by the French Revolution"). Each was seen as a providential man, a symbol of popular sovereignty, and a grand, isolated figure—both as rulers and in their martyrdom. After April 1969, Colombey became the General's Longwood: "Eaten away by grief," as Madame de Gaulle said, he sank into melancholy and died.[29] At the same time, each of the great men's myths had its own slant. Napoleon personified above all the triumph of military glory and the cult of equality, neither of which forms part of the Gaullian imaginative scheme, while the General became the symbol of people's rights to self-determination and their contempt for money—neither of which principles even the most indulgent historian would dare attribute to the Emperor.

But let us return, after this parenthesis, to the General. What were the deep mainsprings of the legend that allowed de Gaulle to equal Napoleon and then to leave him far behind? The Gaullian myth was originally a deliberate ideological and symbolic construct, striking evidence of the intellectual and political creativity of this obscure officer who, from the 18th of June 1940 onward, claimed a past for himself and invented a new future for his country. One could go even further. Coming onto the scene at a moment

when all national traditions of heroism had been pulverized, de Gaulle created a new template of national exemplarity and then occupied it himself.
As Stanley Hoffmann quite rightly says, his greatest contribution to national
life "was the creation of General de Gaulle."[30] This redefinition of the national myth derived in some respects from its context, as we presently note.
But how can one not recognize, in the first place, the prodigiously instructive
character of the Gaullian destiny? His name alone was enough to call to
mind "a thousand years of history,"[31] and his life was a series of battles won
against "the way things are" and against the political hero's most implacable
opponent: fate. Like the Gerbier character in *The Army of Shadows*—written
by Joseph Kessel, as we know, at the behest of the chief of Free France—de
Gaulle always managed to escape the worst; his life was "a series of mira-
cles."[32] The General liked to joke about it. As he said once to Romain Gary,
referring to the seven attempts on his life, "I must be the most shot-at writer
in the history of literature."[33] In more lyrical terms, Malraux stated that the
essence of the Gaullian legend lay in the General's ability to "escape fate."[34] A
sign of this agility was the speed with which the Gaullian myth was able to
shed its "memorially dubious episodes," to quote Pierre Nora: the RPF years,
the return to power in May 1958, the Algerian War, and even May 1968.[35]

At the same time, the new growth of the Gaullian myth was favored by
the ideological vacuum produced by the great turning points of the end of
the twentieth century: the fall of Soviet communism, the changes in the
French Left, the reappearance of a more "realistic" and nation-centered
vision of Europe, the return of religious fundamentalism, the rise in
communitarianisms, and the disillusion with national political elites. In
the face of the fragmentation caused by these various trends, the Jacobin
General could incarnate—and with panache—the principle of national
unity; he was the man who had "totally symbolised the country."[36] That
this wave of enthusiasm for de Gaulle contains a good deal of nostalgia is
also undeniable: nostalgia for greatness and for the last great Frenchman,
as described by the surviving witnesses of the epic; nostalgia for a heroic
age and for a certain political voluntarism, ready to stand against the mediocrity and powerlessness of modern times; nostalgia for a national literary memory, of which the Gaullian voice, filtered through the different
layers of the *War Memoirs,* provides the last echo; and nostalgia, above all,
for the codes and values conveyed through Gaullism at its apogee, which
are constantly invoked in his followers' letters—loyalty, honor, selfless-
ness, and integrity. As one of the General's supporters wrote to him after
his failure in the referendum, "For thirty years you were 'the just man,' and

that was why we followed you and we loved you."[37] De Gaulle was in this sense the last great incarnation of a royalist and republican tradition of public service. Can one imagine today a French statesman insisting, as de Gaulle did, on paying out of his own pocket for the meals of members of his family when he invited them to the Elysée?[38]

But at the same time as turning back, with more than a touch of melancholy, toward a golden age, the Gaullian myth—this is the strength of great legends—also helps us to make sense of the present, notably by endowing the General with one of the most essential political virtues in the French context: the power to symbolize national reconciliation. Indeed, de Gaulle was a key figure—*the* key figure, one might say—in bringing to an end the long and painful history of Franco-French wars. He put an end to two civil wars, which in itself would have been enough to establish his reputation as protector of the nation. But the General did not stop there. He also contributed, by his action after 1958, to settling a certain number of differences that had been tearing the body politic apart since the nineteenth century: the nature of the regime, the conflict between the education system and the Church, the role of the army, the preservation of France's "rank" in the world, and its relations with neighboring countries (especially Germany) and the French-speaking world. One could even turn the problem of France's return to the NATO fold on its head and argue that this decision, which is now being carried out without too much psychological turmoil, proves that the General managed to exorcise twentieth-century France's greatest fear: that the country would die, that it would no longer exist as an independent and sovereign nation.

In this game of balance and pacification, the General's most remarkable historic role was his relation to the essential division created by the Revolution: that between Right and Left. Not that de Gaulle—as a politician—managed to transcend this division, except at the moments of greatest crisis (1940–1944, the Algerian War). One could even say the opposite: In his lifetime he divided the French at least as much as he brought them together. But in a long-term perspective, his contribution to "moving the dividing lines" was none the less decisive. The General redrew the maps inside each of the camps; in a word, he reconciled the Right with the Republic and the Left with the nation. Thanks to him, the modernization of the Right's political culture, which had been begun but not completed under the Third Republic, became an irreversible reality after the Liberation, and the Left's unconditional acceptance of the institutions of the Fifth Republic finally brought about something that none of the previous Republics had been able to accomplish: the full and unreserved incorporation of the French Left into the body politic of the nation. We may add that the same Left has become so completely "Gaullized" since the late 1980s that it has adopted the Man of the 18th of June as its exemplary figure; the General now occupies a privileged position in the progressive pantheon, sometimes displacing even the most classic symbols of the Left like Jean Jaurès, Léon Blum, and Pierre Mendès-France. Sometimes this reappropriation is done in a more oblique manner, as when Bernard-Henri Lévy sums up, at the end of his book, the Christ-like figure of Jean Moulin, calling him a "strange mixture, in the end, of epic and prose, or grandeur and humility—a secular saint in times of tempest, a servant of the State in times of calm."[39] As he wrote those lines, was Lévy not thinking a little, perhaps a lot, about the General?

A fair summing-up of the General's place in the collective imagination[40] must certainly include some negative elements. Great political myths have a strong power of attraction, but they can also give rise to unhealthy passions and obsessions, create unrealistic expectations, or obstruct necessary political changes; the General himself once said that France was "ravaged" by myths.[41] One thinks, for example, of the notion of the *grand soir*, the day of uprising and retribution, and its corrosive effects both on the political strategy of the Left and on its understanding of French society, or the role of the Napoleonic legend in fostering militaristic sentiments in France in the nineteenth century. There can be no doubt that the Gaullian myth had some equally harmful effects. It has often been observed that the insistence on national "greatness" encouraged a general forgetting of less than glorious episodes in recent history; de Gaulle knowingly colluded in some of the "legends, lies, falsifications, denials" that have impeded the search for historical truth in France.[42] And though it is to the eternal honor of the General that he—finally—gave the vote to women in France (and to the eternal shame of the Third Republic that it kept putting off this reform, which would have been the chief symbol of a deepening of republican values), the Gaullian scheme of things was always essentially masculine. There were very few women in his inner circle and—a fundamental symbol—only a handful of women Companions of the Liberation—a mere six in all.[43] One could say that in the epic contest between Gaullism and communism this was the only battle that the latter clearly won. As Mona Ozouf's book highlights, the Communists were the only party to offer real equality to the postwar generation of women.[44]

The schematic quality of Gaullian discourse sometimes led to the demonization of the "Other." A Marseillais writing to the General described the 52 percent of French voters who had rejected him in 1969 like this: "Maoist wreckers, selfish totalitarians, henchmen of 'Anglo-Saxonry,' lackeys of Judaism, holier-than-thou hypocrites, masked gangsters, ballot-box stuffers and other assorted scum."[45] Of course, the General himself would never have used such language, but it was common among some of his supporters, and one must recognize that the Gaullian tendency to oversimplification might have at least tacitly encouraged it. In his eyes Albion, in particular, always remained perfidious; when Paul Reynaud protested against de Gaulle's first veto on Great Britain's entry to the Common Market, the General's reply was an empty envelope marked, "Please forward if necessary to Agincourt (Somme) or Waterloo (Belgium)."[46] A still more serious criticism: Gaullian providentialism also hampered the emergence of a participatory political culture in France—notably by extending the centralizing model of the Fifth Republic to the internal organization of the large political parties, and most of all by focusing the nation's attention on the presidency of the Republic and thus relegating all other groups to a subordinate position. Sarkozy's much-criticized "hyper-presidency" is, in this light, a clear product of the political logic of the founding Father of the Fifth Republic. All the more so since the collective political imagination in France has always been heavily imbued with Rousseauist unanimism and with the revolutionary postulate that a political body could not exist except by the power of the general will. The General's genius was to apply to himself, in an immanent form, this unitary conception of the political sphere, which at the end of the day left little scope for the autonomous action of "civil society"—or for the control of the political sphere by the law. This is not the last of the paradoxes of the Gaullian myth. The incorruptible General (a paragon of probity if ever there was one) opened the way, because of his attachment to the primacy of the political sphere, for the perversion of the res publica by his successors.

But even in its fragility, even in what is questionable about it, the Gaullian myth finally reveals its extraordinary strength. For now that we can take the long view, we see that the General represents the highest point of the French national myth, its most consummate form achieved over time. This perfectibility can be seen first in its historical evolution. The Gaullian myth comes chronologically at the end of a whole series of legends that have marked the French collective imagination since the Enlightenment: Christian monarchy, the Napoleon cult, the Republican ideal, and the Communist utopia, as well as perfectibility, in its inner structure. The Gaullian myth brings together, in a more harmonious whole than any of its predecessors, the five elements that constitute a political legend: the historic moment, the political institution, a symbolic ensemble, a set of ideological and moral values, and their providential incarnation in one person. Let us be clear: The Gaullian myth does not necessary equal all previous legends in what was strongest in each. Gaullian sacredness was not equal to that of traditional royalty; even at its height, his grandeur did not shine so brightly as Napoleon's glory; his moral values never had the national impact of the republican ideal, powerfully transmitted by the education system; and the cult of the General never had the overwhelming planetary power and the historic teleology that gave communism its strength. The General's soul and sensibility were Romantic—that is why he identified with Chateaubriand. But his myth was not: He never promised the sun would rise on glorious tomorrows.

But the comparative superiority of the Gaullian mystique lay—and still lies—in his ability to draw strength from the myths that preceded him and thus to give a contemporary meaning to the transhistoric ideals that marked the collective imagination of the French: heroism, sense of duty, the feeling of belonging, defiance of fate, and contempt for materialism. De Gaulle is often there in the shadows when contemporary writers reflect on the need to go beyond a narrow individualism, to imagine a return to a kind of collective republican sacredness: Regis Debray's recent considerations on fraternity are a fine example of such reflection.[47] Above all, thanks to its rigorous purging of the national political traditions on which it drew, the Gaullian myth is able to offer the nation a synthesis from which the less admirable elements of previous legends have been removed. One striking example is that the Gaullian myth of the Father obviously has some similarities to the communist cult of Stalin in the postwar years—but without ever reaching the most extreme manifestations of that phenomenon.[48] The same restraint can be found in other areas as well. The General is the ideal, achieved at last, of a monarchy without excessive deference; of a Christian ethic kept within limits, neither reactionary nor guilt-inducing; of a republic that is vigorous and fraternal, but without anarchy; of a France respected throughout the world, but without the risk of murderous wars or of servitude imposed on other peoples; of an intransigent conception of public safety, but without terror or despotism; of a leader perfectly holding (well, almost perfectly) the balance between his personal humility and the grandeur of his task. This well-tempered imaginative realm is something that France had been seeking since its earliest days, and it seems that, thanks to Charles de Gaulle, it has finally found it.

NOTES

CHAPTER 1

1. François Mauriac, *De Gaulle* (Paris: Grasset, 1964), p. 326.
2. Pierre Rosanvallon, *La légitimité démocratique* (Paris: Seuil, 2008), pp. 114–115.
3. Ernst Kantorowicz, *The King's Two Bodies: A Study in Medieval Political Theology* (Princeton, NJ: Princeton University Press, 1957).
4. In this context, see the series of surveys "Les voies 'de Gaulle' en France. Le Général dans l'espace et la mémoire des communes," ed. P. Oulmont, *Cahiers de la Fondation Charles de Gaulle* 17 (2009).
5. There is no complete, up-to-date bibliography of works on de Gaulle. Two syntheses by the Institut Charles de Gaulle are still useful: *Essai de bibliographie mondiale des ouvrages consacrés à Charles de Gaulle* (Paris: Institut Charles de Gaulle, 1974) (reoneotyped) and *Nouvelle bibliographie internationale sur Charles de Gaulle* (Paris: Plon, 1990).
6. http://degaulle.ina.fr/
7. Archives Nationales (AN), Paris: The two essential collections are 3 AG (Archives du GPRF) and 5 AG (Archives de la Présidence de la République), as well as the private archives (AP).
8. Notably in the RPF archives, as well as a rich collection of Gaullian manuscripts: http://www.charles-de-gaulle.org/.
9. Of particular interest is the *Fonds Solférino* in the AN, in the 5 AG Series, which includes 1,200 documents, a handlist that is now almost complete, and also the papers of Pierre Lefranc (569 AP), which we were not able to consult for want of the donor's agreement.
10. Jean Charlot, *Le gaullisme d'opposition, 1946–1958* (Paris: Fayard, 1983); Jean-Louis Crémieux-Brilhac, *La France Libre* (Paris: Gallimard, 1996); Jean-Luc Barré, *Devenir De Gaulle* (Paris: Perrin, 2003); Eric Roussel, *Charles de Gaulle* (Paris: Gallimard, 2002). See also two recent works on the Resistance outside France: Sébastien Albertelli, *Les services secrets du général de Gaulle. Le BCRA 1940–1944* (Paris: Perrin, 2009) and Jean-François Muracciole, *Les Français Libres. L'autre Résistance* (Paris: Tallandier, 2009). For a recent biography in English, see Jonathan Fenby, *The General. Charles de Gaulle and the France He Saved* (London, Simon & Schuster, 2010).
11. In this vein, see, for example, the critical observations of Jean-François Revel, "De la légende vivante au mythe posthume," in *Le style du Général* (Brussels: Editions Complexe, 1988), pp. 13–63; Antoine Cassan, *Vivement hier. Tous ringardo-gaullistes* (Paris: JC Lattès, 1996); and Nicolas Tenzer, *La face cachée du gaullisme* (Paris: Hachette, 1998).
12. Emmanuel d'Astier de la Vigerie, *Sept fois sept jours* (Paris: Gallimard, 1961), p. 102.
13. Claude Bouchinet-Serreulles, *Nous étions faits pour être libres* (Paris: Grasset, 2000), p. 197.
14. Pierre-Louis Blanc, *Charles de Gaulle au soir de sa vie* (Paris: Fayard, 1990), p. 310.

15. André Malraux, *Les chênes qu'on abat* (Paris: Gallimard, 1971), pp. 41–42.
16. Claude Mauriac, *Aimer de Gaulle* (Paris: Grasset, 1978); Olivier Guichard, *Mon Général* (Paris: Grasset, 1980); Claude Guy, *En écoutant de Gaulle. Journal 1946–1949* (Paris: Grasset, 1996).
17. Michel Debré, *Mémoires*, 5 vols. (Paris: Albin Michel, 1984–1994); Jacques Foccart, *Journal de l'Elysée*, 5 vols. (Paris: Fayard/Jeune Afrique, 1997–2001); Alain Peyrefitte, *C'était de Gaulle* (Paris, Gallimard, 2002).
18. Philippe de Gaulle, *De Gaulle Mon Père*, 2 vols. (Paris: Plon, 2003–2004).
19. Maurice Agulhon, *De Gaulle. Histoire, symbole, mythe* (Paris: Plon, 2000).
20. On the origins of Gaullian thinking, see the works of Philippe Saint-Robert, *De Gaulle et ses témoins* (Paris: Bartillat, 1999) and Alain Larcan, *De Gaulle inventaire* (Paris: Bartillat, 2003).
21. Bouchinet-Sereulles, *Nous étions faits pour être libres.*
22. See in this context Sudhir Hazareesingh, *La légende de Napoléon* (Paris: Seuil, 2008).
23. Figure mentioned by the General in the course of a meeting with his nephew Bernard de Gaulle at Colombey on September 19, 1970, quoted in Jean Mauriac, *Mort du général de Gaulle* (Paris: Grasset, 1972), p. 130.
24. Charles de Gaulle, *Lettres, notes et carnets*, 13 vols. (Paris: Plon, 1980–1997).
25. See particularly the exchanges between the Count of Paris and General de Gaulle, *Dialogue sur la France, correspondance et entretiens 1953–1970* (Paris: Fayard, 1994).
26. AN, 5 AG1 (308), (309), (310) (Elysée). Letters sent to de Gaulle by notable civil and religious figures (about 200 boxes) are kept in the so-called Fonds Solférino at the AN, which is not yet available to researchers.
27. See Daniel Fabre, *Ecritures ordinaires* (Paris: Editions P.O.L./Bibliothèque du Centre G. Pompidou, 1993).
28. As a general rule, de Gaulle left Paris for Colombey on Saturday evenings, returning to the Elysée on Monday mornings. An article on "Ces messieurs de l'Elysée" published in 1964 reported: "French people write to de Gaulle a great deal on all manner of subjects. De Gaulle replies in his own hand to the most important letters at Colombey on Sundays, sealing and stamping the letters himself" (*Candide*, May 27–June 3, 1964).
29. See Marie-Claire Grassi, *Lire l'épistolaire* (Paris: Dunod, 1998), pp. 92–93.
30. Guillaume Piketty (ed.), "La force du refus," in *Français en résistance. Carnets de guerre, correspondances, journaux personnels* (Paris: Robert Laffont, 2009), p. vi.
31. For a fuller discussion of the concept of myth, see Sudhir Hazareesingh, "Mythe," in *Dictionnaire d'histoire culturelle de la France contemporaine*, ed. C. Delporte, J.Y. Mollier, and J.F. Sirinelli (Paris: PUF, 2010).
32. See Jean-Louis Crémieux-Brilhac, "La France Libre et la symbolique républicaine," in *Actes du colloque sur la symbolique républicaine* (forthcoming).
33. Edmond Michelet, *Le Gaullisme, passionnante aventure* (Paris: Fayard, 1962).
34. Radio and television interview with Michel Droit, June 7, 1968, in Charles de Gaulle, *Discours et messages*, Vol. V (Paris: Plon, 1970), pp. 295–296.
35. Roland Barthes, *Mythologies* (Paris: Seuil, 1970).
36. For representations of the General by cartoonists, see the fine selection from the work of fifty European and American artists in *De Gaulle 300 Caricatures* (Nukerke, Belgium: Editions Cérès, 1967).
37. Raoul Girardet, *Mythes et mythologies politiques* (Paris: Seuil, 1990), pp. 72–73.
38. Sudhir Hazareesingh, "L'histoire politique face à l'histoire culturelle: état des lieux et perspectives," *Revue Historique* 642 (2007).
39. Note the title of Gaetano Quagliariello, *La religion gaulliste* (Paris: Perrin, 2007).
40. Barré, *Devenir de Gaulle*, p. 18.
41. Entry for October 30, 1944. Claude Mauriac, *Aimer de Gaulle*, p. 94.

42. Jean Daniel, *La blessure* (Paris: Grasset, 1992), p. 24.

43. Guichard, *Mon général*, p. 338.

44. Letter from Fernand Braudel to General de Gaulle (Paris: May 3, 1969). Archives of the Fondation Charles de Gaulle [FCDG], AE3/6.

45. On the hatred of de Gaulle in *pied-noir* memory, see Jeannine Verdès-Leroux, *Les Français d'Algérie de 1830 à aujourd'hui* (Paris: Fayard, 2001), pp. 441–471.

46. Debray, "Preface," in de Gaulle, *Les Grands Discours de guerre*.

47. See the enlightening chapter by Stéphane Courtois, "Gaullisme et communisme: la double réponse à la crise d'identité française," in *50 ans d'une passion française. De Gaulle et les communistes*, ed. S. Courtois and M. Lazar (Paris: Balland, 1991), p. 307.

48. Pierre Nora (ed.), "Gaullistes et communistes," in *Les lieux de mémoire*, Vol. III (1) (Paris: Gallimard, 1992).

49. See in this context the work of Alya Aglan, *Le temps de la Résistance* (Arles, France: Actes Sud, 2008).

50. The standard work (highly polemical but extraordinarily well documented on the Second Empire) is Jacques Duclos, *De Napoléon III à de Gaulle* (Paris: Editions Sociales, 1964).

51. Quoted by Claude Estier, *Journal d'un Fédéré* (Paris: Fayard, 1970), p. 129.

52. Letter to General de Gaulle from Toulon, April 29, 1969. FCDG AE3/7.

53. Claude Dulong, *La vie quotidienne à l'Elysée au temps de Charles de Gaulle* (Paris: Hachette, 1974), p. 25.

54. Philippe Oulmont, "Les haut-lieux du Général de Gaulle 1940–44," in *De Gaulle chef de guerre* (Paris: Plon, 2008), pp. 34–46.

55. Nantes, Grenoble, Paris, Vassieux-en-Vercors, and the Ile de Sein.

56. Simon Braillon and Sylvain Parent, "Les hommages des communes du Nord-Pas-de-Calais au général de Gaulle: au grand homme la petite patrie reconnaissante," in P. Oulmont (ed.), *Les voies "De Gaulle" en France*, p. 177.

57. See Pascal Girard, "Le gaullisme d'opposition au miroir de la haine politique, 1947–1958," in Marc Deleplace (ed.), *Le discours de la haine* (Paris: Plon, 2009), pp. 287–305.

58. Letter to General de Gaulle, April 28, 1969. FCDG AE3/5.

59. Letter from J.R. Portalis, Buenos Aires, December 8, 1970. FCDG AE4/1–4 (letter sent to Mrs. de Gaulle after the General's death).

CHAPTER 2

1. Undated letter, received August 20, 1942. FCDG, AE3.

2. In July 1942, *La France Libre* became *La France Combattante*.

3. Guy, *En écoutant de Gaulle*, p. 48. On the first years in London, see Bouchinet-Serreulles, *Nous étions faits pour être libres*, pp. 107–109.

4. Telegram to Adrien Tixier, Londres, December 24, 1941, in de Gaulle, *Lettres, notes et carnets*, July 1941–May 1943 (1982), p. 147.

5. Letter to General de Gaulle, received August 20, 1942. FCDG AE3/4.

6. Jean-François Muracciole, "Les discours de guerre du Général de Gaulle," in *De Gaulle Chef de Guerre, Actes du Colloque International organisé par la Fondation Charles de Gaulle*, October 2006 (Paris: Plon/FCDG 2008), pp. 146–147.

7. AN, 3 AG1 (271), dossier 2 (radio).

8. "A de Gaulle," undated. FCDG AE3/4.

9. Letter to General de Gaulle, dated August 17, 1941. FCDG AE3.

10. Letter to General de Gaulle, dated September 14, 1941. FCDG AE3.

11. Speech of June 18, 1940, in Charles de Gaulle, *Discours et messages*, Vol. I, **Pendant la guerre**, June 1940–January 1946 (Paris: Plon, 1970), p. 4.

12. Speech of June 19, 1940, *Discours et messages*, p. 4.

13. Raymond Aron, "L'Ombre des Bonaparte," in *Chroniques de Guerre* (Paris, Gallimard, 1990), p. 776. On non-Communist resistance mistrust of the General, see Robert Belot, *La Résistance sans de Gaulle* (Paris: Fayard, 2006).
14. Speech of July 13, 1940, *Discours et messages*, p. 16.
15. Speech of August 12, 1940, *Discours et messages*, p. 26.
16. Speech of January 31, 1941, *Discours et messages*, p. 64.
17. Speech of May 12, 1943, *Discours et messages*, pp. 291–293.
18. AN 3 AG1 (271), dossier 2 (radio).
19. Ibid. One should also note the emphasis placed in de Gaulle's youth, in contrast to those de Gaulle called "the old men of Vichy." See, for example, the speech of August 12, 1940, *Discours et messages*, p. 25.
20. Speech at the Albert Hall, June 18, 1942, *Discours et messages*, p. 201.
21. Speech of January 30, 1944, *Discours et messages*, p. 371.
22. On the difficulties regarding the administration of Madagascar after the British invasion in May 1942, see the speeches of May 14 and 25, 1942, *Discours et messages*, pp. 186–189.
23. Speech of February 28, 1941, *Discours et messages*, p. 68.
24. See, for example, the speech of November 11, 1942: "The centre around which national unity is being rebuilt is the struggle of the Free French. To the nation imprisoned we have offered, from the very first day, light and struggle." *Discours et messages*, p. 236.
25. Declaration to the international press, Cairo, April 2, 1941. *Discours et messages*, p. 79.
26. Speech of June 18, 1944, *Discours et messages*, p. 409.
27. Speech of September 18, 1941, *Discours et messages*, pp. 102–103.
28. Speech to the University of Oxford, November 25, 1941, *Discours et messages*, p. 145.
29. Speech of October 2, 1941, *Discours et messages*, Vol. 1, p. 110.
30. Speech of July 14, 1942, *Discours et messages*, pp. 214–215.
31. Speech of July 14, 1941, *Discours et messages*, p. 93.
32. Speech of July 2, 1940, *Discours et messages*, p. 12.
33. Speech of August 1, 1940, *Discours et messages*, p. 21.
34. Rémi Dalisson, *Les fêtes du Maréchal. Propagande et imaginaire dans la France de Vichy* (Paris: Tallandier, 2007), p. 37.
35. Resolution of a small commune in the Gard, September 8, 1940, quoted by Maurice Agulhon, *Les métamorphoses de Marianne* (Paris: Flammarion, 2001), p. 97.
36. Speech of November 25, 1940, *Discours et messages*, p. 43.
37. Speech in the Albert Hall, June 18, 1942, *Discours et messages*, p. 198.
38. Speech of May 10, 1942, *Discours et messages*, pp. 184–185.
39. See Edward Berenson, Vincent Duclert, and Christophe Prochasson (eds.), *The French Republic. History, Values, Debates* (Ithaca, NY: Cornell University Press, 2011).
40. Declaration of January 2, 1943, *Discours et messages*, p. 256. On de Gaulle and the memory of 1970–1971, see Maurice Agulhon, "De Gaulle et le souvenir de Gambetta," in *Charles de Gaulle, du militaire au politique 1920–1940* (Paris: Fondation Charles-de-Gaulle et Plon, 2004).
41. Letter from General de Gaulle to Paul Reynaud, June 3, 1940. AN 3 AG1 (372).
42. Speech of November 11, 1942, *Discours et messages*, pp. 237–238.
43. Speech of April 20, 1943, *Discours et messages*, pp. 280–281.
44. Speech of 1942, *Discours et messages*, p. 180.
45. Address of October 13, 1941, *Discours et messages*, p. 155.
46. Speech of March 4, 1942, *Discours et messages*, p. 173.
47. Nickname given to Clemenceau in 1918.
48. Speech of November 11, 1941, *Discours et messages*, pp. 130–131.
49. Message sent to the United States on the occasion of the fourteenth anniversary of the death of Marshal Foch, March 27, 1943, *Discours et messages*, p. 277.

50. Speech of November 11, 1940, *Discours et messages*, p. 40.

51. Directive of the Minister of the Interior to all prefects, mayors, the gendarmes, and the police. AN, AJ41 (397).

52. Interior Ministry, summary of monthly reports from prefects in the occupied zone, April 1942. AN, F1CIII (1198). The same expression is used in the report of February 1944.

53. See Jean-Louis Crémieux-Brilhac and G. Bensimhon, "Les propagandes radiophoniques et l'opinion publique en France de 1940 à 1944," *Revue d'Histoire de la Deuxième Guerre Mondiale* 101 (January 1976).

54. For examples, see J.L. Crémieux-Brilhac (ed.), *Les voix de la liberté. Ici Londres 1940–1944*, Vol. I (Paris: La Découverte, 1975), pp. 105, 153–155.

55. Maurice Schumann, speech on the BBC, August 7, 1940. AN 3 AG1 (271), dossier 2 (radio).

56. Comité Exécutif de Propagande de la France Libre, meeting of February 8, 1943. AN, Crémieux-Brilhac Papers, 49 Mi 1. This committee, which reported to the Commissariat National à l'Intérieur, met regularly in London during the war; it included Gaullists but also socialists, such as André Philip, and communists, including Fernand Grenier and, later, Waldeck Rochet.

57. Anonymous letter, September 1941. FCDG AE3.

58. Ibid.

59. Letter, Lyon, January 26, 1941. FCDG AE3.

60. Anonymous letter, Haute-Savoie, September 13, 1941. FCDG AE3.

61. Ibid.

62. Anonymous letter, September 1941. FCDG AE3.

63. Stamped "seen by General de Gaulle," it also contains manuscript annotations by the General. FCDG AE3.

64. Speech of December 3, 1941, *Discours et messages*, p. 147.

65. Letter from Gervaise Carminat, Grasse, March 15, 1942. FCDG AE3.

66. Isabelle Flahault-Domergue, "Représenter le Général de Gaulle: photographies et films français libres," in *De Gaulle Chef de Guerre*, pp. 167–172.

67. See the accounts in Pierre Messmer, Pierre Pelissier, and Michel Tauriac, *Nous, les Français combattants de 39–45* (Paris: Tallandier, 2005), pp. 111, 115–116.

68. Collection of envelopes of letters sent to General de Gaulle during the Second World War. FCDG F36 (Fonds Jean Mauriac).

69. Literally, "air mail."

70. Crémieux-Brilhac, *La France Libre*, p. 711.

71. Lucien Neuwirth, *Ma guerre à seize ans* (Paris: Plon, 1986), p. 22.

72. Rémy, *Le livre du courage et de la peur* (Paris: Aux Trois Couleurs, 1945), p. 98.

73. Twenty-five years later, when the General died, she sent the photograph to Madame de Gaulle. Letter from Alice Bornet, November 26, 1970. FCDG AE4.

74. Letter from the Abbé Corolleur to Général de Gaulle, Lampaul-Guimiliau, June 13, 1969. FCDG AE3/1.

75. See Julien Blanc, *Au commencement de la Résistance. Du côté du musée de l'Homme 1940–1941* (Paris: Seuil, 2010).

76. On this day, see Jean-Pierre Azéma, *1940 l'année terrible* (Paris: Seuil, 1990), pp. 335–344.

77. Account by Igor de Schotten, undated. Archives de la Préfecture de Police BA 2361, dossier "November 11, 1940."

78. London, July 14, 1940, in de Gaulle, *Lettres, notes et carnets*, June 1940–July 1941 (1981), p. 35.

79. "General de Gaulle expresses the wish that the anniversary of the 18th of June be celebrated by all French people in an atmosphere of unity and hope." Communiqué, Algiers, June 13, 1943, de Gaulle, *Lettres, notes et carnets*, June 1943–May 1945 (1983), p. 27.

80. This was confirmed to me during an interview with Jean-Louis Crémieux-Brilhac, who was present in London at the time (Paris, April 2009).
81. Messages of December 23, 28, and 31, 1940, *Discours et messages*, pp. 50–53.
82. Speech of April 30, 1942, *Discours et messages*, p. 184.
83. Speech of November 10, 1942, *Discours et messages*, p. 232.
84. Telegram to René Pleven, Brazzaville, April 28, 1941, du Gaulle, *Lettres, notes et carnets*, June 1940–July 1941, p. 308.
85. Incident reported by Dalisson, *Les fêtes du Maréchal*, pp. 378–379.
86. Agulhon, *Les métamorphoses de Marianne*, p. 111.
87. Philippe Barrière, "La Résistance sur les murs: toponymie urbaine et géographie mémorielle (Grenoble 1944–1964), in *Résistants et résistance*, ed. J.-Y. Boursier (Paris: L'Harmattan, 1997), p. 283.
88. Internal memo, General de Gaulle's private office, September 14, 1945. AN 3 AG4 (70).
89. Henri Amouroux, *La vie des français sous l'occupation* (Paris: Fayard, 1990), p. 539.
90. Letter from the mayor of Hochfelden, April 26, 2005. Archives FCDG enquête voies de Gaulle, 67 (Bas-Rhin).
91. Account of Colonel Rémy, quoted by René Hostache, "Bayeux, juin 14, 1944, étape décisive sur la voie d'Alger à Paris," in *De Gaulle et la Libération* (Bruxelles: Editions Complexe, 2004), p. 41.
92. Crémieux-Brilhac, *La France Libre*, p. 908.
93. Quoted by Laurent Douzou and Dominique Veillon, "Les déplacements du Général de Gaulle à travers la France," *De Gaulle et la Libération*, pp. 158–159.
94. Letter from Mme Bâton, Livarot (Calvados), October 6, 1944. FCDG AC1 (voyages, 1944).
95. This request from a Morbihan man, a fervent admirer of the General, who had begun building his boat during the occupation, is mentioned in a letter from Palewski to Senator Rio (Quiberon), July 27, 1945. AN 3 AG4 (70).
96. Letter from the mayor of Courbevoie to Palewski, November 14, 1944. AN 3 AG4 (70).
97. Extracts from the minutes of the municipal commission, December 22, 1944. FCDG Fonds voies de Gaulle, 34 (Hérault).
98. Extract from the minutes of the municipal commission, November 18, 1944. AN 3 AG4 (70).
99. Speech of August 25, 1944, *Discours et messages*, p. 440.
100. Municipal council meeting, September 27, 1944. FCDG Fonds voies de Gaulle, 34 (Hérault).
101. Meeting of the municipal council of Bazas, March 3, 1945. FCDG Fonds voies de Gaulle, 33 (Gironde).
102. Proposal of the president of the municipal commission, Toulouse, September 27, 1944. FCDG Fonds voies de Gaulle, 31 (Haute-Garonne).
103. "Boche" is a French pejorative term for "German." Extract from the minutes of the municipal council of Cappelle, October 29, 1944. AN 3 AG4 (70).
104. Resolution of the municipal commission, September 27, 1944. FCDG Fonds voies de Gaulle, 31 (Haute-Garonne).
105. Letter from the mayor of Cysoing to the prefect of the Nord, February 14, 1945. AN 3 AG4 (70).
106. Letter to General de Gaulle, February 9, 1945. AN 3 AG4 (70).
107. Christian Basque, "Au Général de Gaulle," Lille. FCDG AE3.
108. Letter from the Commissaire de la République to Palewski, October 25, 1944. AN 3 AG4 (70).
109. Speech by the mayor of Hazebrouck, November 15, 1944. AN 3 AG4 (70).
110. Municipal council meeting, November 1, 1944. Fonds voies de Gaulle, 34 (Hérault).

111. AN 3 AG4 (70).
112. Letter from the mayor of Wissant, January 24, 1945. AN 3 AG4 (70).
113. Letter to General de Gaulle, October 3, 1944. FCDG AC1(voyages, 1944).
114. Letter from Madame Maurice Fromont, Lisieux, October 7, 1944. FCDG AC1 (voyages, 1944).
115. Municipal council meeting, June 20, 1945. FCDG, Fonds voies de Gaulle, 33 (Gironde).
116. Speech quoted. AN 3 AG4 (70).
117. Speech of September 12, 1944, *Discours et messages*, p. 448.
118. Radio broadcast by the Commissaire Régional du Nord, September 21, 1944. FCDG AC1 (voyages, 1944).
119. Extract from the minutes book, May 18, 1945. FCDG, Fonds voies de Gaulle, 33 (Gironde).
120. Speech by the mayor of La Réole, October 14, 1944. FCDG, Fonds voies de Gaulle, 33 (Gironde).
121. Alex Faure, "Au Général de Gaulle," September 23, 1944. FCDG AE3.
122. Bouchinet-Serreulles, *Nous étions faits pour être libres*, p. 109.
123. Note in the diary of Diego Brosset, August 23, 1942, quoted in Piketty (ed.), *Français en résistance*, p. 237.
124. Entry of December 17, 1944. Mauriac, *Aimer de Gaulle*, p. 110.
125. Lucien Nachin, *Charles de Gaulle, Général de France* (Paris: Editions Colbert, 1944).
126. Suzanne Delaur, *Une femme raconte la vie extraordinaire du Général de Gaulle* (Paris: Editions S.E.N., 1945).
127. Robert Perrein, *Un grand français, le général de Gaulle* (Paris: Editions Musy, 1944).
128. Ludovic Bron, *Le Général de Gaulle, l'Homme Providentiel* (Le Puy: X. Mappus, 1945).
129. Suzanne Buchot, "La Voix. A Charles de Gaulle," Paris, June 18–24, 1944. FCDG AE3.
130. Anna Clément, "Au Général de Gaulle, sauveur de la France," Saint-Chéron (Seine-et-Oise), undated. FCDG AE3/1.
131. Joseph Adami, "Paris Libéré," Fayence (Var), October 1944; a poem dedicated to General de Gaulle. FCDG AE3/1.
132. Poem by Eugène Cowet, Chars, September 1944. FCDG AE3.
133. Gabriel Cousinou, "Hymne à de Gaulle," Paris, October 25, 1944. FCDG AE3.
134. Angèle Caors, "Gloire à la France," Paris, November 18, 1944. FCDG AE3.
135. C. L. Arnaud, "Au Général de Gaulle," Simiane (Basses-Alpes), September 11, 1944. FCDG AE3.
136. Marie Joseph Brémond, "Vive de Gaulle," Montbrison, September 24, 1944. FCDG AE3.
137. Louise Bordas, "Le Te Deum de Notre Dame," Paris, August 28, 1944. FCDG AE3.
138. Georges Beaumont, "Au Général de Gaulle, libérateur de la patrie," Paris, August 26, 1944. FCDG AE3.
139. Speech of July 13, 1940, *Discours et messages*, p. 15.
140. Alice Boissier, "Au sublime défenseur de notre patrie le Général de Gaulle," Caen, October 8, 1944. FCDG AE3.
141. Jeanne Beaubelicou, "Souvenirs des Trois Guerres," Auvers-sur-Oise (Seine et Oise), October 1944. FCDG AE3.
142. Ginette Berger, "Au Général de Gaulle," Suresnes, September 13, 1944. FCDG AE3.
143. Letter from Sister Marie-Hélène Chesnel to Mme de Gaulle, undated (1970). FCDG AE3.
144. Louis Bousson, "Au Libérateur du territoire," Paris, October 6, 1944. FCDG AE3.
145. "La semaine sainte," a poem to Général de Gaulle, November 1944. FCDG AE3. Many poems noted, in a similar vein, how fitting it was for France to be saved by a warrior whose surname was derived from "Gaul," the old name for France.
146. On this theme, see Aglan, *Le temps de la Résistance*.

147. "Clémenceau," Rouen, June 29, 1940, a poem dedicated to General de Gaulle. FCDG AC 1.
148. Présidence de la République, program for the ceremonies of November 11, 1965. AN 5 AG1 (558), dossier "November 11, 1965."
149. Conversation with Claude Guy in 1946; *En écoutant de Gaulle*, p. 63; author's italics.
150. Charles de Gaulle, *Mémoires de guerre*, Vol. III, ch. 3 (Paris: Plon, 1989), p. 599.

CHAPTER 3

1. Charles de Gaulle, *The Complete War Memoirs* (New York: Carroll and Graf, 1998), p. 3.
2. "Les plus forts tirages depuis 10 ans," *Sud-Ouest* (Bordeaux), May 15, 1955.
3. October 11, 1954, in François Mauriac, *Bloc-notes*, Vol. I (1952–1957) (Paris: Seuil, 1993), p. 209.
4. d'Astier de la Vigerie, *Sept fois sept jours*, p. 109.
5. See, for example, de Gaulle, *Le Fil de l'épée et autres écrits* (Paris: Plon, 1990), p. 181.
6. Declaration of May 6, 1953, in *Discours et messages* (Vol. 2, 1946–1958), p. 582. On this period, see the account of Raymond Triboulet, *Un Gaulliste de la IVe* (Paris: Plon, 1985).
7. *La Depêche de Constantine*, April 18, 1956.
8. Julien Benda's expression. See *Mémoires d'infra-tombe* (Paris: Julliard, 1952), p. 8.
9. Arouet, *Vie et aventures du général de la Perche, d'après les documents ramenés par le suédois Syllog de son voyage en Absurdie* (Paris, 1947).
10. Anonymous letter to General de Gaulle, Marseille, December 4, 1953. FCDG AF5 5.
11. "De Gaulle may go into a monastery," *Sunday Express*, January 8, 1956.
12. de Gaulle, *Mémoires de guerre*, Vol. III, p. 883.
13. On the Rémy affair, see Henry Rousso, *Le syndrome de Vichy* (Paris: Seuil, 1990), pp. 48–55.
14. de Gaulle, *Mémoires de guerre*, Vol. I, p. 82.
15. Ibid., p. 241.
16. Ibid., pp. 239–240.
17. de Gaulle, *Mémoires de guerre*, Vol. II, pp. 304–305.
18. Ibid., p. 352.
19. Letter from Jacqueline Piatier to General de Gaulle, Paris, June 12, 1956. FCDG AE3.
20. *Le Monde*, June 17–18, 1956.
21. Broadcast speech by General de Gaulle, August 29, 1944, *Discours et messages*, Vol. 1, p. 441.
22. "Les Libérateurs: Jeanne d'Arc 1429, les Anglais 1941," a poem addressed to General de Gaulle, Rouen, October 7, 1944. FCDG AC 1.
23. Magdeleine Bommier-Dewarin, "Au général de Gaulle," June 1941, Chateau de Ward-recques, Pas de Calais. FCDG AE3.
24. "Honneur au général de Gaulle," May 11, 1954. FCDG AF50 5.
25. de Gaulle, *Mémoires de guerre*, Vol. I, p. 9.
26. Ibid.
27. Ibid., p. 10.
28. de Gaulle, *Mémoires de guerre*, Vol. III, p. 883.
29. See Pierre Nora, "Les Mémoires d'Etat. De Commynes à de Gaulle," in *Les Lieux de Mémoire I* (Paris: Editions Quarto Gallimard, 1997), pp. 1383–1427.
30. Jean Lacouture, *De Gaulle*, Vol. II: Le politique (Paris: Seuil, 1985), p. 411.
31. Guichard, *Mon Général*, p. 333.
32. Malraux, *Les chênes qu'on abat*, p. 26.
33. Charles de Gaulle, *Mémoires d'espoir* (Paris: Plon, 1996), p. 16.
34. Ibid., p. 24.

35. Ibid., p. 55.
36. Ibid., p. 63.
37. Ibid., p. 239.
38. Ibid., p. 37.
39. Ibid., p. 248.
40. Ibid., p. 214.
41. "Toute ma vie je me suis fait une certaine idée de la France."
42. See, for example, *Le Courrier* (Limoges) October 28, 1954; *Le Berry Républicain* (Bourges), November 3, 1954.
43. Letter to General de Gaulle, Montferrand, May 1969. FCDG AE3/6.
44. Letter to General de Gaulle, Bordeaux, April 30, 1969. FCDG AE3/5.
45. Michel Debré, *Une certaine idée de la France* (Paris: Fayard, 1972); *Une certaine idée*, quarterly review of the neo-Gaullist party, the Rassemblement pour la République (Paris: 1998–2003).
46. Michel d'Ornano, *Une certaine idée de Paris* (Paris: Jean-Claude Lattès, 1977).
47. Olivier Stirn, *Une certaine idée du centre* (Paris: Albin Michel, 1977).
48. Gilles Martinet, *Une certaine idée de la gauche* (Paris: Odile Jacob, 1977).
49. Jean-Pierre Chevènement, *Une certaine idée de la République* (Paris: Albin Michel, 1992).
50. Laurent Fabius, *Une certaine idée de l'Europe* (Paris: Plon, 2004).
51. Gaetan Duval, *Une certaine idée de l'île Maurice* (Port-Louis: Petite Ourse Printing, 1976).
52. Georges Pompidou, *Pour rétablir une vérité* (Paris: Flammarion, 1982), p. 12.
53. Jacques Chirac, *Chaque pas doit être un but. Mémoires.* (Paris: NiL Editions, 2009), p. 11.
54. François Mitterrand, *Ma part de vérité* (Paris: Fayard, 1969), pp. 24–25.
55. Nicolas Sarkozy, *Témoignage* (Paris: XO Editions, 2006), p. 7; emphasis added. Or finally, with a clumsiness characteristic of him, Charles Pasqua's variant: "Ever since I can remember, I have been inoculated with the love of France and the wish to serve her." Charles Pasqua, *Ce que je sais*, Vol. I (Paris: Seuil, 2007), p. 9.
56. January 27, 1978, quoted in Valéry Giscard d'Estaing, *Le pouvoir et la vie*, Vol. I (Paris: France-Loisirs, 1988), p. 401.
57. Roger Belin, *Lorsqu'une République chasse l'autre. 1958–1962: souvenirs d'un témoin* (Paris: Editions Michalon, 1999), p. 278.
58. Pierre Billotte, *Le temps des armes* (Paris: Plon, 1972).
59. Gaston Palewski, *Mémoires d'action 1924–1974* (Paris: Plon, 1988).
60. Claude Hettier de Boislambert, *Les Fers de l'Espoir* (Paris: Plon, 1978).
61. Etienne Burin de Roziers, *Le Retour aux Sources. 1962, l'année décisive* (Paris: Plon, 1986).
62. Jacques Baumel, *De Gaulle, l'Exil Intérieur* (Paris: Albin Michel, 2001).
63. Massu, *Baden 68. Souvenirs*; Méo, *Une fidélité gaulliste à l'épreuve du pouvoir*.
64. Vendroux, *Cette chance que j'ai eue*, p. 357.
65. Guichard, *Mon Général*, p. 8.
66. Messmer, *Après tant de batailles* (Paris: Albin Michel, 1992), p. 431.
67. Lefranc, *Avec de Gaulle*, p. 100.
68. Guéna, *Le temps des certitudes*, p. 353.
69. Debré, *Trois Républiques pour une France*, p. 44.
70. Ibid., pp. 42–43.
71. Michel Debré, *Combattre toujours 1969–1993. Mémoires* (Paris: Albin Michel, 1994), p. 309.
72. Debré, *Trois Républiques pour une France*, p. 43.
73. Debré, *Combattre toujours*, p. 314.
74. Debré, *Trois Républiques pour une France*, p. 60.
75. Ibid., p. 60.
76. Malraux, *Les chênes qu'on abat*, p. 25.

77. de Gaulle, *Mémoires de guerre*, Vol. III, p. 603.

78. de Gaulle, *Mémoires de guerre*, Vol. I, p. 9.

79. Charles de Gaulle, "Du Prestige" (1925), in *Lettres, notes et carnets, 1919–June 1940*, p. 256.

80. de Gaulle, *Mémoires de guerre*, Vol. I, p. 9.

81. Ibid.

82. Ibid., p. 10.

83. Ibid., p. 55.

84. Ibid., p. 68.

85. de Gaulle, *Mémoires de guerre*, Vol. III, pp. 656–657.

86. de Gaulle, *Mémoires de guerre*, Vol. II, p. 352.

87. Philippe de Saint Robert, "Chateaubriand," in *Dictionnaire de Gaulle*, ed. C. Andrieu, P. Braud, and G. Piketty (Paris: Robert Laffont, 2006), p. 201.

88. André Rousseaux, "Les Mémoires du Général de Gaulle," *Le Figaro Littéraire*, October 30, 1954.

89. François-René de Chateaubriand, *Mémoires d'Outre-Tombe*, Vol. I, ed. M. Levaillant (Paris: Flammarion, 1949), p. 4.

90. Ibid., p. 75.

91. de Gaulle, *Mémoires de guerre*, Vol. I, p. 128.

92. Guy, *En écoutant de Gaulle*, p. 335; author's italics.

93. "The War Memoirs have nothing in common with [Chateaubriand's] *Mémoires d'Outre-Tombe*." Quoted in Adrien Le Bihan, *Le Général et son double. De Gaulle écrivain* (Paris: Flammarion, 1996), p. 143.

94. Chateaubriand, *Mémoires d'Outre-Tombe*, Vol. I, p. 469.

95. Ibid., p. 468.

96. de Gaulle, *Mémoires de guerre*, Vol. III, p. 885.

97. Chateaubriand, *Mémoires d'Outre-Tombe*, Vol. I, p. 4.

98. Chateaubriand, *Mémoires d'Outre-Tombe*, Vol. II, pp. 586–587.

99. de Gaulle, *Mémoires de guerre*, Vol. III, p. 800.

100. Chateaubriand, *Mémoires d'Outre-Tombe*, Vol. II, pp. 586–587.

101. de Gaulle, *Mémoires de guerre*, Vol. II, p. 431. On this little-known institution, see the study by Emmanuel Choisnel, *L'Assemblée Consultative Provisoire (1943–1945). Le sursaut républicain* (Paris: L'Harmattan, 2007).

102. Ibid., p. 425.

103. de Gaulle, *Mémoires de guerre*, Vol. III, p. 857.

104. Ibid., pp. 576–578.

105. de Gaulle, *Mémoires de guerre*, Vol. II, p. 445.

106. de Gaulle, *Mémoires de guerre*, Vol. I, p. 28.

107. Ibid., pp. 75–78; my italics.

108. Ibid., p. 39.

109. Speech of November 25, 1940, *Discours et messages*, p. 43.

110. de Gaulle, *Mémoires de guerre*, Vol. II, p. 272.

111. de Gaulle, *Mémoires de guerre*, Vol. I, p. 69.

112. Ibid., p. 240.

113. November 9, 1948; Guy, *En écoutant de Gaulle*, p. 450.

114. de Gaulle, *Mémoires de guerre*, Vol. II, pp. 583–584.

115. See Marc Fumaroli, *Chateaubriand. Poésie et terreur* (Paris: Gallimard, 2003), pp. 612–613.

116. de Gaulle, *Mémoires de guerre*, Vol. II, p. 502.

117. de Gaulle, "Du Prestige," p. 255.

118. de Gaulle, *Mémoires de guerre*, Vol. III, p. 726.

119. Malraux, *Les chênes qu'on abat*, pp. 41, 56.

120. de Gaulle, *Mémoires de guerre*, Vol. I, p. 119.
121. de Gaulle, *Mémoires de guerre*, Vol. III, p. 882.
122. de Gaulle, *Mémoires de guerre*, Vol. I, p. 205.
123. de Gaulle, *Mémoires de guerre*, Vol. II, p. 585.
124. Ibid., p. 353.
125. de Gaulle, *Mémoires de guerre*, Vol. III, p. 645.
126. de Gaulle, *Mémoires de guerre*, Vol. I, p. 55.
127. Malraux, *Les chênes qu'on abat*, pp. 40–42, 50–53.
128. Michel Debré, *Entretiens avec le Général de Gaulle, 1961–1969* (Paris: Albin Michel, 1993), p. 94. I am grateful to my colleague Anne Simonin for having called this saying of the General's to my attention.
129. See *De Gaulle 300 caricatures*, pp. 42, 91–92, 127.
130. P. de Gaulle, *De Gaulle mon père*, Vol. I, p. 399.
131. de Gaulle, "La France et Son Armée" (1938), in de Gaulle, *Le Fil de l'Epée et Autres Ecrits*, pp. 421–422.
132. Malraux, *Les chênes qu'on abat*, pp. 69, 73.
133. Chateaubriand, *Mémoires d'Outre-Tombe*, Vol. II, p. 640.
134. Ibid., p. 653.
135. de Gaulle, *Mémoires de guerre*, Vol. II, p. 575.
136. de Gaulle, *Mémoires de guerre*, Vol. III, p. 834.
137. We have been able to consult two manuscript versions of the third volume of the *Mémoires de guerre*, deposited in the BNF and of which a facsimile is held in the Fondation Charles de Gaulle (AA 6).
138. Guy, *En écoutant de Gaulle*, p. 46.
139. March 20, 1946. Mauriac, *Aimer de Gaulle*, p. 315.
140. See David Reynolds, *In command of history. Churchill fighting and writing the Second World War* (New York: Random House, 2005).
141. Letter to General de Gaulle, undated (1969). FCDG AE3/6.
142. Pierre Nora, "Gaullistes et communistes," in *Les Lieux de Mémoire*, Vol. III (1), p. 357.
143. Jeannelle, *Ecrire ses Mémoires au XXe siècle*, p. 184.
144. See Patrice Gueniffey, *Le Dix-huit Brumaire*, p. 387.
145. Benda, *Mémoires d'infra-tombe*, Vol. I, p. 282.
146. See in particular Michel Winock's study, *13 Mai 1958: l'agonie de la IVe République* (Paris: Gallimard, 2006).
147. Anne Simonin, *Le déshonneur dans la République. Une histoire de l'indignité 1791–1958* (Paris: Grasset, 2008), pp. 29–30.
148. Malraux, *Les chênes qu'on abat*, p. 56.
149. de Gaulle, *Mémoires de guerre*, Vol. III, p. 698.
150. Jacques Chaban-Delmas, *Mémoires pour demain* (Paris: Flammarion, 1997), p. 89.
151. Debré, *Trois Républiques pour une France*, p. 51.
152. On this point, see Anne Simonin's article, "1815 en 1945. Les formes littéraires de la défaite," *Vingtième Siècle* 59 (July–September 1998), pp. 48–61.
153. Jean Mauriac, *Le Général et le journaliste* (Paris: Fayard, 2008), pp. 138–139.
154. Quoted by Henry Rousso, "La Seconde Guerre Mondiale," in *Histoire des Droites en France*, Vol. II, ed. J.F. Sirinelli (Paris: Gallimard, 1992), p. 580.
155. Speech delivered at Douaumont, May 29, 1966. AN 5 AG1 (290).

CHAPTER 4

1. Letter from Paul Roquère to General de Gaulle, Paris, November 22, 1944. FCDG AF24. In his reply, dated January 4, 1945, the General expressed his "heartfelt sympathy" to the

bereaved father. See Charles de Gaulle, *Lettres, notes et carnets,* May 1969–November 1970, Compléments de 1908 à 1968 (Paris: Plon, 1988), p. 384. The tragic death of Paul-Jean Roquère is also mentioned, along with that of many of his comrades, in Romain Gary's memoirs. See *La promesse de l'aube* (Paris: Gallimard, 1980), p. 328.

2. Entry for December 24, 1848, in Victor Hugo, *Choses vues 1830–1848* (Paris: Gallimard, 1972), pp. 761–762.

3. Mauriac, *Aimer de Gaulle,* p. 369.

4. See, for example, the letter from M.-H. Augeard to General de Gaulle, Lozère sur Yvette, December 25, 1944. AN 3AG4 (69).

5. H.D.: "Note pour M. le General Charles de Gaulle. Reflexions sur la démocratie," August 29, 1944. AN 3AG4 (69).

6. Anonymous letter, Nantes, February 5, 1945. AN 3AG4 (69).

7. Letter, Montrouge (Seine), February 6, 1945. AN 3AG4 (69).

8. Letter, December 23, 1944. AN 3AG4 (69).

9. Speech of April 2, 1945, *Discours et messages,* p. 537.

10. Speech by André Le Troquer, president of the Paris Municipal Commission, April 1945. *Bulletin Municipal Officiel de la Ville de Paris,* April 25, 1945.

11. Internal memo, General de Gaulle's office, Paris, September 11, 1945. AN 3AG4 (70).

12. Note from Palewski, undated. AN 3AG4 (70).

13. Internal memo, General de Gaulle's office, Paris, August 14, 1945. AN 3AG4 (70).

14. Letter from Mme L. to General de Gaulle, Le Havre, January 19, 1945. AN 3AG4 (69). The city of Le Havre eventually received (in 1949) the Croix de Guerre, which was awarded to 1,585 towns. See Olivier Ihl, *Le mérite et la République* (Paris: Gallimard, 2007), p. 389.

15. Official ceremony in memory of the dead of the Paris police prefecture during the Liberation of Paris, October 12, 1944. Archives de la Préfecture de police (APP), Paris, FD1 (A) (commémorations 1944–1945).

16. Police note, May 26, 1945. AN 3AG4 (70).

17. Frédéric Turpin, *Le Mont Valérien, de l'histoire à la mémoire* (Paris: Editions du Huitième Jour, 2003), p. 28.

18. Astier de la Vigerie, *Sept fois sept jours,* p. 101.

19. Roger Barberot, "Mes ruminations sur de Gaulle." Unpublished manuscript, Fonds Roger Barberot, FCDG F 24 (46).

20. Serge Berstein, "L'arrivée de de Gaulle à Paris," in *De Gaulle et la Libération,* pp. 136–138.

21. Lacouture, *De Gaulle,* Vol. I, p. 837.

22. Memo from General de Gaulle's office about the ceremonies of November 11, 1944. AN 3AG4 (70).

23. Note of the Gouvernement Militaire de Paris, July 4, 1945. AN 3AG4 (70).

24. De Gaulle, *Mémoires de guerre,* p. 645.

25. Telegram from Winston Churchill, November 16, 1944. AN 3AG4 (70).

26. See Alain Brossat, *Libération, fête folle. 6 juin 44–8 mai 45: mythes et rites ou le grand théâtre des passions populaires* (Paris: Editions Autrement, 1994).

27. Laurent Douzou and Dominique Veillon, "Les déplacements du Général de Gaulle à travers la France," in *De Gaulle et la Libération,* p. 157.

28. Speech of November 11, 1945. AN 3AG4 (70).

29. Gérard Namer, *La commémoration en France* (Paris: Editions Papyrus, 1983); the first part of this work (chapters 1–9) deals only with the year 1945.

30. Alexandre Duval-Stalla, *André Malraux—Charles de Gaulle, une histoire, deux légendes* (Paris: Gallimard, 2008), p. 212.

31. "Projet pour la commémoration le 4 septembre 1945 de la fondation de la IIIe République." AN 3AG4 (70).

32. *L'Humanité,* September 5, 1945.

33. *Le Monde,* September 6, 1945.
34. Speech of September 4, 1945, *Discours et messages,* pp. 610–613.
35. Agulhon, *De Gaulle,* p. 61.
36. Letter to General de Gaulle's office, January 1945. AN 3AG4 (69).
37. See, for example, the photograph of the General's arrival at Périgueux, in *Souvenir de la visite du Général de Gaulle: Limoges—Oradour-sur-Glane—Périgueux, 4–5 mars 1945* (Paris: Limoges, 1945).
38. See in particular the General's message on the occasion of the 18th of June 1943, in de Gaulle, *Lettres, notes et carnets,* June 1943–May 1945 (1983), p. 29.
39. "Projet pour la journée de commémoration nationale du lundi 18 juin 1945," by Colonel Roulier. AN 3AG4 (70).
40. "Célébration de la journée nationale du 18 juin 1945," note of May 28, 1945. APP FD 1.
41. The Appeal of the 18th of June 1940 was not recorded by the BBC: No original sound version of it is extant.
42. Internal memo, General de Gaulle's office, May 24, 1945. AN 3AG4 (70).
43. Ibid.
44. Georges Pompidou, "Note concernant les cérémonies du 18 juin," June 11, 1945. AN 3 AG4 (70).
45. Ibid.
46. *Résistance,* June 19, 1945.
47. "Célébration de la journée nationale du 18 juin 1945," note of May 28, 1945. APP FD 1.
48. Letter from General Méric, May 17, 1956. Fonds Roger Barberot, FCDG F 26 (8).
49. Police report, June 18, 1945. APP FD 1.
50. *La Croix,* June 21, 1945.
51. Léon Blum, "La fête du 18 juin," *Le Populaire,* June 19, 1945.
52. *Combat,* June 19, 1945.
53. Maurice Lacroix, "Après les fêtes du 18 juin," *Résistance,* June 19, 1945.
54. "Note pour le Général de Gaulle," Paris, June 25, 1945. AN 3AG4 (70).
55. Georges Cogniot, *L'Humanité,* June 19, 1945. Rol-Tanguy (and twenty-nine other resistance heroes) received their medals from de Gaulle's own hands—something the PCF newspaper did not see fit to mention. On the twentieth anniversary of the Liberation, Rol-Tanguy was elevated to the rank of Officer of the Legion of Honour by de Gaulle himself. See AN 5 AG1 (556), dossier "Cérémonies du 25 août 1964."
56. Ibid.
57. See "Projet de cérémonie pour la journée nationale du 18 juin 1946." FCDG AC3.
58. *Paris-Matin,* June 19, 1946.
59. *L'Aurore,* June 13, 1945.
60. Serge Barcellini, "Les cérémonies du 11 novembre 1945: une apothéose commémorative gaulliste," in *La France de 1945: résistances, retours, renaissances* (Caen: Presses Universitaires de Caen, 1996).
61. Account by Madame Simone Brunau, Paris, September 2009.
62. Mechtild Gilzmer, *Mémoires de pierre. Les monuments commémoratifs en France après 1944* (Paris: Editions Autrement, 2009), p. 67.
63. Mauriac, *Aimer de Gaulle,* pp. 365–366.
64. Letter from General de Gaulle to Paul Ramadier, June 1, 1947. Fonds 18 Juin (1945–1949), Archives de la Chancellerie de l'Ordre de la Libération.
65. We checked this point in the collection on June 18 (1945–1955 and 1956–1959) in the Archives of the Chancellery of the Order of the Libération in Paris.
66. The year 1947 was the last year in which the president of the Republic took part in the ceremony at the Arc de Triomphe. See Racine-Furlaud, "Mémoire du 18 juin 1940," *De Gaulle en son siècle,* Vol. I.

67. Letter from Paul Ramadier to Admiral d'Argenlieu, Paris, June 5, 1947. Fonds 18 Juin (1945–1955), Archives de la Chancellerie de l'Ordre de la Libération.

68. Danielle Tartakowsky, "Les fêtes de la droite populaire," in *Les usages politiques des fêtes aux XIXe-XXe siècles*, ed. A. Corbin (Paris: Publications de la Sorbonne, 1994), p. 315.

69. Manuscript note by General de Gaulle (1948). FCDG AA (manuscripts).

70. "Message aux Français Libres," 18 Juin 1950, in de Gaulle, *Lettres, notes et carnets*, May 1945–June 1951 (1984), p. 429.

71. See the letter of the president of the section to General de Gaulle, March 18, 1947. FCDG AF24.

72. Thank-you letter from the president of the section to General de Gaulle, November 14, 1951. FCDG AF24.

73. In 1954, de Gaulle canceled his participation in the meeting of resistance medal-holders because of the presence of André Mutter, a minister in the Laniel government. See the correspondence between Boislambert and the General, January 8, 1954, and February 27, 1954. FCDG AA.

74. Press release of the Order of the Liberation, Paris, May 31, 1955. APP FD 4 (1954–1955).

75. See Marc-Olivier Baruch, "Présents d'une commémoration: la Quatrième République face au dixième anniversaire de la Libération," in *Pourquoi Résister? Résister Pour Quoi Faire?* ed. B. Garnier, J.-L. Leleu, J. Quellien, and A. Simonin (Caen: Université de Caen Basse-Normandie, 2006), pp. 165–179.

76. Declaration by General de Gaulle, press conference, April 8, 1954. *France-Soir*, April 9, 1954.

77. Letter from the prefect of police to Captain de Bonneval, undated (May 1954). APP FD 3 (1954), "Dépôt de Gerbe à L'Arc de Triomphe par le Général de Gaulle, 9 mai 1954."

78. Police notes, May 9, 1954. APP FD (1954).

79. See especially Jacques Foccart, *Foccart parle. Entretiens avec Philippe Gaillard*, Vol. 1 (Paris: Fayard, 1995), pp. 74–75, 114.

80. Police reports, May 9 and 10, 1954, APP FD 3 (1954). The crowd in the morning was estimated at 23,000, and in the afternoon, 18,000.

81. *L'Epoque*, June 19, 1946.

82. Telegram from the veterans of the First Army of the Lyonnais region, June 18, 1946. FCDG AF24.

83. In 1948, the AFL comprised 200 regimental or local branches; see Sylvain Cornil-Frerrot, "Le général de Larminat et l'Association des Français Libres," in *Larminat, un fidèle hors série*, ed. P. Oulmont (Paris: Fondation Charles de Gaulle and Editions LBM, 2008), p. 248. See also, for this period, the relevant numbers of the *Revue de la France Libre*, published by the Association des Français Libres, where commemorations carried out by the various branches were systematically listed.

84. Letter from the president of the veterans' association of Valognes, June 26, 1957. FCDG AF24. The campaign quickly produced results: On July 27, 1957, the town council agreed to name the square in front of the town hall "Place du Général de Gaulle." My thanks are due to Madame Agnès Marie, of the Valognes town council, for this information.

85. Letter to General de Gaulle from the branch secretary, Saint-Dié, June 16, 1956. FCDG AF23.

86. Letter to General de Gaulle from the president, Free French War Veterans, and Ladies' Auxiliary, New York, June 17, 1952. FCDG AF24.

87. Telegram, June 26, 1946. FCDG AF24.

88. Letter from the president of the Amicale des FFI de l'Ile de France to General de Gaulle, Paris, June 28, 1949. FCDG AF23.

89. Annual report of the Secretary of the Premiers Compagnons Association, Paris, April 24, 1948. FCDG AF24.

90. Quoted by André Vernier, a comrade of Paimbeuf (and his best man), in a letter to General de Gaulle, Paris, June 14, 1955. FCDG AF24.

91. Daniel Deschamps, "Lettre ouverte à un Général," Foecy (Cher), March 15, 1949. FCDG AF23.

92. Letter from the president of the Premiers Compagnons Association, Paris, June 8, 1948. FCDG AF24.

93. Letter from Edgard Braun, Association des Anciens Combattants de la Division Leclerc, Strasbourg, October 29, 1954. FCDG AF24.

94. Roger Barberot, "Mes ruminations sur de Gaulle." Unpublished manuscript, Fonds Roger Barberot. FCDG F 24 (46).

95. Letter from General Larminat, Paris, May 28, 1956. FCDG AF23.

96. Letter from A. Bougerolle, president of the Chevaliers de la Croix de Lorraine, to General Larminat; Clamart, May 29, 1956. FCDG AF23.

97. Account of the president of the Paris branch of the Fédération Nationale des Amicales d'Anciens de la 9e Division d'Infanterie Coloniale, May 10, 1954. APP FD 3.

98. Edmond Michelet, "Esprit de la Résistance," *Le Monde*, June 19, 1957.

99. Letter to General de Gaulle, November 26, 1956. FCDG AE3–4.

100. René Hostache, *Esprit de la Résistance* 5 (March–April 1958). FCDG AF23.

101. Police reports, Paris, May 8–9, 1958. APP FD 10 (1958) and G/A F18.

102. See the studies by Pierre Miquel, *Compagnons de la Libération* (Paris: Denoël, 1995), and Jean-Christophe Notin, *1061 Compagnons. Histoire des Compagnons de la Libération* (Paris: Perrin, 2000).

103. Letter to Roger Barberot, dated April 14, 1958. Fonds Roger Barberot, FCDG F 24 (8).

104. *Le Monde*, May 18–19, 1958.

105. Letter from General Koenig, May 5, 1958. FCDG AF50.

106. Letter from General Méric, undated. Fonds Roger Barberot, FCDG F 24 (8).

107. Letter from Captain Malin, May 6, 1958. Fonds Roger Barberot, FCDG F 24 (8).

108. Letter from Dr. J.F. Vernier, Conakry, April 24, 1958. Fonds Roger Barberot, FCDG F 24 (8).

109. Letter from Pierre Finet, April 1, 1958. Fonds Roger Barberot, FCDG F 24 (8).

110. Letter from General Koenig, May 5, 1958. FCDG AF50.

111. "Entrevue du 27 mars. Intentions et conceptions." FCDG AF50.

112. Letter from Pierre Finet, April 1, 1958. Fonds Roger Barberot, FCDG F 24 (8).

113. On the general consistency but also the limited character and occasional discordance of the memories of Free French fighters after the war, see Jean-François Muracciole, *Les Français Libres. L'autre Résistance* (Paris: Tallandier, 2009), pp. 335–360.

114. Jacques Vendroux, *Ces grandes années que j'ai vécues* (Paris: Plon, 1975), p. 18.

115. Quoted by Janine Mossuz-Lavau, *André Malraux et le Gaullisme*, 2d ed. (Paris: Presses de la Fondation Nationale des Sciences Politiques, 1982), p. 187.

116. "Discours prononcé Place de la République à Paris," September 4, 1958, *Discours et messages*, May 1958–July 1962, pp. 41–42.

117. Gilzmer, *Mémoires de pierre*, pp. 117–118.

118. Police report, June 19, 1958. APP FD 10 (1958).

119. *L'Aurore*, June 19, 1959.

120. On the day before the 1960 anniversary, the coffins of six fighters and the urn containing the ashes of one person who had been deported were transferred from the temporary crypt to the new France Combattante crypt. The ceremony was presided over by Michel Debré, the prime minister. See reports of June 17–18, 1960. APP FD 16 and FD 17.

121. President of the Republic's office, note by Pierre Lefranc, Paris, March 24, 1959. AN 5AG1(544).

122. Account by Madame Simone Brunau, Paris, September 2009.

123. Letter from Félix Brunau to General de Gaulle, Saint-Cloud, September 29, 1960. Dossier Mont Valérien, Archives de la Chancellerie de l'Ordre de la Libération.

124. The invitation to the mont Valérien ceremony for 1961 was phrased in these terms: "The Grand Chancellor requests the honour of your company at the commemorative ceremony at the Mont Valérien on the 18th of June 1961 at 7 PM, General de Gaulle will preside over the ceremony." AN 5 AG1 (550).

125. Invitation card to the ceremony at the mont Valérien for 1960. AN 5AG1 (544).

126. "I broadcast the commentary on the Mont Valérien ceremony, which is always moving in its spare and austere setting, from which the path starts that leads to the execution ground. De Gaulle seems to me thinner and even paler than usual." Entry for Thursday, June 18, 1959, Droit, Les lueurs de l'aube, p. 171.

127. Letter from the Minister of the Interior to the prefects, Paris, June 2, 1959. APP FD 13.

128. The Arc de Triomphe ceremony was organized by the Association des Français Libres.

129. Manuscript note, Ordre de la Libération, May 22, 1959. AN 5 AG1 (544).

130. Letter from Raymond Triboulet to President de Gaulle, undated (early June 1960). AN 5 AG1 (547).

131. "Cérémonie du 18 juin," notes of the Ordre de la Libération, undated (1960). AN 5AG1 (547).

132. Office of the President of the Republic, note by Pierre Lefranc, May 4, 1960. AN 5AG1 (547).

133. Report of a conference held on Tuesday, April 25, at the Council of the Ordre de la Libération, Paris. APP FD 22.

134. Ibid.

135. Ibid.

136. "Note, au sujet de la prochaine cérémonie au Mémorial du Mont Valérien," in de Gaulle, Lettres, notes et carnets, January 1961–December 1963 (1986), p. 98.

137. Le Parisien Libéré, June 19, 1965.

138. Police report, June 20, 1964. APP FD 41.

139. Police report, June 19, 1960. APP FD 17.

140. Entry for Saturday, June 18, 1966, in Jacques Foccart, "Tous les soirs avec de Gaulle," Journal de l'Elysée I (1965–1967) (Paris: Fayard/Jeune Afrique, 1997), p. 431.

141. Letter from Roger Weill, Ivry hospice, June 8, 1959. AN 5 AG1 (544).

142. Letter from Mme Dagneau, Enghien-les-Bains (S. et Oise), June 9, 1959. AN 5 AG1 (544).

143. Account by Madame Simone Brunau, Paris, September 2009.

144. Letter from Mme Symone Astier, Paris, May 28, 1959. AN 5AG1 (544).

145. Letter from Mme M., Paris, June 4, 1959. AN 5AG1 (544).

146. Police report, June 19, 1960. APP FD 17.

147. L'Aurore, June 17, 1967.

148. Police report, June 18, 1960. APP FD 16.

149. On the occasion of a meeting held in Paris on May 12, 1960, to plan the unveiling of the memorial at the mont Valérien. Fonds 18 Juin (1960–1961), Archives de la Chancellerie de l'Ordre de la Libération.

150. Police telegram, June 17, 1960. APP FD 17. It had been Félix Brunau's idea to strew flowers around the entrance to the crypt in November 1945 when the fifteen coffins were first brought in. He was therefore returning to his own original idea. Information from Madame Simone Brunau, Paris, September 2009.

151. Report of the prefecture of police on the laying of wreaths in the Paris region, Paris, June 18, 1960. APP FD 17.

152. Police report, June 19, 1961, APP FD 22.

153. Police report, Paris, June 20, 1961. APP FD 22.

154. Police report, Paris, June 19, 1958. APP FD 10.
155. Report of the director general of municipal police, Paris, September 5, 1958. APP dossier "4 Septembre 1958, Place de la République."
156. Police report, Puteaux, June 19, 1960. APP FD 17.
157. Police telegram, Suresnes, June 18, 1968. APP FD 73.
158. *L'Aurore*, June 19, 1958.
159. This (nonexhaustive) list has been reconstituted on the basis of letters sent by Companions or by Free French veterans to the Grand Chancellor of the Ordre de la Libération apologizing for being unable to come to the mont Valérien because of ceremonies that were taking place at the same time in their own towns. Fonds 18 Juin (1960–1961 and 1962–1968), Archives de la Chancellerie de l'Ordre de la Libération.
160. Letter from Geoffroy de Courcel to the Grand Chancellor of the Ordre de la Libération, London, June 4, 1964. Fonds 18 Juin (1964), Archives de la Chancellerie de l'Ordre de la Libération.
161. *Le Figaro*, June 20, 1966.
162. This claim was inaccurate in two senses: First, the PCF "appeal" came some months later and was antedated, and second, the text is exclusively directed at the Vichy regime and the British; it does not really challenge German occupation. See Nicole Racine-Furlaud, "18 juin 1940 ou 10 juillet 1940. Batailles de mémoires," in *50 ans d'une passion française. De Gaulle et les communistes*, ed. S. Courtois and M. Lazar (Paris: Balland, 1991), pp. 202–203.
163. Police report, Paris, June 20, 1964. APP FD 41.
164. *La mémoire des Français. Quarante ans de commémorations de la Seconde guerre mondiale* (Paris: Editions du CNRS, 1986); the second part (pp. 113–367) is devoted to a "tour of the France of commemorations."
165. On the participation of the SAC in the "orderly management" of the 18th of June, see the letter from Ch. Mattéi, a national official of the SAC, to Jules Muracciole, secretary to the Chancellery of the Ordre de la Libération, Paris, June 9, 1964. Fonds 18 Juin (1964), Archives de la Chancellerie de l'Ordre de la Libération.
166. La Croix, June 20, 1964.
167. Police note, Paris, June 18, 1968. APP FD 73.
168. Note of the security service, presidency of the Republic, June 7, 1968. AN 5 AG1 (563).
169. "Premier 18 juin sans de Gaulle," *Le Parisien*, June 19, 1969.
170. He would enter the crypt only once, in 1973.
171. Jean Mauriac, *L'après de Gaulle. Notes confidentielles 1969–1989* (Paris: Fayard, 2006), p. 54.
172. Jacques Foccart, "Dans les bottes du Général," *Journal de l'Elysée* III (1969–1971) (1999), p. 57.
173. Police report, Nanterre, June 18, 1969. APP FD 81.
174. See particularly the internal memo of the Chancellery of the Ordre de la Libération, "Critique sur la cérémonie du 18 juin 1957," which stressed that the stand prepared for delegations was far from full. Fonds 18 Juin (1956–1959), Archives de la Chancellerie de l'Ordre de la Libération.
175. Some, like Jean d'Escrienne, even spoke of a "profanation" of the 18th of June in 1958; see *De Gaulle de loin et de près* (Paris: Plon, 1978), pp. 176–177.
176. See, for example, the letter from Roger Barberot to the Grand Chancellor Hettier de Boislambert, Paris, June 23, 1975. Dossier Mont Valérien, Archives de la Chancellerie de l'Ordre de la Libération.
177. Letter from Hettier de Boislambert to Georges Galichon (director of the Office of the President of the Republic), Paris, April 13, 1966. Fonds 18 Juin (1966), Archives de la Chancellerie de l'Ordre de la Libération.

178. Foccart, "Tous les soirs avec de Gaulle," *Journal de l'Elysée* I, p. 171.
179. On this planned journey, see Mauriac, *Mort du Général de Gaulle*, pp. 91–104.
180. Letter from General de Gaulle, Londres, August 18, 1944, in de Gaulle, *Lettres, notes et carnets,* May 1969–November 1970, Compléments de 1908 à 1968, p. 382.
181. The president usually left the Elysée about 5:40 and was back before 8 P.M. See, for example, the official program for the ceremony of the 18th of June 1965. AN 5 AG1 (558), dossier "Mont Valérien, 18 Juin 1965."
182. Note of the Office of the President, Paris, April 7, 1965. 5 AG1 (558), dossier "Messe des Déportés, 25 avril 1965."
183. Program of the ceremony of the 8th of May 1965. 5 AG1 (558), dossier "20e anniversaire de l'armistice."
184. Confidential note of the Office of the President, Paris, October 8, 1968. AN 5 AG1 (564), dossier "50e anniversaire de l'armistice, 10–11 novembre 1968."
185. He would say a few words at the Elysée, at the reception for the Compagnons de la Libération.
186. Program of the ceremony of the 18th of June 1951. Fonds 18 Juin (1950–1955), Archives de la Chancellerie de l'Ordre de la Libération.
187. Olivier Ihl, *La fête républicaine* (Paris: Gallimard, 1996), p. 374.
188. My thanks to Claire Andrieu for this stimulating thought.
189. Debray, "Preface," in de Gaulle, *Les grands discours de guerre.*
190. Gilzmer, *Mémoires de pierre,* pp. 109–113.
191. Speech by André Malraux, December 19, 1964. AN 5 AG1 (556), dossier "Transfert au Panthéon des cendres de Jean Moulin."
192. Peyrefitte, *C'était de Gaulle* (Paris: Editions Quarto Gallimard, 2002), pp. 512–513.
193. Claude Guy, "L'Homme," in *En écoutant de Gaulle,* p. 239.
194. "Note sur la cérémonie du 18 Juin" (1950). Fonds 18 Juin (1950–1955), Archives de la Chancellerie de l'Ordre de la Libération.
195. Letter from J. Laurent, Neuilly-sur-Seine, October 26, 1964. AN 5 AG1 (291) commemoration 1939–1945, dossier "Anniversaire de l'Appel du 18 Juin."
196. See AN 5 AG1 (546) (Sorties du président de la République), dossier "Cérémonies du 8 Mai 1960."
197. Alain de Boissieu, quoted by Mauriac, *L'après de Gaulle,* p. 173.
198. See, for example, André Passeron's article in *Le Monde,* June 20, 1967.
199. Letter to General Boud'hors, June 27, 1950, in Charles de Gaulle, *Lettres, notes et carnets,* May 1945–June 1951, p. 431.
200. *Le Parisien,* June 18–19, 1970.

CHAPTER 5

1. AN 5AG1 (287), Voyages officiels du Président de la République en France (1962–1969), dossier "Voyage dans les Charentes (Juin 1963)."
2. de Gaulle, *Lettres, notes et carnets.* As we noted in chapter 1, these are only a small fraction of the General's complete letters.
3. Frédérique Dufour, "Colombey et le gaullisme sous la Ve République," in *Gaullisme et gaullistes dans la France de l'Est sous la IVe République,* ed. F. Audigier and F. Schwindt (Rennes, Presses Universitaires de Rennes, 2009), pp. 361–362.
4. Dulong, *La vie quotidienne à l'Elysée au temps de Charles de Gaulle,* p. 189.
5. AN 5 AG1 308, 309, 310 (physionomie du courrier, 1959–1969).
6. See in this context Frédéric Monier's study on Daladier and clientelism in the Vaucluse, *La politique des plaintes* (Paris: La Boutique de l'Histoire, 2007).
7. Letter of April 1967. AN 5 AG1 (310).

8. Daniel Cordier, *Alias Caracalla* (Paris: Gallimard, 2009), p. 130.
9. Letter of January 1961, Juzennecourt. Archives départementales de la Haute-Marne (ADHM), 819 W 26219, "Interventions auprès du Général de Gaulle (1958–69)."
10. Letter, St. Dizier, September 16, 1968. ADHM, 819 W 26219.
11. Letter, Heuilley-Cotton, August 1964. ADHM, 819 W 26219.
12. For example, letter of April 30, 1969. FCDG AE3/5.
13. "Pépère," Roger Tessier, *J'étais le gorille du Général 1947–1970* (Paris: Perrin, 2002), p. 195.
14. Pierre Lefranc, *Gouverner selon de Gaulle. Conversations avec Geneviève Moll* (Paris: Fayard, 2008), p. 32.
15. Reports of June 1965. AN 5 AG1 (310).
16. Letter, Vanves, April 30, 1969. FCDG AE4 (5).
17. Pierre Viansson-Ponté, *Les Gaullistes: rituel et annuaire* (Paris: Seuil, 1963), p. 52.
18. Report of September 1960. AN 5AG1 (308).
19. Thirteen percent of French households had television in 1960. See Anne Simonin and Hélène Clastres, *Les idées en France 1945–1988, une chronologie* (Paris: Gallimard, 1989), p. 170.
20. Report of April 1960. AN 5 AG1 (308).
21. See, for example, the letter of thanks from the mayor of Decazeville (Aveyron), September 24, 1961. 5 AG1 (286), dossier "Voyage dans l'Aveyron, la Lozère et l'Ardèche (21–24 septembre 1961)."
22. Reports May–June 1959. AN 5AG1 (308).
23. Reports of April 1962. AN 5 AG1 (309).
24. On this episode, and on the historic evolution of French attitudes toward de Gaulle, according to the surveys of the IFOP, see Jean Charlot, *Les Français et de Gaulle* (Paris: Plon, 1971).
25. Letter of April 1962. AN 5 AG1 (309). Between 1953 and 1962, de Gaulle's lieutenant (and presidential successor) Georges Pompidou worked for the Rothschild Bank in France.
26. Letter of October 1962. AN 5 AG1 (309).
27. Report of January 1– February 15, 1960. AN 5 AG1 (308).
28. Report of August 1–15, 1961. AN 5 AG1 (308).
29. Report of January 1962. AN 5 AG1 (309).
30. Report of July 1962. AN 5 AG1 (309).
31. *Pied-noirs* (literally "black feet") is a term used to designate European settlers in Algeria; by the time of Algerian independence they numbered more than a million. They bitterly opposed de Gaulle's negotiated settlement with the Algerian nationalists.
32. Declaration made at a luncheon in the Sarthe, May 22, 1965; quoted by Alain Peyrefitte, *C'était de Gaulle*, p. 684.
33. Quoted by Rainer Hudemann, "Voyage en Allemagne," in *Dictionnaire de Gaulle*, p. 1171.
34. See Maurice Vaïsse, *La grandeur. Politique étrangère du Général de Gaulle 1958–1969* (Paris: Fayard, 1998).
35. Malraux, *Les chênes qu'on abat*, p. 37.
36. Report of October 1965. AN 5 AG1 (310).
37. Letter from Frère A.M. Henry, Paris, April 28, 1969. FCDG AE4 (5).
38. Folder of drawings from the school at Civrieux d'Azergue (Rhône). FCDG AE4 (5).
39. De Gaulle, *Mémoires d'espoir*.
40. Communal condolence book, Douai, November 1970. FCDG AG79 Nord (Douai).
41. See AN 5 AG1 (287), dossier "Voyage en Bretagne (janvier–février 1969)."
42. Nicolas Mariot, *Bains de foule. Les voyages présidentiels en France 1888–2002* (Paris: Belin, 2006).

43. See the police report, June 10, 1959. 5AG1 (286), dossier "Voyage en Auvergne (Cantal, Haute Loire, Puy-de-Dôme, Loire), 5–7 Juin 1959."

44. From the council minutes of Dieue, June 29, 1961. AN 5 AG1 (286), dossier "Voyage en Lorraine (28 juin au 2 juillet 1961)."

45. Bonneval was de Gaulle's aide, and he was responsible for keeping de Gaulle on schedule during these official visits. Letter of April 1963. AN 5 AG1 (309).

46. Letter of May 1963. AN 5 AG1 (309).

47. Letter of March 1960. AN 5 AG1 (308).

48. For examples, see Lefranc, *Avec de Gaulle*, pp. 151–157.

49. Letter from the prefect of the Haut-Rhin to Olivier Guichard, Colmar, November 25, 1959. AN 5 AG1 (286), dossier "Voyage en Alsace 18–22 novembre 1959."

50. See, for example, André Passeron's article in *Le Monde*, June 19, 1965, on country people's response between Provins and Melun.

51. Letters of October 1964. AN 5AG1 (309).

52. Letter of May 1963. AN 5 AG1 (287), dossier "Voyage dans les Charentes (Juin 1963)."

53. Letter from the General's office to the mayor of Reims, Mai 1963. AN 5 AG1 (287), dossier "Voyage en Champagne (mai 1963)."

54. Note from the General's office to Mme de Gaulle. AN 5 AG1 (287), dossier "Voyage dans l'Ouest (Vendée, Maine et Loire, Mayenne, Sarthe), 19–23 mai 1965."

55. See the various letters from the prefect of the Bouches-du-Rhône to the General's principal private secretary, 1961–1963. AN 5 AG1 (286), dossier "Voyage en Corse, dans le Var et dans les Bouches-du-Rhône (7–10 novembre 1961)."

56. Letter from General de Gaulle to Mgr. Rastouil, bishop of Limoges, July 11, 1962. AN 5 AG1 (286).

57. Letter from the Minister of Public Works to General de Gaulle's office, May 22, 1962. AN 5 AG1 (286), dossier "Pont Bailey, Saint Mihiel."

58. Manuscript note by General de Gaulle, February 19, 1962: "Next Sunday is for the people of the commune and nothing else. Drinks, I'll pay." AN 5 AG1 (552), dossier "Inauguration Centre Culturel Colombey (1962)."

59. Letters of thanks from mayors, May 1963. AN 5AG1 (287), dossier "Voyage en Champagne Mai 1963."

60. See, for example, Galichon's letter to Mgr Henri Vion, bishop of Poitiers, June 17, 1963. AN 5AG1 (287).

61. Letter from General de Gaulle's office to Abbé Michel Catteau, parish priest of Ebblinghem (Nord), July 4, 1966. AN 5 AG1 (287), dossier "Voyage dans la région du Nord (avril 1966)."

62. Letter to General de Gaulle, Paris, July 4, 1969. FCDG AE4 (5).

63. Letter of March 1966. AN 5AG1 (310).

64. Letter of April 1966. AN 5 AG1 (310).

65. Drawing reproduced in *De Gaulle 300 caricatures*, p. 81.

66. See, for example, the batch of letters received in April 1967. AN 5 AG1 (310).

67. Information from Jean d'Escrienne, the General's last aide-de-camp (who talked to her); see his *De Gaulle sans frontières* (Paris: Thélès, 2007), pp. 92–93.

68. Letter of December 1967. AN 5 AG1 (310).

69. Letter of June 1968. AN 5 AG1 (310).

70. François Flohic, *Souvenirs d'Outre-Gaulle* (Paris: Plon, 197), p. 196.

71. Mauriac, *Mort du général de Gaulle*, p. 33.

72. Flohic, *Souvenirs d'Outre-Gaulle*, p. 204.

73. Mauriac, *Mort du général de Gaulle*, p. 60.

74. Flohic, *Souvenirs d'Outre-Gaulle*, p. 221.

75. Blanc, *Charles de Gaulle au soir de sa vie*, p. 61.

76. Letter, Paris, April 29, 1969. FCDG AE4 (5).

77. Letters, Marseille, April 28, 1969, and Paris, May 8, 1969. FCDG AE3/5.
78. Letter, Paris, May 1, 1969. FCDG AE4 (5).
79. Letter, Paris, April 30, 1969. FCDG AE4 (5).
80. Letter, Clamart (Hauts-de-Seine), May 1, 1969. FCDG AE3/5.
81. Quoted in a letter to General de Gaulle, Montfermeil, July 27, 1969. FCDG AE4 (5).
82. Letter, Paris, April 28, 1969. FCDG AE4 (5).
83. Letter, Paris, undated (April 1969). FCDG AE4 (5).
84. Letter, Paris, April 28, 1969. FCDG AE3/6.
85. Letter, Sèvres, April 30, 1969. FCDG AE4 (5).
86. Letter, Clichy, April 28, 1969. FCDG AE4 (5).
87. Letter, Saint-Denis-de-Cabanne, April 28, 1969. FCDG AE3/7.
88. Letter, Burbure, May 5, 1969. FCDG AE4 (5).
89. Letter, Paris, April 24, 1969. FCDG AE3/5.
90. Letter, Paris, Versailles, May 2, 1969. FCDG AE3/6.
91. Letter, Paris, April 28, 1969. FCDG AE3/6.
92. Letter, Bourg-en-Bresse, April 28, 1969. FCDG AE3/8.
93. Letter, Vaison-la-Romaine, April 28, 1969. FCDG AE4 (5).
94. Letter, Paris, April 28, 1969. FCDG AE3/6.
95. Letter, La Teste, May 3, 1969. FCDG AE3/5.
96. Letter, Vanves, April 30, 1969. FCDG AE4 (5).
97. Jean Daniel, "L'habit de lumière," *Le Nouvel Observateur*, November 16, 1970.
98. Michel Cazenave, "Le roi et le héros. Fragment pour une mythanalyse future du général de Gaulle," *Cadmos* (Spring/Summer 1982), p. 61.
99. See Evelyne Cohen and André Rauch, "Le corps souverain sous la Cinquième République. Les funérailles télévisées du général de Gaulle et de François Mitterrand," *Vingtième Siècle* 88 (October–December 2005).
100. Julien Roux-Champion, *Colombey Novembre 1970* (Paris: Editions Le Serpentaire, 1970).
101. The collection includes 340 bound volumes from France and abroad, received by the Institut de Gaulle in the months following the death of the General.
102. She was born on December 29, 1869. FCDG AG77 Nièvre (Nevers).
103. FCDG AG1 Basses-Alpes (Castellane).
104. "You will live forever." FCDG AG5 and AG6 Bouches-du-Rhône (Aix-en-Provence et Marseille).
105. FCDG register of FFL veterans, Douai. AG79 Nord (Douai).
106. FCDG AG13 Corrèze (Brive).
107. FCDG AG137 Seine-Maritime (Rouen).
108. Ibid.
109. For example, FCDG AG29 Marne (Châlons-sur-Marne).
110. Ibid.
111. FCDG AG137 Seine-Maritime (Rouen).
112. FCDG AG1 Aisne (Laon).
113. FCDG AG37 (Seine-Maritime).
114. FCDG AG3 Alpes-Maritimes (Menton).
115. FCDG AG44 Vienne (Lussac les Chateaux).
116. *Le Barde, Son fabuleux destin* (Paris: Grassin, 1970).
117. FCDG AG44 Vienne (Loudun).
118. FCDG AG14 Côtes-du-Nord (Pléneuf).
119. FCDG AG1 Basses-Alpes (Castellane).
120. FCDG AG14 Corse (Ajaccio) and AG14 Côte d'Or (Beaune).
121. Message of a former soldier who had served in Chad, the French Congo, and Gabon between 1945 and 1952. FCDG AG1 Aisne (Laon).

122. FCDG AG5 Bouches-du-Rhône (Aix-en-Provence).

123. Ibid.

124. FCDG AG79 Nord (Douai).

125. FCDG AG3 Alpes-Maritimes (Menton).

126. Message of the PCF branch, Les Mées. FCDG AG1 Alpes/Provence (Les Mées).

127. FCDG AG13 Corrèze (Tulle).

128. FCDG AG8 Bouches-du-Rhône (Saint-Cannat).

129. FCDG AG3 Alpes-Maritimes (Menton).

130. FCDG AG6 Bouches-du-Rhône (Marseille).

131. FCDG AG8 Bouches-du-Rhône (Salon-de-Provence).

132. FCDG AG137 Seine-Maritime (Rouen).

133. FCDG AG5 Bouches-du-Rhône (Aubagne).

134. FCDG AG37 Seine-Maritime.

135. FCDG AG44 Vienne (Loudun).

136. FCDG AG6 Bouches-du-Rhône (Marseille).

137. FCDG AG137 Seine-Maritime (Rouen).

138. Ibid.

139. FCDG AG5 Bouches-du-Rhône (Aubagne); AG1 Aisne (Laon); AG44 Vienne (Lavoux).

140. FCDG AG14 Corse (Ajaccio).

141. FCDG AG29 Marne (Châlons-sur-Marne).

142. FCDG AG13 Corrèze (Brive).

143. Ibid.

144. FCDG AG3 Alpes-Maritimes (Menton).

145. FCDG AG137 Seine-Maritime (Rouen).

146. Letter, Saint-Denis (La Réunion), April 28, 1969. FCDG AE4 (5).

147. "Sortir de l'Histoire," Saint-Germain, June 4, 1969. FCDG AE4 (6).

148. Letter, Saumont, May 2, 1969. FCDG AE3/8.

149. Letter, Villers-Ecalles, April 28, 1969. AE3/8.

150. Letter to General de Gaulle, April 28, 1969. FCDG AE3/5.

151. Ibid.

152. Letter, May 2, 1969. FCDG AE3/7.

153. Letter from B. Ducamin (member of General de Gaulle's secretariat) to Michel Jobert (principal private secretary to the prime minister), Paris, July 1967. AN 5AG1 (91).

154. Note from the General's office, Paris, December 1967. AN 5AG1 (91).

155. The prince wished his name to appear directly after the prime minister's and before those of all the other ministers, which was not the protocol. De Gaulle decided in the end that the list of members of the Committee would not be made public. Internal memo of the General's office, January 1969. AN 5AG1 (91).

156. Letter from General de Gaulle, Paris, February 18, 1969. AN 5AG1 (91).

157. Memo of the General's office, January 1969. AN 5AG1 (91).

158. Malraux, *Les chênes qu'on abat,* p. 40.

159. See, for example, FCDG AG44 Vienne (Lencloitre).

160. FCDG AG1 Aisne (Pinon).

161. FCDG AG14 Corse (Ajaccio).

162. FCDG AG5 Bouches-du-Rhône (Allauch).

163. FCDG AG77 Nièvre (Nevers).

164. FCDG AG29 Marne (Châlons-sur-Marne).

165. FCDG AG77 Nièvre (Nevers).

166. FCDG AG5 Bouches-du-Rhône (Aubagne).

167. FCDG AG38 Seine-Maritime (Saint-Valéry-en-Caux).

CHAPTER 6

1. Paris, December 1970. Archives du Cabinet du préfet de la Haute-Marne, Archives Départementales de la Haute-Marne (ADHM) 1524 W11.
2. de Gaulle, *Mémoires de guerre*, pp. 884–886.
3. Malraux, *Les chênes qu'on abat*, p. 129.
4. See Sébastien Danchin and François Jenny, *De Gaulle à Colombey. Refuge d'un romantique* (Nancy: Presses Universitaires de Nancy, 1990). See also Michel Cazenave, *De Gaulle et la terre de France* (Paris: Plon, 1988).
5. Dufour, "Colombey et le gaullisme," p. 371.
6. Jacques Soustelle, *Vingt-huit ans de gaullisme* (Paris: Editions J'ai Lu, 1971), p. 45.
7. Jean Mauriac, "Le Général de Gaulle et Colombey-les-Deux-Eglises," in Charles de Gaulle, *1890–1970, Comité national du mémorial du général de Gaulle* (Paris: Imprimerie Nationale, 1973), pp. 41–53.
8. See Jean-Paul Ollivier, *De Gaulle à Colombey* (Paris: Plon, 1998).
9. Telegrams from the Renseignements Généraux, May 20, 21, and 22, 1958. ADHM 819 W26357 (surveillance de La Boisserie).
10. Information provided by Professor Alain Corbin.
11. Memo of the Office of the President, May 24, 1961. ADHM 1524 W11 (protection de La Boisserie). The batteries were installed, but de Gaulle discovered them when walking in the forest of the Dhuits and had them removed. See Tessier, *J'étais le gorille du Général*, p. 101.
12. Letter, Saint-Cloud, September 1, 1969. FCDG AE4 (5).
13. Story told by de Gaulle to Alain Peyrefitte, *C'était de Gaulle* (DVD).
14. "Madame de Gaulle sort de sa solitude," *Le Californien*, January 12, 1973.
15. This material is partly in the archives of the Mémorial de Colombey (Series J) and partly in two collections of press cuttings. The first, which consists of about fifty boxes (Series I), was collected and kept updated by Mme Louise de Béa (1911–1999), who worked at the Institut Charles de Gaulle. She was a Free French veteran and edited the journal *France Libre*. Since her death, her work had been carried on by Monsieur Martial Gout, the concierge of the Charles de Gaulle Foundation, who was kind enough to let me draw on his material, for which I am extremely grateful.
16. She was born with Down syndrome and died in 1948 at the age of twenty.
17. Jacques Foccart, "Dans les bottes du Général," *Journal de l'Elysée* III, 1969–1971 (Paris: Fayard/Jeune-Afrique, 1999), pp. 754–755.
18. The archives of the Préfecture de Police (APP) hold an extremely interesting dossier on this affair. My thanks are due to Monsieur Olivier Accarie, archivist at the APP, who pointed it out to me and allowed me to consult it.
19. *L'Aurore*, December 2, 1970.
20. Philippe Nivet, "L'attribution contestée du nom 'Charles-de-Gaulle' à la Place de l'Etoile, à Paris," in *Les voies "De Gaulle" en France*, p. 91.
21. Police report, Paris, December 15, 1970. APP, dossier "Place de l'Etoile."
22. Police report, Paris, December 19, 1970. APP, dossier "Place de l'Etoile."
23. See, for example, *L'Aurore*, December 16, 1970.
24. Based on the second floor of 5 rue de Solférino, this movement had about 15,000 members at the end of 1971; it was a continuation of the earlier association of supporters of General de Gaulle. See Patrice Desaubliaux, "Les gardiens de la fidélité," *Le Figaro*, January 31, 1972.
25. *L'Echo Municipal d'Epinay-sur-Orge*, June 1975.
26. "Pèlerinage à Colombey," *Le Déporté*, October 1971.
27. On the national and departmental organization of the Committee, see the circular of the Ministre des Anciens Combattants to all prefects, Paris, June 15, 1971. FCDG Archives du Mémorial de Colombey, Série J (box 1).

28. Communiqué of Henri Duvillard, Ministre des Anciens Combattants, Paris, June 18, 1971. ADHM 1524 W2.

29. Minutes of the meeting of the Presidents of the Departmental Committees, Paris, September 30, 1971. ADHM 1524 W2.

30. Gaston Palewski, Claude Hettier de Boislambert, Pierre Lefranc, Gaston de Bonneval, Geoffroy de Courcel.

31. Memo to the architects, Cabinet du Ministre des Anciens Combattants, Paris, June 21, 1971. FCDG Archives du Mémorial de Colombey, Série J (box 1).

32. Letter from the prefect of the Haute-Marne to the Ministre des Anciens Combattants, Chaumont, June 1971. ADHM 1524 W2.

33. The architect was chosen through a national competition. Letter from Nebinger to the Ministre des Anciens Combattants, Boulogne, November 22, 1971. FCDG Archives du Mémorial de Colombey, Série J (box 1).

34. Marc Nebinger and Michel Mosser, "Mémorial du Général de Gaulle: note sur le mode de construction de la Croix de Lorraine." ADHM 1524 W2.

35. "In the end, 900 million old francs. That's not bad, and I think we can be pleased and proud of ourselves." Memo of the Ministre des Anciens Combattants, Paris, August 22, 1972. FCDG Archives du Mémorial de Colombey, Série J (box 1).

36. Report of the Renseignements Généraux, 19 juin 1972. ADHM 1524 W7 (Inauguration of the Mémorial du Général de Gaulle, 1972).

37. Lefranc, *Gouverner selon de Gaulle*, p. 35.

38. Jacques Foccart, *Journal de l'Elysée IV, La France Pompidolienne, 1971–1972* (Paris: Fayard/ Jeune Afrique, 2000), p. 388.

39. *Valeurs Actuelles*, June 22, 1972.

40. Entry for June 12, 1972. Jean Mauriac, *L'après de Gaulle*, p. 88.

41. Minutes of the meeting of the presidents of the Departmental Committees, Paris, September 30, 1971. ADHM 1524 W2.

42. Account of money raised by the Departmental Committees, end of July 1972. FCDG Archives du Mémorial de Colombey, Série J (box 1).

43. *L'Est Républicain*, November 6, 1971. One month later—on November 9—Jeanneney resigned from the UDR. See Jean-Marcel Jeanneney, *A mes amis gaullistes* (Paris: Presses-Pocket, 1973), p. 19.

44. Minutes of the extraordinary meeting of the Conseil Général de la Haute-Marne, May 10, 1971. ADHM 1524 W2.

45. Letter dated April 5, 1971. FCDG Archives du Mémorial de Colombey, Série J (box 1).

46. "La Boisserie ouverte au public le 9 novembre," *L'Union*, October 3, 1979.

47. Quoted in F. Mauerhan, "La Boisserie a reçu ses premiers visiteurs," *L'Est Républicain*, December 18, 1979.

48. They were regarded in this light in the official accounts of the memorial. See "Nombre de pèlerins au Mémorial 1972–79." FCDG Archives du Mémorial de Colombey, Série J (box 6).

49. Jacques Marion, "Colombey, dix ans après," *La Croix*, November 7, 1980.

50. "Nombre de pèlerins au Mémorial 1972–79." FCDG Archives du Mémorial de Colombey, Série J (box 6).

51. *L'Union*, August 31, 1976.

52. Interview with Christian Paul, *L'Est Républicain*, January 6, 1983.

53. "Les gaullistes lorrains à pied de Nancy à Colombey-les-Deux-Eglises," *L'Est Républicain*, November 11, 1974.

54. André Frossard, "Pèlerinage," *Le Figaro*, November 10, 1975.

55. "Mireille Mathieu a chanté à La Boisserie," *La Haute-Marne Libérée*, October 19, 1990.

56. "Massu est arrivé à cheval à Colombey," *L'Espoir*, June 24, 1971.

57. Reports of the prefecture of police, Paris, and of the R.G., Chaumont, June 1972. ADHM 1524 W7 Inauguration du Mémorial du GDG (1972).

58. "Norodom Sihanouk en pèlerinage à Colombey," *Est Éclair*, March 31, 1980.

59. "Les Médaillés de la Résistance en pèlerinage à Colombey," *Essonne Matin*, November 14, 1979.

60. Press release of the Grenoble branch of the Association Nationale d'Action pour la Fidélité au Général de Gaulle, Le Dauphiné Libéré, November 3, 1979.

61. Déclaration reprise dans l'Union, November 15, 1979.

62. Chirac would only achieve this objective in 1995. On the politics of neo-Gaullism, see Andrew Knapp, *Le gaullisme après de Gaulle* (Paris: Seuil, 1997).

63. For example, on the 18th of June 1977. See *Voix du Nord*, June 20, 1977.

64. *Le Midi Libre*, June 19, 1978.

65. *La Haute-Marne Libérée*, November 10, 1977.

66. *VSD*, September 4, 1980.

67. *Le Journal du Dimanche*, November 10, 1975.

68. Chirac, *Chaque pas doit être un but*, p. 205.

69. *VSD*, December 21, 1978.

70. Some twenty former ministers of General de Gaulle walked in the procession, but neither Jacques Chaban-Delmas nor Michel Debré was present. *Le Midi Libre*, June 16, 1980.

71. See various reports of the gendarmerie, November and December 1970. ADHM 1524 W11.

72. *Le Parisien Libéré*, June 17, 1977.

73. "Vous, vos vacances et les souvenirs du Général," *Paris-Match*, June 1972.

74. Ibid.

75. Ibid.

76. Quoted by Jean Mauriac, to whom it was sent, entry for January 5, 1973. *L'après de Gaulle*, p. 102.

77. This place was set aside for visitors to leave flowers; no wreath was to be laid on the General's grave.

78. *La Liberté de l'Est*, November 10, 1975.

79. Ibid.

80. She stayed for week at the Hôtel des Dhuits before returning to Bordeaux with the same taxi driver, who had waited for her; no doubt it was the journey of her life. Information from M. Richard Dobros, Chaumont, a former ancien gendarme who did several tours of duty at Colombey between 1974 and 1977.

81. *La Haute-Marne Libérée*, January 6, 1983.

82. *La Haute-Marne Libérée*, July 20, 1980.

83. "Les graviers de la Boisserie pillés," *Le Meilleur*, July 4, 1980.

84. Letter from the prefect of the Haute-Marne to the military governor of Metz, Chaumont, January 12, 1980. ADHM 1524 W8.

85. Memo from the préfecture, Chaumont, June 16, 1972. ADHM 1524 W7.

86. *Ici-Paris*, November 1976.

87. Article by François Luizet, *Le Figaro*, November 9, 1984.

88. Telegram from the gendarmerie, Chaumont, June 16, 1985. ADHM 1524 W3.

89. J.-M. Théolleyre, "La tanière du Général," *Le Monde*, November 21–22, 1982.

90. Michel Cordier, "La Boisserie," *Le Guide Pratique de l'Habitat en Lorraine* (Alsace: Vosges, 1980).

91. *La Haute-Marne Libérée*, November 10, 1988.

92. Reports of the gendarmerie on visitors to Colombey (1978–1991). ADHM 1524 W3.

93. "Pèlerinage à Colombey," *Le Monde*, February 15, 1988.

94. *L'Aurore*, November 10, 1989.

95. "Les parlementaires RPR à Colombey: De Gaulle nous a appris l'opposition," *Le Quotidien de Paris*, November 16, 1982.
96. Françoise Berger, "Un train de pèlerins pour Colombey," *Libération*, November 21, 1986.
97. See, for example, "Le seizième anniversaire," *Sud-Ouest*, November 10, 1986.
98. "Visite surprise de M. Toubon à Colombey-les-deux-Eglises," *La Haute-Marne Libérée*, December 9, 1985.
99. François Luizet, *Le Figaro*, November 9, 1984.
100. "Show Tour de France à Colombey-les-Deux-Eglises," *La Haute-Marne Libérée*, July 8, 1987.
101. *Le Figaro*, July 6, 1987.
102. As Edouard Balladur, his prime minister from 1993 to 1995, explains: "Mitterrand often spoke of de Gaulle with jealousy, even spitefully, criticising his role and his achievements, and even sometimes indecently refusing to mention them at all, as in the speech he gave in Normandy in 1994 on the 40th anniversary of D-Day." Edouard Balladur, *Le pouvoir ne se partage pas. Conversations avec François Mitterrand* (Paris: Fayard, 2009), p. 51.
103. Jean-Michel Royer, "Colombey Bis," *Les Dépêches de Dijon*, July 14, 1986.
104. Jacques Julliard, "De de Gaulle à Mitterrand," in *La mort du roi. Essai d'ethnographie politique comparée*, ed. J. Julliard (Paris: Gallimard, 1999), p. 34.
105. "Sur la tombe du Général: une gerbe de trop," *La Haute-Marne Libérée*, November 12, 1981. Because in France the president is always right, the gendarmes put Mitterrand's wreath back on the General's grave after the Companions had left.
106. "M. Mitterrand à Colombey?" *La Haute-Marne Libérée*, November 1, 1982.
107. Press release from the Institut Charles de Gaulle to the AFP, Paris, November 2, 1982.
108. "Pas de rue Mitterrand à Colombey!" *Le Figaro*, January 16, 1996.
109. "Le jour où Mitterrand et Chirac ont refusé de se serrer la main," *Paris-Match*, July 4, 1986.
110. Apart from extreme right-wing titles like Minute or Rivarol, or satirical papers like *Le Canard Enchaîné* or *Charlie Hebdo*, which took over from Hara Kiri.
111. Gendarmerie report, Colombey-les-deux-Eglises, November 20, 1979. ADHM 1524 W8.
112. Eric Favereau, "Le suicidé et la folle de Colombey," *Libération*, November 5, 1981.
113. Philippe Nourry, "De Gaulle intime," *Le Figaro*, November 5, 1981.
114. Michel Droit, "De Gaulle, chez lui à la Boisserie," *L'Aurore*, November 3, 1981.
115. "Philippe de Gaulle raconte Colombey," *La Haute-Marne Libérée*, November 18–20, 1981.
116. "A la place de Mitterrand mon père serait déjà parti." Interview with Philippe de Gaulle by Jean-Louis Remilleux, *Le Figaro-Magazine*, April 20, 1985.
117. *Le Canard Enchaîné*, April 24, 1985. "Sosthène" was the Admiral's nickname.
118. "Le sort de la Boisserie," *Le Figaro-Magazine*, May 11, 1985. This last idea was taken up again by minister of culture Jack Lang, but the Admiral rejected it out of hand.
119. *Les Dernières Nouvelles d'Alsace*, April 23, 1985.
120. Alain de Boissieu, *Pour servir le Général* (Paris: Plon 1982), p. 199. These studies of the General as a private man had begun to appear in the late 1970s. See in particular Jean d'Escrienne, *De Gaulle de loin de près*; François Flohic, *Souvenirs d'Outre-Gaulle*; and Bernard Marin, *De Gaulle de ma jeunesse* (Paris: Le Cercle-d'Or, 1984).
121. Robert Lassus, *Le mari de Madame de Gaulle* (Paris: JC Lattès, 1990).
122. Francine Tinguely, *La vie d'Honorine, du couvent jusqu'aux cuisines du Général* (Genève: Editions de l'Hèbe, 1997).
123. For the thirtieth anniversary of the Fifth Republic, the Bank of France struck a one-franc piece with de Gaulle's portrait. See *Le Dauphiné Libéré*, October 24, 1988.
124. "RMC: le Général embrigadé dans la publicité," *Le Figaro*, October 7, 1985.
125. Luc Bernard, "Citroën reconstitue l'attentat du Petit-Clamart," *L'Evènement du Jeudi*, January 11–17, 1996. In September 2009, for Citroën's ninetieth anniversary, another advertisement showed de Gaulle approaching a microphone, raising his arms in his usual greeting, before crying out "I want a DS!"

126. Yannick Delneste, "La passion du Général," *Nord Littoral*, June 2, 1995.
127. "Alain Gournac: une bibliothèque de 574 titres," *Le Figaro*, September 30, 1999. The present figure, supplied by the senator's parliamentary office, has reached 715.
128. Association Ecouen Reconnaissant à Charles de Gaulle. Président M. Jacques Chemeton, 4 rue Victor Hugo, 95440 Ecouen.
129. "Barre: les souvenirs de De Gaulle seront sauvegardés," *Le Figaro*, April 24, 1979.
130. "Même dactylographié, de Gaulle a toujours la côte," *France-Soir*, November 24, 1984.
131. *Le Figaro*, June 19, 1986.
132. "De Gaulle, homme de lettres, fait du chiffre," *France-Soir*, October 10, 1987.
133. Stéphane Gaillet, "La 15 CV Citroën de Charles de Gaulle a pris place près du Mémorial," *L'Union*, June 14, 1982.
134. "La traction du Général de Gaulle exposée au Mémorial," *La Haute-Marne Libérée*, June 13, 1982.
135. "La voiture de l'attentat du Petit-Clamart est entrée au musée de Gaulle à Lille," *La Voix du Nord*, December 29, 1982.
136. "De Gaulle y a dormi: c'est le berceau de la Ve République," *France-Soir*, March 2, 1983.
137. "On a volé l'acte de naissance du Général de Gaulle," *La Haute-Marne Libérée*, October 27, 1989.
138. Philippe Le Guillou, *Stèles à de Gaulle* (Paris: Gallimard, 2000), p. 48.
139. "Conclusion en forme d'appel," in Henri de Miscault, *De la Boissière à la Boisserie: suivre la Croix de Lorraine* (Nancy: Imprimerie J. Rubrecht, 1988), p. 8.
140. Caroline Tossan, "Colombey conseille Jarnac," *VSD*, February 11, 1996.
141. Article by Sébastien Le Fol, *Le Figaro*, September 30, 1999. The average number of annual visitors for the years 2000 to 2008 was similar (40,000); after the opening of the new Colombey educational museum, the number rose to 60,000 in 2009. My thanks to Madame Aurore Jacquinot, the manager of the La Boisserie site, for kindly supplying these figures.
142. http://www.memorial-charlesdegaulle.fr/
143. Olivier Biffaud, "L'hommage de la France chiraquienne au général de Gaulle," *Le Monde*, November 11, 1995.
144. Bruno Seznec, "L'amiral de Gaulle ne veut plus de pèlerinage," *Le Parisien*, October 31, 1999.
145. Maurice Agulhon, "Colombey-les-Deux-Eglises," *Dictionnaire de Gaulle*, pp. 232–233.
146. Simone Hoffmane, "Au Mémorial Charles de Gaulle, poème à l'occasion du 40e anniversaire de l'appel du 18 Juin," *Etudes Gaulliennes*, June 30, 1980, p. 137.
147. Speech by Nicolas Sarkozy, Colombey-les-Deux-Eglises, October 11, 2008.

CHAPTER 7

1. *La Voix du Nord*, September 12, 1995.
2. *Le Figaro*, June 24, 1993.
3. The two monuments were the work of the same sculptor, Jean Cardot.
4. One may reasonably wonder whether the General would have approved of this proximity with his old English colleague and rival. In the cabinet meeting of November 23, 1966, when Couve de Murville announced that de Gaulle would have "the honour" of inaugurating the new Avenue Winston Churchill, the General had seemed "frankly grumpy" and had even criticized the "bad habit [. . .] of naming Paris streets after foreigners." Quoted in Peyrefitte, *C'était de Gaulle*, p. 1253.
5. See Charlot, *Les Français et de Gaulle*.
6. *Le Journal du Dimanche*, October 16, 1988.

7. *Le Monde,* November 9, 1990.
8. The difference between the positive and negative ratings.
9. *Le Monde,* November 9, 1990.
10. More generally on this question, see François Broche, *Histoire de l'anti-gaullisme* (Paris: Bartillat, 2007).
11. For more detailed surveys, see the collection of surveys conducted for the November 1990 colloquium at UNESCO and then published in one volume by the Institut Charles de Gaulle, *De Gaulle en son siècle, Sondages et enquêtes d'opinion* (Paris: 1992).
12. Established by the Charles de Gaulle Foundation after inquiries made from the French postal service, the figures are the following: Leclerc thoroughfares, 2,075 communes; Jaurès, 2,046; Clemenceau, 1,095; Gambetta, 1,284; Jeanne d'Arc, 1,802; Jean Moulin, 1,965. *Les voies "de Gaulle" en France,* p. 238.
13. For more details, see Philippe Oulmont, "L'hommage municipal: continuités et fluctuations, 1940–2007," *Les voies "de Gaulle" en France,* pp. 21–45.
14. Extract from the minutes book of the commune of Vendenheim, November 17, 1970. FCDG, Fonds voies de Gaulle, 67 (Bas-Rhin).
15. Extract from the minutes book of the town council of Colmar, December 7, 1970. FCDG, Fonds voies de Gaulle, 68 (Haut-Rhin).
16. Extract from the minutes book of the commune of Altkirch, January 18, 1971. FCDG, Fonds voies de Gaulle, 68 (Haut-Rhin).
17. Extraordinary meeting of the town council of Bischwiller, November 11, 1970. FCDG, Fonds voies de Gaulle, 67 (Bas-Rhin).
18. Memo of the mayor of Ribeauvillé, February 2, 1972. FCDG, Fonds voies de Gaulle, 68 (Haut-Rhin).
19. Report on the 14th of July celebrations and the inauguration of the Place du Général de Gaulle, Ammerschwihr, July 15, 1971. FCDG, Fonds voies de Gaulle, 68 (Haut-Rhin).
20. Letter from Jean-Marie Fritsch, mayor of Ammerschwihr, to the Fondation Charles de Gaulle, April 19, 2006.
21. Extract from the minutes book of the town council of Auch, May 4, 1990. FCDG, Fonds voies de Gaulle, 32 (Gers).
22. Extract from the minutes book of the city council of Rennes, November 27, 1990. FCDG, Fonds voies de Gaulle, 35 (Ille et Vilaine).
23. Information supplied by the town hall of Le Bouscat in 2003. FCDG, Fonds voies de Gaulle, 33 (Gironde).
24. Note from Henri Duvillard, president of the Commission du Mémorial, June 1980. FCDG, Série J, (box 1) (construction du Mémorial).
25. Letter from the Nîmes committee of the ANACR to the mayor of Nîmes, October 16, 1979. FCDG, Fonds voies de Gaulle, 30 (Gard).
26. Contribution by M. Codvelle, recorded in the minutes of the council of Bron, June 28, 1990. FCDG, Fonds voies de Gaulle, 69 (Rhône).
27. FCDG, Fonds voies de Gaulle, 30 (Gard).
28. Quoted by Oulmont, "L'hommage municipal: continuité et fluctuations, 1940–2007," *Les voies "de Gaulle" en France,* p. 44.
29. Louis Aragon, *Le Général de division* (Paris: Editions du Nouveau Clarté, 1968).
30. Speech by Marcel Houël, Communist deputy mayor of Vénissieux, November 17, 1979. *Le Progrès,* December 1979.
31. Inauguration of new street names, Place de la Nation, Vaulx en Velin, January 28, 1978. FCDG, Fonds voies de Gaulle, 69 (Rhône).
32. Marie-Claire Lavabre, "Mémoire, souvenirs et images de De Gaulle chez les militants communistes," in *50 ans d'une passion française,* p. 225.
33. La vie municipale (Grigny), June 1979. FCDG, Fonds voies de Gaulle, 69 (Rhône).

34. Cartoon in *L'Express*, May 22, 1979, reproduced in Mitelberg, *De Gaulle de France* (Paris: Olivier Orban, 1990).

35. "Pétain: commémoration place de Gaulle," *Le Figaro*, June 18, 1990.

36. "Anniversaire du 18 Juin: commémoration mitigée," *L'Echo du Centre*, June 19, 1990.

37. "Vols de plaques de l'Appel du 18 juin," *Le Figaro*, June 18, 1991.

38. "18 Juin à côté de la plaque," *Var Matin*, June 20, 1990.

39. *Le Figaro*, January 1, 1990.

40. *Le Figaro*, April 27, 1991.

41. *Le Quotidien de Paris*, June 19, 1990. Prime Minister Michel Rocard did not agree to make the 18th of June a bank holiday, despite Jacques Chirac's request based on a unanimous motion passed by the Paris city council. See *L'Aurore*, March 17, 1990.

42. "Un mémorial pour le centenaire du Général de Gaulle," *Le Figaro*, November 23, 1990.

43. Philippe Séguin, *Louis Napoléon le Grand* (Paris: Grasset, 1990), pp. 63–67.

44. "Hommage à de Gaulle," *VSD*, June 14, 1990.

45. *Le Quotidien de Paris*, September 22, 1990.

46. *La Haute-Marne Libérée*, November 12, 1990.

47. "Oudot et le Grand Charles," *L'Alsace*, June 12, 1990.

48. *La Haute-Marne Libérée*, November 10, 1990.

49. *Vie de Biarritz*, June 1990; *Nice-Matin*, October 30, 1990.

50. "Le Général en mosaïque," *L'Est Républicain*, May 26, 1990.

51. *L'Est Républicain*, June 3, 1990.

52. *Ici Londres*, "Le rap du 18 Juin," published in Paris by Flarenasch, distributed by Carrère Music (1990).

53. *De Gaulle*, text by Jacques Marseille, illustrations by Lucien Nortier and Christian Gaty, general ed. Alain Plessis (Paris: Hachette, 1990).

54. Henri Amouroux, *De Gaulle raconté aux enfants* (Paris: Perrin, 1990).

55. *Presse Océan*, June 19, 1990.

56. "L'Année de Gaulle," *Le Courrier Picard*, May 10, 1990.

57. "De Gaulle raconté par les enfants de Colombey," *La Haute-Marne Libérée*, May 24, 1990.

58. "Plantation de l'arbre de la liberté à Monthélie," *Les Dépêches de Dijon*, March 5, 1990.

59. Claire Andrieu, "Charles de Gaulle, héritier de la Révolution française," in *De Gaulle en son siècle*, Vol. 2 (Paris: La Documentation Française/Plon, 1992), pp. 43–68.

60. (1) *Dans la mémoire des hommes et des peuples* (2) *La République* (3) *Moderniser la France* (4) *La sécurité et l'indépendance de la France* (5) *L'Europe* (6) *Liberté et dignité des peuples* (7) *De Gaulle et la culture*. As noted earlier, an eighth volume was devoted to surveys and opinion polls.

61. "Le Colonel Kadhafi décore de Gaulle," *Le Monde*, October 4, 1989.

62. *Le Figaro*, June 24, 1993.

63. *Le Figaro*, May 25, 1996.

64. "Le cadeau du général de Gaulle," *Le Monde*, October 24–25, 1993. In an interview in *Le Nouvel Observateur* (January 11, 2001), the president of the Palestinian Authority declared: "I am proud to wear this Cross of Lorraine."

65. The Institut became the Fondation Charles de Gaulle in 1990.

66. Pierre Lefranc, "Les vingt-cinq ans de l'Institut Charles-de-Gaulle," *Le Figaro*, March 19, 1996.

67. Peyrefitte, *C'etait de Gaulle*, published by Fallois/Fayard; Gallimard published a single-volume edition in 2002, which we have used here.

68. Peyrefitte, *C'était de Gaulle*, pp. 190–191.

69. Ibid., pp. 55, 1237–1244.

70. Ibid., p. 1140.

71. Ibid., p. 1693.

72. Ibid., p. 68.

73. Ibid., pp. 68, 1057.

74. Ibid., p. 40.

75. Ibid., pp. 61, 175, 307.

76. Ibid., p. 131.

77. Ibid., p. 117.

78. Ibid., p. 1828.

79. This monarchical interpretation is also used by Fabrice Bouthillon, "Les schèmes qu'on abat. A propos du gaullisme, I," *Commentaire* 63 (Autumn 1993), pp. 467–475.

80. Fernand Grenier, "1943: ma rencontre avec lui," *La Marseillaise,* June 18, 1990.

81. Jean Lacouture, "Où j'en suis avec de Gaulle," *De Gaulle en son siècle,* Vol. I, p. 511.

82. Alain Krivine, "Où j'en suis avec de Gaulle," *De Gaulle en son siècle,* Vol. I, p. 505.

83. Michel Winock, "Où j'en suis avec de Gaulle," *De Gaulle en son siècle,* Vol. I, p. 523.

84. Claude Bourdet, *L'aventure incertaine: De la Résistance à la Restauration* (Paris: Stock, 1975), p. 427.

85. Bourdet, "Où j'en suis avec de Gaulle," pp. 486–487.

86. Winock, "Où j'en suis avec de Gaulle," p. 523.

87. See chapter 3.

88. François Mitterrand, *Le coup d'état permanent* (Paris: Presses de la Cité, 1993).

89. Pierre de Boisdeffre, *Le lion et le renard. De Gaulle-Mitterrand* (Paris: Editions du Rocher, 1998), p. 240.

90. Frédéric Mitterrand, *Les années de Gaulle* (Paris: Edition No.1, 1995).

91. Jean Daniel, *Les religions d'un président* (Paris: Grasset, 1988), p. 168.

92. Henri Lerner, *De Gaulle et la gauche* (Limonest: Editions de l'Interdisciplinaire, 1994), pp. 249–261.

93. Alain Duhamel, *De Gaulle-Mitterrand. La marque et la trace* (Paris: Flammarion, 1991), p. 232.

94. Pierre Péan, *Une jeunesse française* (Paris: Fayard, 1994).

95. Patrick Jarreau, "La gauche désorientée," *Le Monde,* September 14, 1994.

96. André Glucksmann, *De Gaulle où es-tu?* (Paris: Jean-Claude Lattès, 1995), p. 203.

97. Régis Debray, *A demain de Gaulle* (Paris: Gallimard, 1990).

98. Ibid., p. 26.

99. Ibid., p. 87.

100. Ibid., p. 139.

101. Ibid., pp. 36–37.

102. Ibid., p. 75.

103. Ibid., p. 84.

104. Ibid., p. 16.

105. Ibid., pp. 88–89.

106. Ibid., pp. 123–125.

107. Ibid., p. 126.

108. Régis Debray, *Loués soient nos seigneurs. Une éducation politique* (Paris: Gallimard, 1996), p. 326.

109. Chevènement left the Socialist Party to found the Mouvement des Citoyens in 1993.

110. See particularly Jean-Pierre Chevènement, *Le courage de décider* (Paris: Robert Laffont, 2002). He dismisses the claims of both Lionel Jospin and Jacques Chirac and praises the "immense contribution" made by General de Gaulle.

111. For more details, see Lefranc, *Avec de Gaulle,* pp. 288–289.

112. Max Gallo, *De Gaulle,* 4 vols. (Paris: Robert Laffont, 1998). Volume titles are (1) *L'Appel du destin,* (2) *La solitude du combattant,* (3) *Le premier des Français,* (4) *La statue du commandeur.*

113. Jacques Julliard, *La Reine du monde* (Paris: Flammarion, 2008), p. 126.

114. Agulhon, *De Gaulle.*

115. Ibid., pp. 12–13, 18.

116. Ibid., pp. 58–59.

117. Ibid., p. 143.

118. Philippe Séguin, *Discours pour la France* (Paris: Grasset, 1992).

119. Georges-Marc Benamou, *C'était un temps déraisonnable* (Paris: Laffont, 1999).

120. "Charles de Gaulle scandalise sa famille." *Le Figaro*, May 6, 1999. On the attempts made by the Front National, particularly by the FN councils of Marignane and Toulon, to claim de Gaulle for themselves at the end of the 1990s, see Jean-Marie Guillon, "De Gaulle en Provence," in *Les voies "de Gaulle" en France*, p. 132.

121. Marion Thébaud, "Un salle historique pour de Gaulle," *Marianne*, October 11, 1999.

122. In 2002 the RPR dissolved itself into the new party created by Jacques Chirac, the UMP. See Christine Clerc, "L'adieu sans nostalgie des gaullistes historiques," *Le Figaro*, September 21, 2002.

123. P. de Gaulle, *De Gaulle mon père*. Entretiens avec Michel Tauriac.

124. P. de Gaulle, *Mémoires accessoires*, 2 vols. (Paris: Plon, 1997/2000).

125. *L'Union*, March 5, 2005.

126. *Le Parisien*, February 28–29, 2004.

127. Angelo Rinaldi, "Sur la route nationale," *Le Figaro*, November 20, 2003.

128. Jean-Luc Barré, "De Gaulle, l'homme de personne," *Le Monde*, March 5, 2004; Laurent Greilsamer, "Un triomphe pour le Général," *Le Monde*, March 14, 2004.

129. *L'Express*, November 27, 2003.

130. Jean Daniel, "La passion du Général," *Le Nouvel Observateur*, March 11, 2004.

131. P. de Gaulle, *De Gaulle mon père*, Vol. I, p. 371.

132. P. de Gaulle, *De Gaulle mon père*, Vol. II, p. 221.

133. Philippe Alexandre, "De Gaulle: un trou dans la légende du père," *France-Soir*, March 15, 2004.

134. P. de Gaulle, *De Gaulle mon père*, Vol. I, pp. 445–446.

135. Ibid., p. 295.

136. Ibid., pp. 550–552.

137. See, for example, Vol. I, p. 493; Vol. II, p. 222.

138. P. de Gaulle, *De Gaulle mon père*, Vol. II, pp. 407–408.

139. P. de Gaulle, *De Gaulle mon père*, Vol. I, p. 393.

140. Ibid., p. 398.

141. Ibid., p. 401.

142. P. de Gaulle, *De Gaulle mon père*, Vol. II, p. 81.

143. P. de Gaulle, *De Gaulle mon père*, Vol. I, p. 355.

144. Ibid., p. 207.

145. P. de Gaulle, *De Gaulle mon père*, Vol. II, p. 470.

146. P. de Gaulle, *De Gaulle mon père*, Vol. I, p. 212.

147. P. de Gaulle, *De Gaulle mon père*, Vol. II, p. 19.

148. P. de Gaulle, *De Gaulle mon père*, Vol. I, pp. 181–200.

149. P. de Gaulle, *De Gaulle mon père*, Vol. II, pp. 296–316.

150. P. de Gaulle, *De Gaulle mon père*, Vol. I, p. 328.

151. Ibid., p. 327.

152. P. de Gaulle, *De Gaulle mon père*, Vol. II, p. 76.

153. Stéphane Denis, "De Gaulle II," *Le Figaro Magazine*, February 28, 2004.

154. François Reynaert, "Twist à Colombey," *Le Nouvel Observateur*, March 25, 2004.

155. Jacques le Groignec, *Philippique contre des mémoires gaulliens* (Paris: Nouvelles Editions Latines, 2004).

156. Jean Mauriac, "Les erreurs de l'amiral de Gaulle," *Le Monde*, March 28, 2004.
157. Henri-Christian Giraud, *Réplique à l'amiral de Gaulle* (Paris: Editions du Rocher, 2004).
158. Jean Lacouture, "Un général bleu et blanc," *Le Débat* 134 (March–April 2005), pp. 158–166.
159. Eric Roussel, "Les étranges vérités de l'amiral de Gaulle," *Le Débat* 134 (March–April 2005), pp. 167–175.
160. Pierre Nora, "Du général à l'amiral," *Le Débat* 134 (March–April 2005), pp. 156–157.
161. Pierre Nora, "Gaullistes et communistes," in *Lieux de Memoire*, Vol. III (1), p. 362.
162. William Faulkner, *De Gaulle: Scénario* (Paris: Gallimard, 1989).
163. Pierre Champalle, "Les malheurs du Général," *Paris-Match*, November 15, 1990.
164. "La famille de Gaulle s'insurge," *Le Figaro*, February 1, 1990.
165. "Jean Moulin, une affaire française," *TF1*, January 2003; "Ils voulaient tuer de Gaulle," *TF1*, May 2005.
166. *Le Parisien*, July 1, 2005.
167. Nathalie Simon, "Bernard Farcy, un 'admirable' général de Gaulle," *Le Figaro*, May 9, 2008.
168. *Le Figaro*, October 10, 2008.
169. Hervé Bentégeat, *La fuite à Baden* (Paris: Ramsay, 2006).
170. As a politician, de Gaulle of course fascinated writers; there is a fine range of perspectives on the General in Jean-Claude Perrier, *De Gaulle vu par les écrivains* (Paris: La Table Ronde, 2000). On literary admiration for de Gaulle, see also Stéphane Giocanti, *Une histoire politique de la littérature* (Paris: Flammarion, 2009).
171. Jacques Kermoal, *Procès en canonisation de Charles de Gaulle* (Paris: Balland, 1970).
172. Maurice Cury, *De Gaulle est mort* (Paris: Editions de l'Athanor, 1975).
173. Alain Lorne, *Le petit gaulliste* (Paris: Actes Sud, 2000). We note also two novels bearing the name of the General in their titles: Gérard de Cortanze, *De Gaulle en maillot de bain* [De Gaulle in a bathing-costume] (Paris: Plon, 2007); and Robert Yessouroun, *La tondeuse du général de Gaulle* [General de Gaulle's lawn mower] (Fontaine: Editions ThoT, 2007).
174. Bernard Fauconnier, *L'Etre et le géant* (Paris: Edition des Syrtes, 2000).
175. Jean-Christophe Notin, *Nom de code La Murène* (Paris: Seuil, 2008), p. 226.
176. Daniel Picouly, *68, mon amour* (Paris: Grasset, 2008).
177. Stéphane Zagdanski, *Pauvre de Gaulle!* (Paris: Editions Pauvert, 2000).
178. Benoît Duteurtre, *Le retour du Général* (Paris: Fayard, 2010).
179. See the stimulating study by Nicolas Rouvière, *Astérix ou les lumières de la civilisation* (Paris: PUF, 2006).
180. Jean-Yves Ferri, *De Gaulle à la plage* (Paris: Dargaud, 2007), p. 22.

CONCLUSION

1. Works already in print include: Raphael Dargent, *De Gaulle: portrait en douze tableaux d'histoire de France* (Paris: Bayol, 2009); Laurent de Gaulle, *Une vie sous le regard de Dieu. La foi du Général de Gaulle* (Paris: Editions de l'Oeuvre, 2009); Henri Lerner, *De Gaulle, tel qu'en lui-même* (Paris: Editions Autres Temps, 2009); Benjamin Stora, *Le mystère de Gaulle. Son choix pour l'Algérie* (Paris: Robert Laffont, 2009); and Jean-Louis Crémieux-Brilhac, *Georges Boris, Trente ans d'influence: Blum, de Gaulle, Mendès France* (Paris: Gallimard, 2010).
2. Quoted in Lerner, *De Gaulle et la gauche*, p. 10.
3. "Les transformations du Général," in Mitelberg, *Le pouvoir civil* (Paris: Julliard, 1960).
4. A recent example was given at a roundtable discussion organized by Régis Debray in Paris in March 2010, at which Stéphane Hessel, Jean-Louis Crémieux-Brilhac, Yves Guéna, and Daniel Cordier celebrated the memory of the General. See the article by Thomas Wieder, "Les retrouvailles de la France Libre," *Le Monde*, March 19, 2010.

5. On the decline in the tradition of republican festivals after 1945, see Rémi Dalisson, *Célébrer la nation. Les fêtes nationales en France de 1789 à nos jours* (Paris: Nouveau Monde, 2009), pp. 357–468.

6. Letter to General de Gaulle, Saint-Martin du Var, undated. FCDG AE3/8.

7. Letter to General de Gaulle, Paris, April 28, 1969. FCDG AE3/8.

8. "Charles le Seul," documentary in the series *La légende du siècle*, directed by Claude Santelli and shown on French television in November 1975. Bnf NUMAV—45009.

9. Michel Tauriac, *Vivre avec de Gaulle. Les derniers témoins racontent l'homme* (Paris: Plon, 2008).

10. Robert Skidelsky, "Vladimir Putin, the New de Gaulle?" *The Guardian*, December 5, 2007.

11. Letter from Claude Caneri to General de Gaulle, Paris, April 28, 1969. FCDG AE3/5.

12. For some recent examples of this branch of literature, see particularly André Figueras, *Pétain, c'était de Gaulle!* (Paris: Editions Déterna, 2000); Claude Foussé, *L'anti-mythe. De Gaulle était-il bien la France?* (Paris: Editions du Panthéon, 2002); Guy Forzy, *ça aussi c'était de Gaulle*, 2 vols. (Issy-les-Moulineaux: Muller, 2002); Florent Gintz, *Autopsie du mythe gaulliste* (Paris: Godefroy de Bouillon, 2003); and Louis-Christian Michelet, *La légende gaullienne* (Paris: Godefroy de Bouillon, 2008).

13. "Le Général de Gaulle a trouvé sa place," *Nice-Matin*, June 19, 2011. The statue represents the General in full stride; it is the work of Jean Cardot, who created the effigies of de Gaulle and Churchill at the Champs-Elysées in Paris.

14. See particularly Pierre Maillard's editorial, "A propos de la réintégration de la France dans l'OTAN," *Espoir* 156 (March 2009), pp. 73–76.

15. François Bayrou, *Abus de pouvoir* (Paris: Plon, 2009), p. 11.

16. Girardet, *Mythes et mythologies politiques*.

17. Renault was the leading French car manufacturer who collaborated with the Germans during the occupation. "Carton Rouge au Capitalisme" [Show Capitalism the Red Card]. Leaflet by the Communists of the 12th arrondissement, Paris, April 4, 2009.

18. Michel Marcq, *Charles de Gaulle. La légende du Nord* (Paris: Renaudot, 1988).

19. *Catalogue of the Mémorial Charles de Gaulle* [Haute-Marne] (Paris: Nouveau Monde Editions, 2008).

20. Bernard Lachaise, "De Gaulle en Acquitaine, hier et aujourd'hui," in *Les voies "de Gaulle" en France*, p. 149.

21. On the cult of Mao in contemporary China, see Claude Hudelot and Guy Gallice, *Le Mao* (Paris: Editions du Rouergue, 2009).

22. David Smith, "Rise and rise of the Mandela industry," *The Guardian*, July 18, 2009.

23. It was Jacques Chirac in person who settled the choice of the Invalides in 2004 and found the extra money needed to finish the work in the last days of his second term of office in 2007. See the memoirs of the Secretary-General of the Fondation Charles de Gaulle, Jean Méo, *Une fidélité gaulliste à l'épreuve du pouvoir*, pp. 410–413.

24. Barthes, *Mythologies*, p. 202.

25. Mariot, *Bains de foule*, pp. 306–311.

26. "Le génie et le prophète: entretien avec Abel Gance," in *Charles de Gaulle*, ed. M. Cazenave and O. Germain-Thomas (Paris: Editions de l'Herne, 1973), pp. 355–356.

27. Charles de Gaulle, *Le flambeau* (Paris: Editions Plon et Saurat, 2000).

28. Mauriac, *Mort du général de Gaulle*, p. 53.

29. Peyrefitte, *C'était de Gaulle*, p. 1829.

30. Stanley Hoffmann, *De Gaulle artiste de la politique* (Paris: Seuil, 1973), p. 112.

31. Debray, *Loués soient nos seigneurs*, p. 339.

32. Joseph Kessel, *L'Armée des ombres* (Paris: Plon, 1963), p. 171.

33. Quoted in "A Mon Général: adieu, avec amour et colère" (May 1969), reprinted in Romain Gary, *Ode à l'homme qui fut la France* (Paris: Calmann-Lévy, 1997), p. 112.

34. Malraux, *Les chênes qu'on abat*, pp. 41–42.

35. Nora, "Gaullistes et communistes," p. 355.

36. Letter to General de Gaulle, May 4, 1969. FCDG AE3/5.

37. Letter to General de Gaulle, April 28, 1969. FCDG AE3/5.

38. Lefranc, *Gouverner selon de Gaulle*, pp. 152, 344.

39. Bernard-Henri Lévy, *Ce grand cadavre à la renverse* (Paris: Grasset, 2007), p. 413.

40. This must of course be kept distinct from the General's purely political inventory, which we cannot remake here.

41. Malraux, *Les chênes qu'on abat*, p. 113.

42. Pierre Nora, "Malaise dans l'identité historique," in *Liberté pour l'histoire*, ed. P. Nora and F. Chandernagor (Paris: CNRS Editions, 2008), p. 21.

43. Even though two of them, Bertie Albrecht and Simone Michel-Lévy, are among the sixteen persons buried in the crypt of the Mémorial de la France Combattante at the mont Valérien.

44. Mona Ozouf, *Composition française* (Paris: Gallimard, 2009), p. 177.

45. Letter to General de Gaulle, Marseille, April 28, 1969. FCDG AE3/8.

46. Barré, *Devenir de Gaulle*, p. 77.

47. Régis Debray, *Le moment fraternité* (Paris: Gallimard, 2009).

48. Notably on the death of Stalin in 1953. See Jean Marie Goulemot, *Pour l'amour de Staline. La face oubliée du communisme français* (Paris: CNRS Editions, 2009), pp. 167–208.

SOURCES AND BIBLIOGRAPHY

ARCHIVES OF THE CHANCELLERY OF THE ORDER OF THE LIBERATION, PARIS

Anniversary of 18th of June Series

Organization of Ceremonies: Folders for years 1945–1949, 1950–1955, 1956–1959, 1960–1961, and 1962–1968

Mont Valérien Memorial: Folder on construction and inauguration (1958–1960); correspondence for the 1960s and 1970s

ARCHIVES NATIONALES, PARIS

3 AG Series: Archives of the Provisional Government of the French Republic and Archives of General de Gaulle, 1940–1958

3 AG1 (271) Press, radio, cinema, decorations (Order of the Liberation)

3 AG4 (63) Official events 1944–1946

3 AG4 (69) Medals, investigations, and opinions

3 AG4 (70) Streets, public squares, and commemorative plaques; homages to General de Gaulle; festivals and ceremonies

5 AG Series: Archives of the Presidency of the Republic (General de Gaulle)

5 AG1 (91) Commemorations 1967–1969 (Napoleon bicentenary)

5 AG1 (94) Monuments, ceremonies, war veterans (1963–1969)

5 AG1 (286) Official visits of General de Gaulle (1959–1962)

5 AG1 (287) Official visits of General de Gaulle (1962–1969)

5 AG1 (290) War commemorations 1914–1918

5 AG1 (291) War commemorations 1939–1945

5 AG1 (308) Correspondence received from the public (1959–1961)

5 AG1 (309) Correspondence received from the public (1962–1964)

5 AG1 (310) Correspondence received from the public (1965–1969)

5 AG1 (544) Ceremony at the mémorial de la France Combattante, June 18, 1959

5 AG1 (546) Anniversary of the death of Napoleon

5 AG1 (547) Ceremony at the mémorial de la France Combattante, June 18, 1960

5 AG1 (550) Ceremony at the mémorial de la France Combattante, June 18, 1961

5 AG1 (552) Ceremony at the mémorial de la France Combattante, June 18, 1962

5 AG1 (554) Ceremony at the mémorial de la France Combattante, June 18, 1963

5 AG1 (556) Cérémonies: Twentieth anniversary of the liberations, Paris; Clemenceau monument (November 11, 1964); mémorial de la France Combattante, June 18, 1964

5 AG1 (558) Cérémonies: Twentieth anniversary of the victory in 1945; mémorial de la France Combattante, June 18, 1965

5 AG1 (559) Ceremony at the mémorial de la France Combattante, June 18, 1966

5 AG1 (561) Ceremony at the mémorial de la France Combattante, June 18, 1967

5 AG1 (563) Ceremony at the mémorial de la France Combattante, June 18, 1968
5 AG1 (564) Fiftieth anniversary of the Armistice of November 11, 1968
5 AG1 (826–832) *Mémoires de guerre*. Vol. 1 and 2: Press cuttings (1954–1958)
AJ Series: Various collections
AJ 41 Reports from organizations created after the 1940 Armistice
F1C Series: Public attitudes, elections
F1CIII (1198) Monthly prefectoral reports (1942–1944)
Mi Series: Microfilms
49 Mi 1 Jean-Louis Crémieux-Brilhac papers (1942–1944)

ARCHIVES OF THE FONDATION CHARLES DE GAULLE, PARIS
A Series: Collection of documents concerning General de Gaulle
AA Manuscripts personally annotated by de Gaulle (including a version of the *Mémoires de guerre*)
AC (1–3) Visits in France and abroad (1941–1947)
AE3 (1) Letters and poems sent to de Gaulle (1944)
AE3 (4) Letters to de Gaulle, London 1940–1942; France 1952–1957
AE3 (5–8) Letters to de Gaulle (1969)
AE4 (1–4) Letters to Madame de Gaulle after the death of General de Gaulle (1970)
AE4 (5–6) Letters to de Gaulle after the referendum (April–September 1969)
AF (1–50) Documents from the RPF years
AG (1–340) Condolence books, France and abroad (1970)
F Series: Personalities' papers
F15 papers of Julien Roux, known as Roux-Champion
F26 Roger Barberot papers
F28 Catroux-Dellschaft papers
F33 Léon Delbecque papers
F35 Jacques Narbonne papers
F36 Jean Mauriac papers
I Series: Press cuttings and documents concerning General de Gaulle and his memory, assembled by Madame Louise de Béa (1970–1999)
J Series: Archives of the Colombey Memorial
Series on "de Gaulle thoroughfares" (responses from local authorities to the questionnaire from the Foundation; filed by department)

ARCHIVES OF THE PRÉFECTURE DE POLICE, PARIS
Dossier "September 4, 1958, Place de la République"
BA Series
BA 2361 dossier "November 11, 1940." Testimony of Igor de Schotten
F/D Series: Commemorations
Folder 1 Commemoration 18 June 1945
Folder 1 (A) Commemorations 1944–1945
Folder 1 (bis) Commemoration 18 June (1944–1949)
Folder 3 Victory festivities and anniversary of 18 June 1954; laying of wreath at the Arc de Triomphe by General de Gaulle, 9 May 1954
Folder 4 Anniversary of the Liberation of Paris: Victory festival, anniversary of 18 June (1954 and 1955)
Folders 5–6 Idem (1955)
Folders 7–8 Idem (1956)
Folders 9–10 Idem (1957 and 1958)
Folders 11–12 Idem (1958, cont.)
Folder 13 Jeanne d'Arc festival, commemoration of 18 June (May–June 1959)

Folder 14 Anniversary of the Liberation of Paris (August 1959)
Folder 15 Jeanne d'Arc festival, ceremony of 8 May (1960)
Folder 16 Ceremony of 8 May (cont.), commemoration of 18 June (1960)
Folder 17 Commemoration of 18 June (cont.) (1960)
Folders 18–19 Commemoration of the Liberation of Paris
Folder 21 Ceremony of 8 May (1961)
Folder 22 Jeanne d'Arc festival (14 May), commemoration of 18 June (1961)
Folders 24–25 Commemoration of the Liberation of Paris (1961)
Folder 27 Inauguration by General de Gaulle of the crypt of the martyrs of deportation (12 April), ceremonies of 8 May (1962)
Folder 28 Commemoration of Victory, Jeanne d'Arc festival, 13 May (1962)
Folder 29 Commemoration of 18 June (1962)
Folder 31 Commemoration of the Liberation of Paris (1962)
Folder 33 Ceremony of 8 May (1963)
Folder 34 Jeanne d'Arc festival, commemoration of 18 June (1963)
Folders 36–37 Commemoration of the Liberation of Paris (1963)
Folder 39 Ceremony of 8 May, Jeanne d'Arc festival, 10 May (1964)
Folder 40 Jeanne d'Arc festival (cont.), eighth centenary of Notre Dame (1964)
Folder 41 Commemoration of 18 June (1964)
Folders 44–47 Twentieth anniversary of the Liberation of Paris
Folders 50–51 Jeanne d'Arc festival, commemoration of 8 May
Folder 52 Commemoration of 18 June (1965)
Folder 55 Photographic albums and documents, anniversary of the Liberation of Paris (August 1965)
Folder 59 Commemoration of 8 May, Jeanne d'Arc festival, commemoration of 18 June (1966)
Folders 61–63 Anniversary of the Liberation of Paris (1966)
Folder 65 Ceremony of 8 May (1967)
Folders 66 Ceremony of 8 May (cont.), Jeanne d'Arc festival, 14 May, commemoration of 18 June (1967)
Folder 70 Anniversary of the Liberation of Paris (1967)
Folder 73 Commemoration of 18 June (1968)
Folder 76 Anniversary of the Liberation of Paris (1968)
Folder 81 Ceremony of 8 May, Jeanne d'Arc festival, commemoration of 18 June (1969)
Folder 82 Commemoration of 18 June (1969) (cont.)
F/E Series: Funerals
Folder No.1 funeral of Marshal Leclerc
G/A F18 Reports of the Renseignements généraux
Jeanne d'Arc festivals, dossiers 1954–1971
World Deportation Day, dossiers 1961–1967

DÉPARTEMENTAL ARCHIVES OF THE HAUTE-MARNE, CHAUMONT

819 W 26219 Local requests to General de Gaulle (1958–1969)
819 W26357 Surveillance of la Boisserie (May 1958, January 1960, April 1961)
1090 W105 Public attendance at Colombey (1972–1978)
1382 W203 Organization of security at Colombey
1524 W2 National and departmental Committee for the Colombey Memorial (1971)
1524 W3 Public attendance at Colombey (1979–1991)
1524 W7 Inauguration of the Memorial (1972)
1524 W8 De Gaulle Memorial: maintenance of order (1970–1978)
1524 W11 Death of General de Gaulle and Madame de Gaulle (1970–1979); archives from the Office of the Prefect

NEWSPAPERS AND PERIODICALS CITED

L'Aurore
Le Berry Républicain (Bourges)
Bulletin Municipal Officiel de la Ville de Paris
Le Californien
Le Canard Enchaîné
Candide
Combat
Le Courrier (Limoges)
Le Courrier de la Colère
Le Courrier Picard (Amiens)
La Croix
Le Dauphiné Libéré
La Depêche de Constantine
Les Dépêches de Dijon
Le Déporté
Les Dernières Nouvelles d'Alsace (Strasbourg)
L'Echo du Centre (Limoges)
L'Echo Municipal d'Epinay-sur-Orge
L'Epoque
Espoir
Esprit de la Résistance
Essonne Matin
Est Éclair (Troyes)
L'Est Républicain (Nancy)
Etudes Gaulliennes
L'Evènement du Jeudi
L'Express
Le Figaro
Le Figaro-Magazine
France-Soir
La Haute-Marne Libérée (Chaumont)
L'Humanité
Ici-Paris
Le Journal du Dimanche
Libération
La Liberté de l'Est (Epinal)
Marianne
La Marseillaise
Le Midi Libre (Montpellier)
Le Monde
Nice-Matin
Nord Littoral (Calais)
Le Nouvel Observateur
Le Parisien
Le Parisien Libéré
Paris-Match
Paris-Matin
Le Point
Le Populaire
Le Quotidien de Paris

Résistance
Revue de la France Libre
Sud-Ouest (Bordeaux)
Sunday Express
L'Union (Reims)
Valeurs Actuelles
Var Matin (Toulon)
Vie de Biarritz
La vie municipale (Grigny)
La Voix du Nord (Lille)
VSD

WORKS CITED

Aglan, Alya. *Le temps de la Résistance*. Arles: Actes Sud, 2008.

Agulhon, Maurice. "De Gaulle et le souvenir de Gambetta," in *Charles de Gaulle, du militaire au politique 1920–1940*. Paris: Fondation Charles-de-Gaulle et Plon, 2004.

———. *De Gaulle: Histoire, symbole, mythe*. Paris: Plon, 2000.

———. *Les métamorphoses de Marianne*. Paris: Flammarion, 2001.

Albertelli, Sébastien. *Les services secrets du général de Gaulle. Le BCRA 1940–1944*. Paris: Perrin, 2009.

Amouroux, Henri. *De Gaulle raconté aux enfants*. Paris: Perrin, 1990.

———. *La vie des français sous l'occupation*. Paris: Fayard, 1990.

Aragon, Louis. *Le Général de division*. Paris: Editions du Nouveau Clarté, 1968.

Aron, Raymond. "L'Ombre des Bonaparte," in *Chroniques de Guerre*. Paris: Gallimard, 1990.

Arouet. *Vie et aventures du général de la Perche, d'après les documents ramenés par le suédois Syllog de son voyage en Absurdie*. Paris: 1947.

Astier de la Vigerie, Emmanuel. *Sept fois sept jours*. Paris: Gallimard, 1961.

Azéma, Jean-Pierre. *1940 l'année terrible*. Paris: Seuil, 1990.

Balladur, Edouard. *Le pouvoir ne se partage pas. Conversations avec François Mitterrand*. Paris: Fayard, 2009.

Barcellini, Serge. "Les cérémonies du novembre 11, 1945: une apothéose commémorative gaulliste," in *La France de 1945: résistances, retours, renaissances*. Caen: Presses Universitaires de Caen, 1996.

Barré, Jean-Luc. *Devenir De Gaulle*. Paris: Perrin, 2003.

Barrière, Philippe. "La Résistance sur les murs: toponymie urbaine et géographie mémorielle (Grenoble 1944–1964)," in *Résistants et résistance*, ed. J.-Y. Boursier. Paris: L'Harmattan, 1997.

Barthes, Roland. *Mythologies*. Paris: Seuil, 1970.

Baruch, Marc-Olivier. "Présents d'une commémoration: la Quatrième République face au dixième anniversaire de la Libération," in B. Garnier, J.-L. Leleu, J. Quellien, and A. Simonin (eds.), *Pourquoi Résister? Résister Pour Quoi Faire?* Caen: Université de Caen Basse-Normandie, 2006.

Baumel, Jacques. *De Gaulle, l'Exil Intérieur*. Paris: Albin Michel, 2001.

Bayrou, François. *Abus de pouvoir*. Paris: Plon 2009.

Belin, Roger. *Lorsqu'une République chasse l'autre. 1958–1962: souvenirs d'un témoin*. Paris: Editions Michalon, 1999.

Belot, Robert. *La Résistance sans de Gaulle*. Paris: Fayard, 2006.

Benamou, Georges-Marc. *C'était un temps déraisonnable*. Paris: Laffont, 1999.

Benda, Julien. *Mémoires d'infra-tombe*. Paris: Julliard, 1952.

Bentégeat, Hervé. *La fuite à Baden*. Paris: Ramsay, 2006.

Berenson, Edward, Vincent Duclert, and Christophe Prochasson (eds.). *The French Republic. History, values, debates*. Ithaca, NY: Cornell University Press, 2011.

Billotte, Pierre. *Le temps des armes*. Paris: Plon, 1972.

Blanc, Julien. *Au commencement de la Résistance. Du côté du musée de l'Homme 1940–1941*. Paris: Seuil, 2010.

Blanc, Pierre-Louis. *Charles de Gaulle au soir de sa vie*. Paris: Fayard, 1990.

Boisdeffre, Pierre de. *Le lion et le renard. De Gaulle-Mitterrand*. Paris: Editions du Rocher, 1998.

Boissieu, Alain de. *Pour servir le Général*. Paris: Plon 1982.

Bouchinet-Serreulles, Claude. *Nous étions faits pour être libres*. Paris: Grasset, 2000.

Bourdet, Claude. *L'aventure incertaine. De la Résistance à la Restauration*. Paris: Stock, 1975.

Bouthillon, Fabrice. "Les schèmes qu'on abat. A propos du gaullisme, I." *Commentaire* 63 (Autumn 1993).

Broche, François. *Histoire de l'anti-gaullisme*. Paris: Bartillat, 2007.

Bron, Ludovic. *Le Général de Gaulle, l'Homme Providentiel*. Le Puy: X. Mappus, 1945.

Brossat, Alain. *Libération, fête folle. 6 juin 44–8 mai 45: mythes et rites ou le grand théatre des passions populaires*. Paris: Editions Autrement, 1994.

Burin de Roziers, Etienne. *Le Retour aux Sources. 1962, l'année décisive*. Paris: Plon, 1986.

Cassan, Antoine. *Vivement hier. Tous ringardo-gaullistes*. Paris: JC Lattès, 1996.

Cazenave, Michel. *De Gaulle et la terre de France*. Paris: Plon, 1988.

———. "Le roi et le héros. Fragment pour une mythanalyse future du général de Gaulle." *Cadmos* (Spring/Summer 1982).

Cazenave, Michel, and O. Germain-Thomas (eds.). *Charles de Gaulle*. Paris: Editions de l'Herne, 1973.

Chaban-Delmas, Jacques. *Mémoires pour demain*. Paris: Flammarion, 1997.

Charlot, Jean. *Les Français et de Gaulle*. Paris: 1971.

———. *Le gaullisme d'opposition, 1946–1958*. Paris: Fayard, 1983.

Chateaubriand, François-René de. *Mémoires d'Outre-Tombe*. 2 vols., ed. M. Levaillant. Paris: Flammarion, 1949.

Chevènement, Jean-Pierre. *Le courage de décider*. Paris: Robert Laffont, 2002.

———. *Une certaine idée de la République*. Paris: Albin Michel, 1992.

Chirac, Jacques. *Chaque pas doit être un but. Mémoires*. Paris: NiL Editions, 2009.

Choisnel, Emmanuel. *L'Assemblée Consultative Provisoire (1943–1945). Le sursaut républicain*. Paris: L'Harmattan, 2007.

Cohen, Evelyne, and André Rauch. "Le corps souverain sous la Cinquième République. Les funérailles télévisées du général de Gaulle et de François Mitterrand." *Vingtième Siècle* 88 (October–December 2005).

Comte de Paris, and Général de Gaulle. *Dialogue sur la France, correspondance et entretiens 1953–1970*. Paris: Fayard, 1994.

Cordier, Daniel. *Alias Caracalla*. Paris: Gallimard, 2009.

Cordier, Michel "La Boisserie," in *Le Guide Pratique de l'Habitat en Lorraine*. Alsace: Vosges, 1980.

Cornil-Frerrot, Sylvain. "Le général de Larminat et l'Association des Français Libres," in *Larminat, un fidèle hors série*, ed. P. Oulmont. Paris: Fondation Charles de Gaulle et Editions LBM, 2008.

Cortanze, Gérard de. *De Gaulle en maillot de bain*. Paris: Plon, 2007.

Courtois, Stéphane. "Gaullisme et communisme: la double réponse à la crise d'identité française," in S. Courtois and M. Lazar (eds.), *50 ans d'une passion française. De Gaulle et les communistes*. Paris: Balland, 1991.

Crémieux-Brilhac, Jean-Louis. *Georges Boris, Trente ans d'influence: Blum, de Gaulle, Mendès France*. Paris: Gallimard, 2010.

———. *La France Libre*. Paris: Gallimard, 1996.

———. "La France Libre et la symbolique républicaine," in *Actes du colloque sur la symbolique républicaine* (forthcoming).

———. (ed.). *Les voix de la liberté. Ici Londres 1940–1944.* Paris: La Découverte, 1975.

Crémieux-Brilhac, Jean-Louis, with G. Bensimhon. "Les propagandes radiophoniques et l'opinion publique en France de 1940 à 1944." *Revue d'Histoire de la Deuxième Guerre Mondiale* 101 (January 1976).

Cury, Maurice. *De Gaulle est mort.* Paris: Editions de l'Athanor, 1975.

Dalisson, Rémi. *Célébrer la nation. Les fêtes nationales en France de 1789 à nos jours.* Paris: Nouveau Monde, 2009.

———. *Les fêtes du Maréchal. Propagande et imaginaire dans la France de Vichy.* Paris: Tallandier, 2007.

Danchin, Sébastien, and Jenny, François. *De Gaulle à Colombey. Refuge d'un romantique.* Nancy: Presses Universitaires de Nancy, 1990.

Daniel, Jean. *La blessure.* Paris: Grasset, 1992.

———. *Les religions d'un président.* Paris: Grasset, 1988.

Dargent, Raphael. *De Gaulle: portrait en douze tableaux d'histoire de France.* Paris: Bayol, 2009.

Debray, Régis. *A demain de Gaulle.* Paris: Gallimard, 1990.

———. *Le moment fraternité.* Paris: Gallimard, 2009.

———. *Loués soient nos seigneurs. Une éducation politique.* Paris: Gallimard, 1996.

———. "Preface," in C. de Gaulle, *Les Grands Discours de guerre. Une Anthologie.* Paris: Perrin, 2010.

Debré, Michel. *Entretiens avec le Général de Gaulle, 1961–1969.* Paris: Albin Michel, 1993.

———. *Trois Républiques pour une France: Mémoires.* 5 vols. Paris: Albin Michel, 1984–1994.

———. *Une certaine idée de la France.* Paris: Fayard, 1972.

De Gaulle. Text by Jacques Marseille, illustrations by Lucien Nortier and Christian Gaty, under the direction of Alain Plessis. Paris: Hachette, 1990.

de Gaulle, Charles. *Discours et messages.* 5 vols. Paris: Plon, 1970.

———. *Le Fil de l'épée et autres écrits.* Paris: Plon, 1990.

———. *Le flambeau.* Paris: Plon et Saurat, 2000.

———. *Lettres notes et carnets.* 13 vols. Paris: Plon, 1980–1997.

———. *Mémoires de guerre.* Paris: Plon, 1989.

———. *Mémoires d'espoir.* Paris: Plon, 1996.

———. *The Complete War Memoirs.* New York: Carroll and Graf, 1998.

De Gaulle Chef de Guerre, Actes du Colloque International organisé par la Fondation Charles de Gaulle, Octobre 2006. Paris: Plon-FCDG, 2008.

De Gaulle en son siècle, Actes du colloque international de 1990. 8 vols. Paris: La Documentation Française/Plon, 1992.

De Gaulle et la Libération. Bruxelles: Editions Complexe, 2004.

de Gaulle, Laurent. *Une vie sous le regard de Dieu. La foi du Général de Gaulle.* Paris: Editions de l'Oeuvre, 2009.

de Gaulle, Philippe. *De Gaulle Mon Père.* 2 vols. Paris: Plon, 2003/2004.

———. *Mémoires accessoires.* 2 vols. Paris: Plon, 1997/2000.

De Gaulle 300 caricatures. Nukerke, Belgium: Editions Cérès, 1967.

Delaur, Suzanne. *Une femme raconte . . . la vie extraordinaire du Général de Gaulle.* Paris: Editions S.E.N., 1945.

d'Escrienne, Jean. *De Gaulle de loin et de près.* Paris: Plon, 1978.

———. *De Gaulle sans frontières.* Paris: Thélès, 2007.

Dictionnaire de Gaulle. C. Andrieu, P. Braud, and G. Piketty (eds.). Paris: Robert Laffont, 2006.

d'Ornano, Michel. *Une certaine idée de Paris:* Paris: Jean-Claude Lattès, 1977.

Droit, Michel. *Les lueurs de l'aube.* Paris: Plon, 1981.

Duclos, Jacques. *De Napoléon III à de Gaulle.* Paris: Editions Sociales, 1964.

Dufour, Frédérique. "Colombey et le gaullisme sous la Ve République," in F. Audigier and F. Schwindt (eds.), *Gaullisme et gaullistes dans la France de l'Est sous la IVe République.* Rennes, Presses Universitaires de Rennes, 2009.

Duhamel, Alain. *De Gaulle-Mitterrand. La marque et la trace.* Paris: Flammarion, 1991.

Dulong, Claude. *La vie quotidienne à l'Elysée au temps de Charles de Gaulle.* Paris: Hachette, 1974.

Duteurtre, Benoît. *Le retour du Général.* Paris: Fayard, 2010.

Duval, Gaetan. *Une certaine idée de l'ile Maurice.* Port-Louis: Petite Ourse Printing, 1976.

Duval-Stalla, Alexandre. *André Malraux—Charles de Gaulle, une histoire, deux légendes.* Paris: Gallimard, 2008.

Essai de bibliographie mondiale des ouvrages consacrés à Charles de Gaulle. Paris: Institut Charles de Gaulle, 1974.

Estier, Claude. *Journal d'un Fédéré.* Paris: Fayard, 1970.

Fabius, Laurent. *Une certaine idée de l'Europe.* Paris: Plon, 2004.

Fabre, Daniel. *Ecritures ordinaires.* Paris: Editions P.O.L./Bibliothèque du Centre G. Pompidou, 1993.

Fauconnier, Bernard. *L'Etre et le géant.* Paris: Edition des Syrtes, 2000.

Faulkner, William. *De Gaulle: Scénario.* Paris: Gallimard, 1989.

Fenby, Jonathan. *The General. Charles de Gaulle and the France He Saved.* London, Simon & Schuster, 2010.

Ferri, Jean-Yves. *De Gaulle à la plage.* Paris: Dargaud, 2007.

Figueras, André. *Pétain, c'était De Gaulle!* Paris: Editions Déterna, 2000.

Flohic, François. *Souvenirs d'Outre-Gaulle.* Paris: Plon, 1979.

Foccart, Jacques. *Foccart parle. Entretiens avec Philippe Gaillard.* 2 vols. Paris: Fayard, 1995/1997.

———. *Journal de l'Elysée.* 5 vols. Paris: Fayard/Jeune Afrique, 1997–2001.

Forzy, Guy. *ça aussi . . . c'était de Gaulle.* 2 vols. Issy-les-Moulineaux: Muller, 2002.

Foussé, Claude. *L'anti-mythe. De Gaulle était-il bien la France?* Paris: Editions du Panthéon, 2002.

Fumaroli, Marc. *Chateaubriand. Poésie et terreur.* Paris: Gallimard, 2003.

Gallo, Max. *De Gaulle.* 4 vols. Paris: Robert Laffont, 1998.

Gary, Romain. *La promesse de l'aube.* Paris: Gallimard, 1980.

———. *Ode à l'homme qui fut la France.* Paris: Calmann-Lévy, 1997.

Gilles, Martinet. *Une certaine idée de la gauche.* Paris: Odile Jacob, 1977.

Gilzmer, Mechtild. *Mémoires de pierre. Les monuments commémoratifs en France après 1944.* Paris: Editions Autrement, 2009.

Gintz, Florent. *Autopsie du mythe gaulliste.* Paris: Godefroy de Bouillon, 2003.

Giocanti, Stéphane. *Une histoire politique de la littérature.* Paris: Flammarion, 2009.

Girard, Pascal. "Le gaullisme d'opposition au miroir de la haine politique, 1947–1958," in *Le discours de la haine,* ed. Marc Deleplace. Paris: Plon, 2009.

Giraud, d'Henri-Christian, ed. *Réplique à l'amiral de Gaulle.* Paris: Editions du Rocher, 2004.

Girardet, Raoul. *Mythes et mythologies politiques.* Paris: Seuil, 1990.

Giscard d'Estaing, Valéry. *Le pouvoir et la vie.* Paris: France-Loisirs, 1988.

Glucksmann, André. *De Gaulle où es-tu?* Paris: Jean-Claude Lattès, 1995.

Goulemot, Jean-Marie. *Pour l'amour de Staline. La face oubliée du communisme français.* Paris: CNRS Editions, 2009.

Grassi, Marie-Claire. *Lire l'épistolaire.* Paris: Dunod, 1998.

Guéna, Yves. *Le temps des certitudes 1940–1969.* Paris: Flammarion, 1982.

Gueniffey, Patrice. *Le Dix-huit Brumaire. L'épilogue de la Révolution française.* Paris: Gallimard, 2008.

Guichard, Olivier. *Mon Général.* Paris: Grasset, 1980.

Guy, Claude. *En écoutant de Gaulle. Journal 1946–1949.* Paris: Grasset, 1996.

Hazareesingh, Sudhir. *La légende de Napoléon.* Paris: Seuil, 2008.

———. "L'histoire politique face à l'histoire culturelle: état des lieux et perspectives," *Revue Historique* 642 (2007).

———. "Mythe," in C. Delporte, J.Y. Mollier, and J.F. Sirinelli (eds.), *Dictionnaire d'histoire culturelle de la France contemporaine.* Paris: PUF, 2010.

Hettier de Boislambert, Claude. *Les Fers de l'Espoir.* Paris: Plon, 1978.

Hoffmann, Stanley. *De Gaulle artiste de la politique*. Paris: Seuil, 1973.

Hudelot, Claude, and Guy Gallice. *Le Mao*. Paris: Editions du Rouergue, 2009.

Hugo, Victor. *Choses vues 1830–1848*. Paris: Gallimard, 1972.

Ihl, Olivier. *La fête républicaine*. Paris: Gallimard, 1996.

———. *Le mérite et la République*. Paris: Gallimard, 2007.

Jeannelle, Jean-Louis. *Ecrire ses Mémoires au XXe siècle*. Paris: Gallimard, 2008.

Jeanneney, Jean-Marcel. *A mes amis gaullistes*. Paris: Presses-Pocket, 1973.

Julliard, Jacques. "De de Gaulle à Mitterrand," in *La mort du roi. Essai d'ethnographie politique comparée*, ed. J. Julliard. Paris: Gallimard, 1999.

———. *La Reine du monde*. Paris: Flammarion, 2008.

Kantorowicz, Ernst. *The King's Two Bodies: A Study in Medieval Political Theology*. Princeton, NJ: Princeton University Press, 1957.

Kermoal, Jacques. *Procès en canonisation de Charles de Gaulle*. Paris: Balland, 1970.

Kessel, Joseph. *L'Armée des ombres*. Paris: Plon, 1963.

Knapp, Andrew. *Le gaullisme après de Gaulle*. Paris: Seuil, 1997.

Lacouture, Jean. *De Gaulle*. 3 vols. Paris: Seuil, 1984–1986.

———. "Un général bleu et blanc." *Le Débat* 134 (March–April 2005).

La mémoire des Français. Quarante ans de commémorations de la Seconde guerre mondiale. Paris: Editions du CNRS, 1986.

Larcan, Alain. *De Gaulle inventaire*. Paris: Bartillat, 2003.

Lassus, Robert. *Le mari de Madame de Gaulle*. Paris: JC Lattès, 1990.

Le Barde, Son fabuleux destin. Paris: Grassin, 1970.

Le Bihan, Adrien. *Le Général et son double. De Gaulle écrivain*. Paris: Flammarion, 1996.

Lefranc, Pierre. *Avec de Gaulle. Pendant et après. 1947–2005*. Paris: F.-X. de Guibert, 2007.

———. *Gouverner selon de Gaulle. Conversations avec Geneviève Moll*. Paris: Fayard, 2008.

Le Groignec, Jacques. *Philippique contre des mémoires gaulliens*. Paris: Nouvelles Editions Latines, 2004.

Le Guillou, Philippe. *Stèles à de Gaulle*. Paris: Gallimard, 2000.

Lerner, Henri. *De Gaulle et la gauche*. Limonest: Editions de l'Interdisciplinaire, 1994.

———. *De Gaulle, tel qu'en lui-même*. Paris: Editions Autres Temps, 2009.

"Les voies 'de Gaulle' en France. Le Général dans l'espace et la mémoire des communes," ed. P. Oulmont, *Cahiers de la Fondation Charles de Gaulle* 17 (2009).

Lévy, Bernard-Henri. *Ce grand cadavre à la renverse*. Paris: Grasset, 2007.

Lorne, Alain. *Le petit gaulliste*. Paris: Actes Sud, 2000.

Malraux, André. *Les chênes qu'on abat . . .* Paris: Gallimard, 1971.

Marcq, Michel. *Charles de Gaulle. La légende du Nord*. Paris: Renaudot, 1988.

Marin, Bernard. *De Gaulle de ma jeunesse*. Paris: Le Cercle-d'Or, 1984.

Mariot, Nicolas. *Bains de foule. Les voyages présidentiels en France 1888–2002*. Paris: Belin, 2006.

Massu, Jacques. *Baden 68. Souvenirs d'une fidélité gaulliste*. Paris: Plon, 1983.

Mauriac, Claude. *Aimer de Gaulle*. Paris: Grasset, 1978.

Mauriac, François. *Bloc-notes*. 2 vols. Paris: Seuil, 1993.

———. *De Gaulle*. Paris: Grasset, 1964.

Mauriac, Jean. *L'après de Gaulle. Notes confidentielles 1969–1989*. Paris: Fayard, 2006.

———. "Le Général de Gaulle et Colombey-les-Deux-Eglises," in *Charles de Gaulle 1890–1970*. Paris: Comité national du mémorial du général de Gaulle, 1973.

———. *Le Général et le journaliste*. Paris: Fayard, 2008.

———. *Mort du général de Gaulle*. Paris: Grasset, 1972.

Méo, Jean. *Une fidélité gaulliste à l'épreuve du pouvoir*. Panazol: Lavauzelle 2008.

Messmer, Pierre. *Après tant de batailles . . . Mémoires*. Paris: Albin Michel, 1992.

Messmer, Pierre. Pierre Pelissier, and Michel Tauriac. *Nous, les Français combattants de 39–45*. Paris: Tallandier, 2005.

Michelet, Edmond. *Le Gaullisme, passionnante aventure*. Paris: Fayard, 1962.

Michelet, Louis-Christian. *La légende gaullienne*. Paris: Godefroy de Bouillon, 2008.

Miquel, Pierre. *Compagnons de la Libération*. Paris: Denoël, 1995.

Miscault, Henri de. *De la Boissière à la Boisserie: suivre la Croix de Lorraine*. Nancy: Imprimerie J. Rubrecht, 1988.

Mitelberg, Louis [Tim]. *De Gaulle de France*. Paris: Olivier Orban, 1990.

——. *Le pouvoir civil*. Paris: Julliard, 1960.

Mitterrand, François. *Le coup d'état permanent*. Paris: Presses de la Cité, 1993.

——. *Ma part de vérité*. Paris: Fayard, 1969.

Mitterrand, Frédéric. *Les années de Gaulle*. Paris: Edition No. 1, 1995.

Monier, Frédéric. *La politique des plaintes*. Paris: La Boutique de l'Histoire, 2007.

Mossuz-Lavau, Janine. *André Malraux et le Gaullisme*. 2d ed. Paris: Presses de la Fondation Nationale des Sciences Politiques, 1982.

Muracciole, Jean-François. *Les Français Libres. L'autre Résistance*. Paris: Tallandier, 2009.

Nachin, Lucien. *Charles de Gaulle, Général de France*. Paris: Editions Colbert, 1944.

Namer, Gérard. *La commémoration en France*. Paris: Editions Papyrus, 1983.

Neuwirth, Lucien. *Ma guerre à seize ans*. Paris: Plon, 1986.

Nora, Pierre. "Du général à l'amiral." *Le Débat* 134 (March–April 2005).

——, ed. *Les lieux de mémoire*. Paris: Editions Quarto Gallimard, 1997.

Nora, Pierre, and F. Chandernagor. *Liberté pour l'histoire*. Paris: CNRS Editions, 2008.

Notin, Jean-Christophe. *Nom de code La Murène*. Paris: Seuil, 2008.

——. *1061 Compagons. Histoire des Compagnons de la Libération*. Paris: Perrin, 2000.

Nouvelle bibliographie internationale sur Charles de Gaulle. Paris: Plon, 1990.

Ollivier, Jean-Paul. *De Gaulle à Colombey*. Paris: Plon, 1998.

Ozouf, Mona. *Composition française*. Paris: Gallimard, 2009.

Palewski, Gaston. *Mémoires d'action 1924–1974*. Paris: Plon, 1988.

Pasqua, Charles. *Ce que je sais*. 2 vols. Paris: Seuil, 2007.

Péan, Pierre. *Une jeunesse française*. Paris: Fayard, 1994.

Perrein, Robert. *Un grand français, le général de Gaulle*. Paris: Editions Musy, 1944.

Perrier, Jean-Claude. *De Gaulle vu par les écrivains*. Paris: La Table Ronde, 2000.

Peyrefitte, Alain. *C'était de Gaulle*. Paris: Gallimard, 2002.

Picouly, Daniel. *68, mon amour*. Paris: Grasset, 2008.

Piketty, Guillaume, ed. "La force du refus," in *Français en résistance: Carnets de guerre, correspondances, journaux personnels*. Paris: Robert Laffont, 2009.

Pompidou, Georges. *Pour rétablir une vérité*. Paris: Flammarion, 1982.

Quagliariello, Gaetano. *La religion gaulliste*. Paris: Perrin, 2007.

Racine-Furlaud, Nicole. "18 juin 1940 ou 10 juillet 1940. Batailles de mémoires," in *50 ans d'une passion française. De Gaulle et les communistes*, eds. S. Courtois and M. Lazar. Paris: Balland, 1991.

Rémy. *Le livre du courage et de la peur*. Paris: Aux Trois Couleurs, 1945.

Revel, Jean-François. "De la légende vivante au mythe posthume," in *Le style du Général*. Brussels: Editions Complexe, 1988.

Reynolds, David. *In Command of History. Churchill Fighting and Writing the Second World War*. New York: Random House, 2005.

Rosanvallon, Pierre. *La légitimité démocratique*. Paris: Seuil, 2008.

Roussel, Eric. *Charles de Gaulle*. Paris: Gallimard, 2002.

——. "Les étranges vérités de l'amiral de Gaulle." *Le Débat* 134 (March–April 2005).

Rousso, Henry. "La Seconde Guerre Mondiale," in *Histoire des Droites en France*, ed. J.F. Sirinelli. Paris: Gallimard, 1992.

——. *Le syndrome de Vichy*. Paris: Seuil, 1990.

Rouvière, Nicolas. *Astérix ou les lumières de la civilisation*. Paris: PUF, 2006.

Roux-Champion, Julien. *Colombey Novembre 1970*. Paris: Editions Le Serpentaire, 1970.

Saint-Robert, Philippe. *De Gaulle et ses témoins*. Paris: Bartillat, 1999.

Sarkozy, Nicolas. *Témoignage*. Paris: XO Editions, 2006.

Séguin, Philippe. *Discours pour la France*. Paris: Grasste, 1992.

———. *Louis Napoléon le Grand*. Paris: Grasset, 1990.

Simonin, Anne. "1815 en 1945. Les formes littéraires de la défaite." *Vingtième Siècle* 59 (July–September 1998).

———. *Le déshonneur dans la République. Une histoire de l'indignité 1791–1958*. Paris: Grasset, 2008.

Simonin, Anne, and Hélène Clastres. *Les idées en France 1945–1988, une chronologie*. Paris: Gallimard, 1989.

Soustelle, Jacques. *Vingt-huit ans de gaullisme*. Paris: Editions J'ai Lu, 1971.

Souvenir de la visite du Général de Gaulle: Limoges—Oradour-sur-Glane—Périgueux, 4–5 mars 1945. Paris: Limoges, 1945.

Stirn, Olivier. *Une certaine idée du centre*. Paris: Albin Michel, 1977.

Stora, Benjamin. *Le mystère de Gaulle: Son choix pour l'Algérie*. Paris: Robert Laffont, 2009.

Tartakowsky, Danielle. "Les fêtes de la droite populaire," in *Les usages politiques des fêtes aux XIXe–XXe siècles*, ed. A. Corbin. Paris: Publications de la Sorbonne, 1994.

Tauriac, Michel. *Vivre avec de Gaulle. Les derniers témoins racontent l'homme*. Paris: Plon, 2008.

Tenzer, Nicolas. *La face cachée du gaullisme*. Paris: Hachette, 1998.

Tessier, Roger. *J'étais le gorille du Général 1947–1970*. Paris: Perrin, 2002.

Tinguely, Francine. *La vie d'Honorine, du couvent jusqu'aux cuisines du Général*. Genève: Editions de l'Hèbe, 1997.

Triboulet, Raymond. *Un Gaulliste de la IVe*. Paris: Plon, 1985.

———. *Un ministre du Général*. Paris: Plon, 1985.

Turpin, Frédéric. *Le Mont-Valérien, de l'histoire à la mémoire*. Paris: Editions du Huitième Jour, 2003.

Vaïsse, Maurice. *La grandeur. Politique étrangère du Général de Gaulle 1958–1969*. Paris: Fayard, 1998.

Vendroux, Jacques. *Ces grandes années que j'ai vécues*. Paris: Plon, 1975.

———. *Cette chance que j'ai eue. Souvenirs de famille et journal politique 1920–1957*. Paris: Plon, 1974.

Verdès-Leroux, Jeannine. *Les Français d'Algérie de 1830 à aujourd'hui*. Paris: Fayard, 2001.

Viansson-Ponté, Pierre. *Les Gaullistes: rituel et annuaire*. Paris: Seuil, 1963.

Winock, Michel. *13 Mai 1958: l'agonie de la IVe République*. Paris: Gallimard, 2006.

Yessouroun, Robert. *La tondeuse du général de Gaulle*. Fontaine: Editions ThoT, 2007.

Zagdanski, Stéphane. *Pauvre de Gaulle!* Paris: Editions Pauvert. 2000.

INDEX